# FEMINIST RESPONSES TO INJUSTICES OF THE STATE AND ITS INSTITUTIONS

Politics, Intervention, Resistance

Edited by
Kym Atkinson, Úna Barr, Helen Monk
and Katie Tucker

BRISTOL
UNIVERSITY
PRESS

First published in Great Britain in 2023 by

Bristol University Press
University of Bristol
1–9 Old Park Hill
Bristol
BS2 8BB
UK
t: +44 (0)117 374 6645
e: bup-info@bristol.ac.uk

Details of international sales and distribution partners are available at bristoluniversitypress.co.uk

© Bristol University Press 2023

British Library Cataloguing in Publication Data
A catalogue record for this book is available from the British Library

ISBN 978-1-5292-0728-6 hardcover
ISBN 978-1-5292-0731-6 ePdf
ISBN 978-1-5292-0732-3 ePub

The right of Kym Atkinson, Úna Barr, Helen Monk and Katie Tucker to be identified as editors
of this work has been asserted by them in accordance with the Copyright, Designs and Patents
Act 1988.

Cover design: Nicky Borowiec
Front cover image: filo - iStock.com
Bristol University Press uses environmentally responsible print partners.
Printed and bound in Great Britain by CPI Group (UK) Ltd,
Croydon, CR0 4YY

FSC
www.fsc.org
MIX
Paper | Supporting
responsible forestry
FSC® C013604

# Contents

# Notes on Contributors

**Kym Atkinson** is Lecturer in Criminology and Human Rights at Sheffield Hallam University. She joined Sheffield Hallam in 2021 having previously worked as Lecturer in Criminology at Liverpool John Moores University. She completed her PhD in 2020 at Liverpool John Moores University which explored women students' experiences of sexual violence at university and institutional responses to this violence.

**Anette Ballinger** retired from the School of Sociology and Criminology at Keele University in 2016. She is the author of the award-winning book *Dead Woman Walking: Executed Women in England & Wales 1900–1955* (Ashgate, 2000; winner of the Hart Socio-Legal Prize 2001). She has written several book chapters and journal articles on the subject of gender and punishment in modern history. More recently her research interests have also included contemporary issues – particularly in relation to state responses to violence against women. Her most recent book is *Gender, Truth and State Power: Capitalising on Punishment* (Routledge, 2016).

**Úna Barr** is Lecturer in Criminology at Liverpool John Moores University. She completed her PhD in 2017 at the University of Central Lancashire. Prior to this, she attended the University of Manchester and Queens University, Belfast for her MRes and LLB respectively. Úna also taught at the University of Manchester and Manchester Metropolitan University. In 2019, *Desisting Sisters: Gender, Power and Desistance in the Criminal (In)Justice System*, based on Úna's PhD research, was published by Palgrave Macmillan.

**Victoria Canning** is Senior Lecturer in Criminology at the University of Bristol. She co-coordinates the European Group for the Study of Deviance and Social Control, is an associate director at Border Criminologies, Oxford University, and trustee of Statewatch. Vicky is co-creator of the Right to Remain Asylum Navigation Board (with Lisa Matthews) ESRC Future Research Leader fellow (2016–18) and winner of the 2018 British Society of Criminology Book Prize.

**Aisha K. Gill** is Professor of Criminology at University of Roehampton. Her main areas of interest and research are health and criminal justice responses to violence against Black, racially minoritized, refugee women in the UK, Afghanistan, Georgia, Libya, Iraqi Kurdistan, India, Pakistan and Yemen. She has been involved in addressing the problem of violence against women and girls, 'honour' crimes and forced marriage at the grassroots level for the past 22 years. Her recent publications include articles on crimes related to the murder of women/femicide, 'honour' killings, coercion and forced marriage, child sexual exploitation and sexual abuse in Black and racially minoritized communities, female genital mutilation, sex selective abortions, intersectionality and women who kill. In 2019, she was appointed co-chair of the End Violence Against Women Coalition.

**Emily Luise Hart** is Lecturer in Criminology at the University of Liverpool. Her research takes a critical and abolitionist approach to the study of prisons, women offenders, resettlement and desistance from crime. She is co-editor of *Resist the Punitive State: Grassroots Struggles Across Welfare, Hosing, Education and Prisons* (Pluto Press, 2020) and *New Perspectives on Desistance: Theoretical and Empirical Developments* (Palgrave, 2017). She is also an anti-prison and trade union activist and campaigner.

**Jodie Hodgson** is Lecturer in Criminology at Manchester Metropolitan University and is based in the Manchester Centre for Youth Studies. Jodie has previously worked as a lecturer at Leeds Beckett University and the University of Liverpool. Jodie is the author of *Gender, Power and Restorative Justice: A Feminist Critique* (Palgrave, 2022). Her research interests are situated within the areas of youth justice, feminism and critical criminology.

**Adrian Howe** was Foundational Professor of Criminology at the University of Central Lancashire. Her current work, the Othello Theatre in Education project, builds on her criminological research by repurposing Shakespeare's *Othello* to highlight continuing high levels of intimate partner femicide in all Western jurisdictions. The project's first play, *Othello on Trial*, has been performed in Melbourne and London. Her most recent book (co-edited with Daniela Alaattinoğlu) is *Contesting Femicide: Feminism and the Power of Law Revisited* (Routledge, 2019).

**Will Jackson** is Senior Lecturer in Criminology at Liverpool John Moores University. His research is concerned with policing, protest and political activism with a particular emphasis on women's experiences of police. He is co-editor of *Destroy Build Secure: Readings in Pacification* (Red Quill, 2017) and his work has recently been published in *Critical Social Policy*, *Policing and Society*, *Feminist Review*, *Journal of Gender Based Violence* and *Social Justice*.

**Maev McDaid** is Graduate Teaching and Research Assistant at the University of Sheffield where she has just completed her PhD on Irish migration. Originally from Ireland, she has been an activist with Alliance for Choice Derry for almost 20 years and continues to campaign for full reproductive rights and bodily choice. Maev also writes occasionally for Pluto Press and other blogs and is working on a book about the breakup of the 'United Kingdom'.

**Helen Monk** is Senior Lecturer in Criminology at Liverpool John Moores University where she also acts as Co-Director of the Centre for the Study of Crime, Criminalisation and Social Exclusion. Her research interests include feminist theory, sexual coercion, men's violence against women and the policing of women. She is co-editor (with Professor Joe Sim) of *Women, Crime and Criminology: A Celebration* (CCSE and EG Press Limited, 2017) and is widely published in academic journals such as *Feminist Review*.

**Brian Christopher Nelis** is a teacher, trade unionist and activist in London. Originally from Derry, he studied law at University of Glasgow, education at Canterbury Christchurch and UCL, holds an MA in Leadership from the Institute for Education and has been involved in the movement for bodily autonomy for over 15 years. Brian writes occasionally for Pluto Press and other current affairs blogs and is working on a book about decolonizing the school curriculum.

**Pragna Patel** is an activist and consultant in her fields of expertise, namely violence against women and girls, particularly those from Black and minority communities, and related issues of racial and other forms of discrimination, poverty, immigration insecurities and religious coercion. She is currently a member of Feminist Dissent and has written extensively on race, gender and religion. Until January 2022, she was the director of Southall Black Sisters (SBS) advocacy and campaigning centre which she founded in 1982 and steered through the intervening 40 years, save for a break in 1993 when she left to train and practice as a solicitor. Throughout this time, she led some of the most important cases and campaigns run by SBS.

**Joe Sim** is Professor of Criminology and Co-Director of the Centre for the Study of Crime, Criminalisation and Social Exclusion at Liverpool John Moores University. He has published a number of books including *Medical Power in Prisons, Punishment and Prisons, British Prisons* (Open University Press, 1990, with Mike Fitzgerald) and *Prisons Under Protest* (Open University Press, 1991, with Phil Scraton and Paula Skidmore). He is a trustee of the charity INQUEST, which supports the families of those who die in the custody of the state as well as the families of those who have died outside of state custody such as at Grenfell.

**Katie Tucker** is currently undertaking her PhD at Liverpool John Moores University and her research focuses on the discursive framing of child sexual abuse. Katie is also Associate Lecturer at the Open University. Before this she undertook both her undergraduate degree and master's by research at the University of Central Lancashire in Preston, England. Katie is involved with the Centre for Crime Criminalisation and Social Exclusion through Liverpool John Moores University and an active member of the European Group for the Study of Deviance and Social Control.

# Acknowledgements

On 16 March 2016, the Centre for the Study of Crime, Criminalisation and Social Exclusion (CCSE) at Liverpool John Moores University (LJMU) hosted a seminar to celebrate the 40th anniversary of the publication of Carol Smart's seminal text, *Women, Crime and Criminology*. The event provided a critical reflection on the historical significance of the book and its contemporary relevance for those of us working on the politics of gender in relation to criminalization and victimization. It was a pivotal moment in our friendship and working relationship and raised significant questions about the future work of feminist criminology. We dedicate this collection to Carol and the myriad feminist thinkers who have gone before us, many of whom we have cited in the Introduction and throughout the collection. We are indebted beyond words to Professor Joe Sim who was instrumental in connecting our research interests. Joe's retirement at the end of 2021 was a huge loss to LJMU, the CCSE and critical criminology more widely. The influence Joe has had in all our work cannot be underestimated. Joe has been involved in all stages of production of this collection and his continued guidance, advice and chats about music and Celtic are sources of joy in all our lives. Thank you so much Joe.

Thank you to all the contributors to the collection, for your patience in bearing with us throughout the pandemic where all our working conditions were drastically altered, and during periods of maternity leave, new jobs and PhD submissions. Your diligence and enthusiasm for the collection has been a huge source of motivation and the excellent range of submissions has been above even our expectations at the outset. Thank you in particular to Pragna Patel for writing the Afterword to the collection. Pragna's fearless campaigning with Southall Black Sisters will forever be inspirational to us all. Thank you also to all our colleagues at the CCSE and in particular to Lindsey Metcalf McGrath for organizing the 'Shut Up and Write' sessions which gave space and time to the production of many of the chapters in this collection. Finally, we would collectively like to thank Bristol University Press, particularly Rebecca and Freya, for their guidance, support and patience during the editing of this collection.

Helen would like to thank colleagues, family and friends for their mix of support, encouragement, inspiration, distraction and company – in particular, Ashton, Joe, Jude, Katie, Kym, Sarah, Una and Will. Special thanks to Danny and Seb for bringing much needed joy and light – as always, this was a team effort.

Katie would like to echo the thanks to Joe Sim and further thank her fellow editors for all of their support and guidance and the collective vision to bring this book to life. As always a gigantic thank you to Will Jackson for his mentorship, I am beyond lucky to have you on my team. A huge thanks also goes to my ever-patient partner Daniel and our wonderful son Myles – you are my reasons. I would finally like to thank my wonderful parents for their everlasting and unwavering support and faith in my abilities, this is dedicated to you both, especially you mum, it's all your fault.

Kym would like to thank friends, family and colleagues in Newcastle, Liverpool, Sheffield and Manchester for their constant support and distraction. Thanks to my co-editors and all contributors for their hard work and patience. As always, a special thank you to Joe for your belief, support and encouragement.

Úna would like to thank co-editors, friends and colleagues in Liverpool, Manchester, Sheffield, Preston and Derry. As always thanks to mammy, daddy, Dermot, Éimear, Tom and, of course, wee Nóra, I love you to the moon and back.

# PART I

# Feminist Epistemology

# Introduction: Denying Oppression a Future[1] – Gender, the State and Feminist Praxis

*Kym Atkinson, Úna Barr and Helen Monk*

It is over 40 years since the publication in paperback of the seminal, feminist text *Violence against Wives: A Case against the Patriarchy* (Dobash and Dobash, 1979). Alongside other important feminist-inspired texts produced in the 1970s, *Violence against Wives* contributed to a critical, feminist praxis through its analysis of power, men's violence, gender relations and the state. The book provided a feminist-based, analytical framework for addressing three key areas: the historical context of male dominance and the prevailing cultural norms which uphold and maintain the dominant social order; the realities of interpersonal violence and the systematic loss of power experienced by women at an institutional level, in this instance, the institution of marriage; and the incompetent response of state support systems for women in need which were underpinned by victim-blaming narratives. The text concluded by warning that unless the legal, political, economic and family structures which pervade every aspect of cultural life were challenged and disassembled, the systemic subordination of women and the endemic nature of violent practices against them would continue.

In 2022, *all* of these arguments remain depressingly familiar. While there are many causes for celebration with regard to feminist gains made over the last 40 years, these are neither secure nor protected. Rampant, toxic masculinity and violent, structural power relations such as 'race', ethnicity, nationality, sexuality, faith, socio-economic status and disability, bind together enduring and remorseless acts of violence against women and children, perpetrated at individual, institutional and state levels. Against a backdrop of a global health pandemic, an urgent movement for racial justice, Brexit, the decimation of the public sector through the onslaught of austerity, and the continued role of state institutions in policing and punishing vulnerable women, and in reinforcing patriarchal social relations, the future looks bleak.

However, we appear to be at a critical juncture in relation to the ongoing disruption of accepted academic narrative, popular common sense and political complacency around particular gendered social issues. In breaking the silence around sexual harassment and abuse, various disclosures and different campaigns have sought to frame men's violence as an issue that is pervasive, overlooked and ignored. Recently, the tireless work of survivors and activists, in particular, have succeeded in exposing the continuum of violence (Kelly, 1988) faced by women and children in a range of contexts – the home, state institutions, the sporting arena, the entertainment industry, the education system and aid agencies, for example – and, importantly, they have done so on an international scale, penetrating dominant cultural and political discourses as well as the public consciousness. The centrality of the White voice in the #MeToo era has also been subject to analysis and rightly positioned as an enduring practice, which will no longer be tolerated (Phipps, 2019).

Discussions of permissive spaces and themes of (re)victimization and the power of silence have also opened up other urgent debates. The Police, Crime, Sentencing and Courts Bill and Nationality and Borders Bill represent a threat to the various gains made through feminist activism and the space in which the exercise of state power can be resisted. Moreover, the treatment and detainment of incarcerated women and the use of punitive and discriminatory immigration controls within the 'hostile environment' manufactured by the British state (see Canning, Chapter 7, this volume); the continued control over female bodies through denial of abortion by devolved powers in Northern Ireland (discussed by McDaid and Nelis in Chapter 3 in this volume); and the ongoing inquiry into undercover policing, examining the highly publicized practice of deceiving women into intimate relationships with male police officers (discussed by Jackson and Monk in Chapter 6 in this volume), for example, highlight the distinctly gendered approach state abuses are currently taking. At the same time, they also highlight the distinctly gendered nature of resistance and the inroads that women are making in attempting to hold the state to account.

For these reasons, this is a book concerned with documenting a series of *feminist* interventions into criminology; examining the injustices discussed in the contributions as *feminist* issues and outlining responses built on *feminist* praxis. The argument here is that the complex social structures, multiple and interlocking inequalities, state-defined forms of acceptable femininity, common-sense and state-defined definitions of acceptable, ultimately repressive and regressive, forms of hegemonic masculinity and violent mechanisms of social control, through which these injustices are produced and sustained, require rigorous feminist analysis in order to dispute and displace deeply embedded gender norms and misogynies, many of which have recently come to the fore in public and political discourses. Thus, this book makes the case for continued and revitalized political and structural analysis to make the operations of the state and its institutions clear as a precursor to contesting their workings. The book is designed to contribute to the development of a counter-discourse to resist the politics of gendered subjugation and victimization and document survival strategies in the 21st century.

All of this will be aimed at making a case for extending a feminist criminology which is equipped to contest and dismantle the hetero-patriarchal state, the hegemonic, militarized form of masculinity on which its institutions are based, and the social harms which it produces and maintains. We wish to celebrate the vitality and productivity of five decades worth of feminist work in criminology while extending, rather than repeating, feminist analysis. This edited collection brings together academics and activists seeking to document the politics of feminist interventions and responses to injustices in the criminal justice system (CJS), broadly conceived. It also highlights and challenges the endless capacity of the state to close things down, to cynically incorporate spheres of resistance and contestation and to disentangle the connections we can make within and across the theory–policy–practice nexus. It is designed, therefore, to explore the radical space opened up by feminist interventions into criminology in order to ask key questions about the conceptualization of gender, the complacent state response to women's victimization and the punitive state response to women's criminality.

In this introduction, we first sketch out where we are currently in relation to issues outlined 40 years or so ago, addressing what has been achieved by feminist praxis and tracing significant theoretical and methodological developments. Next, we consider what issues still persist through an exploration of prevailing cultural norms, contemporary regimes of truth and the role of the state. Finally, we attempt to map the ground for resistance and consider the (necessarily limited) harms towards women and girls which the collection discusses, and the vision of justice articulated, indeed demanded, by the contributors.

## Feminist praxis and intersectional ideas

Carol Smart (1995) famously queried whether criminology had anything to offer those engaged in feminist scholarship and we are unsure whether there was ever a sufficient answer given to this question. What we do know is that feminist thinking and feminist praxis have added much to the general terrain of criminological inquiry and that radical, counter-discursive spaces have been opened up by feminist interventions into the discipline.

It is not our intention to thoroughly review the range of developments in feminist criminologies (see Daly, 2010; Carrington, 2018 for contemporary overviews). We acknowledge and celebrate the ground-breaking intrusions made by the convergence of feminist activism and feminist theory into criminology. From a variety of different and distinctive approaches, feminist criminologies have sought to dismantle and rebuild criminological frames of reference and traditional methodologies, making room for women as producers of knowledge and acknowledging and working with the varied relationships women have with victimization, criminalization and social harm.

It is our contention that the way forward for feminist criminology, research and activism, in terms of intervention, contestation and resistance to the injustices outlined in this collection, requires responses which are built on feminist praxis. In practice, this means asking the question, what is this research and knowledge for? For feminist research, and a feminist praxis, the production of knowledge which contributes to the radical transformation of the social world is key. Stanley (1990) suggests the use of the term 'feminist praxis' is important for three central reasons. First, it signifies a feminist commitment to 'a political position in which "knowledge" is not simply defined as "knowledge *what*" but also as "knowledge *for*"' (Stanley, 1990: 15, emphasis in original). Second, a feminist praxis rejects the divide between theory and research. Instead, they are understood as symbiotically related activities which are mutually beneficial in the production of purposeful knowledge. Third, feminist praxis centralizes methodological and epistemological concerns and asserts that the 'how' and 'what' of research 'are indissolubly interconnected and that the shape and nature of the "what" will be a product of the "how" of its investigation' (Stanley, 1990: 15). The approach outlined by Stanley allows for an analysis of issues of power, violence, gender relations and the state as *feminist* issues. It also values the relationship between theory and method in terms of their connections to the production of purposeful knowledge. Finally, the value in feminist praxis is to move beyond critique and to forge a path forward which intervenes and resists injustices which, as this collection documents, span a range of state institutions.

What Smart (1976) and others were calling for nearly 50 years ago, which remains as pressing and as prescient today, is the adoption of perspectives which understand 'the *different* ways in which the state and state apparatus define, respond to, and control men and women and reproduce the dominant social order' (Monk and Sim, 2017: 8, emphasis in original). To understand the material and ideological conditions under which masculinity and femininity are constructed, maintained and reproduced, and their interaction with intersecting systems of power is fundamental to any progressive critical social theory and, as such, we maintain that a feminist take on criminology, built upon feminist praxis, is essential.

However, to capture and attend to the specificity, variability and multiplicity of women's experiences of criminal and social (in)justice, feminist criminologies must address cross-cutting regimes of inequality and the effects that these systems of power, and the role of state institutions, have on each other. Appeals, emerging from predominantly Black and racially minoritized women,[2] to end the compartmentalization of identity and experience and to understand social divisions as relational, interactive, intermeshed and dynamic gave rise to a broad approach which insisted that historical, cultural, socio-economic, ethnic and racial diversity mattered (Davis, 1983; King, 1988; Mohanty, 1988; Rice, 1990; Crenshaw, 1991).

Referring to what Collins (2000: 18) calls the 'matrix of domination', applying an intersectional lens (Crenshaw, 1991) insists that people are characterized by a multitude of social divisions, that these divisions are socially constructed and modified by other systems of power, and that they create specific social locations (hooks, 1992; Burgess-Proctor, 2006). The interplay of hierarchies of power and difference takes place on structural, subjective and discursive levels (Yuval-Davis, 2006) occupying both productive and compounding space. This positions women differently in relation to criminal law, criminal justice and social justice (Spivak, 1990; Carrington, 2018). It is imperative, therefore, that feminists working with questions of justice seek to explore the ways in which 'race', ethnicity, social class, age, sexuality and disability impact upon experience and state and institutional discrimination and power. Feminists who work from this perspective would be advocating an intersectional approach to studying gender (Burgess-Proctor, 2006).

Potter suggests that 'despite the relevance of an intersectional perspective to *most questions* within criminology, its implementation has remained at the conceptual level' (Potter, 2015, in Parmar, 2017: 37, emphasis added). Much criminological work on intersectionality and crime has sought to understand how the lived experiences of offenders and victims complicate analyses focusing on 'race', class, gender, place or sexuality, rather than exploring how these systems of power work together to produce specific effects. However, some feminist criminologies have adopted versions of an intersectional approach for some time to examine the interlaced impacts of social divisions and how these constructs map onto criminological contexts (see, for example, Carlen, 1983, 1998; Richie, 1996, 2005).

The CJS, and its associated institutions, are an integral part of state apparatus which is able to reinforce, transform and reproduce social inequalities (Daly and Stephens, 1995). To do this 'the state itself enshrines White supremacy, heteropatriarchy, and transmisogyny into its legal codes – a structure that operates through non-consensual imposition, coercion, and at many times, brute force' (Whalley and Hackett, 2017: 4). The only way to effectively grapple with the complexities and messiness of these vectors of power, and to contribute to their dismantlement, is to tackle them as co-producing forces and ones which are inscribed into our conceptualizations of social location, privilege and oppression. In the context of women's treatment by the state, the 'call to take an intersectional approach is more than an intellectual exercise: it is literally a matter of life and death' (Paik, 2017: 4). Nonetheless, these discussions remain 'fairly scarce' in mainstream debates (Thiara and Gill, 2010: 33). This point is made persuasively by Gill in this collection (Chapter 9). We join her, Potter and others in advocating for an expanded use of an intersectional framework 'in all forms of inquiry and most certainly in any form of criminology that designates itself as critical' (Potter, 2013: 316; 2015).

## Cultural norms and contemporary regimes of truth

On 24 November 2020, the 'Counting Dead Women' project commemorated UK women and girls killed by men in the previous 12 months, naming them on Twitter, one at a time, every five minutes. It took nine hours to commemorate all those killed. On the same day, the Femicide Census report was also published (Long et al, 2020). The report detailed levels of fatal violence against women across a ten-year period, 2009–18, stating that at least 1,425 women were killed by men in that period (Long et al, 2020: 3). This means that a man killed a woman every three days. Why, given the ostensible increase in economic, social and personal freedoms for women, investment from successive governments through a plethora of initiatives, consistent and vehement campaigning from activists, survivors and the academy, and claims by the police, and other state institutions, that they have changed, has men's violence against women continued to be exercised fatally at such an alarming and devastating rate? There are, we suggest, a number of answers to this question, many of which remain unresolved and unchanged despite consistent dissenting actions and voices, some of which are covered in the first section of this book by Anette Ballinger (Chapter 2). We wish to concentrate first, here, on one of the issues identified by Dobash and Dobash (1979), which centralizes the role that cultural norms play in the stability and maintenance of the gendered social order. To do this, we examine the 'regimes of truth' (Foucault, 1980: 133) which endure with regard to sexual violence.

The reasons, excuses and justifications of the violent man are well known and documented, in academic and activist work, case law and the cultural narratives of victim-blaming. They do not need to be rehearsed in detail here, but they are important in pointing to the longevity of reductive, narrow cultural discourses with which contemporary society can make sense of gendered, sexed and racialized culpability. Despite the transitory and contestable nature of these regulatory tropes, the meaning we attach to social divisions as they intersect and modify each other and as they produce material, symbolic and violent effects, persists.

In December 2018, Grace Millane was murdered. The man convicted of her murder choked her so hard and for so long that she died. He claimed that this was a case of 'sex games gone wrong', a term gaining traction as a specific defence to murder and one which takes place against a cultural backdrop of 'consensual rough sex' (We Can't Consent To This, 2020). There is much to learn from the narrative that weaved its way through all elements of this case about prevailing cultural norms and the relentless acts of victim-blaming which circulate around acts of sexual violence and gendered culpability. Ballinger picks this up in this collection, arguing that the case, alongside others, exemplifies the clock 'turning backwards' in terms of how we deal with violence against women and the themes of individualization and responsibilization (see also Atkinson, Chapter 5, for a discussion of how these themes produce dominant institutional truths around sexual violence).

Despite the outcome of the trial, systemic misunderstandings around the case and a reliance on tired interpretations may actually serve to reinscribe problematic social attitudes, particularly in a technology-mediated world. A series of discursive manoeuvres (Howe, 2008), which systematically attempt to present a utopian sexual terrain, full of freedom, liberation and choice, masks, a feminist analysis of the case would suggest, a culture-wide obligation for young women to embrace the 'progressive' and agency-led sexual demands of the 21st century (Gavey, 2005; Levy, 2005). While this may be true for some, and happily so, the Millane case typifies what we know from years of feminist research and praxis – that many women are forced or coerced into, or acquiesce to, sexual relationships, and still encounter issues when trying to exercise full autonomy over their gendered performance, sexed bodies and subjectivity. At the heart of many women's relationship to sex, and to gender relations, gender regimes and the gender order, is the normalization of sexed violence.

For Gavey (2019), the trial of Grace Millane's killer and the unprecedented media coverage that it generated 'unfolded as a crucible of modern gender and sexual politics'. She continues:

> The perils of blame and shame was a key theme in lawyer Ron Mansfield's speech to introduce the defence evidence. 'The younger generation,' he was reported saying, 'does not adhere to this "pressure on us to appear normal", and they can teach us about their refusal to accept these old concepts.' On the surface, his words sound progressive. They resonate with feminist 'sex positive' discourse, which calls for women's rights to sexual pleasure and experimentation without judgement and shame. They fit with queer theory's critique of the oppressive grip of societal ideas about what is 'normal'. And they appear to embrace inclusion, as they reject the way that some sexual practices and identities have historically been marginalized and stigmatised. …

But this picture of a happy new sexual landscape is woefully blind to the ways it remains shaped by gendered dynamics of power and domination. (Gavey, 2019)

This interpretation by the legal defence team and by several media outlets when 'reporting' on the case fundamentally ignores the *violence* at the centre of this crime and the normalization of violence against women during sex. Thirty-eight per cent of UK women under the age of 40 report being assaulted during otherwise consensual sex (Harte, 2019). These acts of assault include being choked, slapped, gagged and spat on. These acts of violence are presented in dominant discourse as elements of modern sexual culture, that is, until this violence is contested in some way. At this point, established regimes of truth are deployed to dissect appropriate sexual behaviour for women and to undermine women's experiences. Grace Millane was constructed as having received what she asked for – rough sex, strangulation – and the victim-blaming narratives deployed in both media and legal discourse throughout the trial served to rework old provocation defences to fit contemporary excuses for men who kill women (see also Howe, Chapter 11, this volume). Grace's case is one which ultimately demonstrates how little we understand, or are willing to understand, about men's violence against women and how dominant discourses still prevail in the production of common-sense ideas, and in the media's sensationalist and titillating coverage, of sex, violence and crime.

Contemporary regimes of truth, therefore, not only demonstrate a limited level of understanding of these issues, but also, the reproduction of these discourses work to mystify the realities of injustice at the hands of the state and its institutions. Challenging these truths, as Foucault (1977: 13) states, requires 'a battle about the status of truth and the economic/political role it plays'. This battle for truth is, however, a challenge, given the stubborn persistence of discourses which work to mystify, deny, deflect and responsibilize gendered harms. Over 25 years ago, Lees (1997) and Ussher (1997) identified medical discourses which operate in the legal process to construct women's bodies in rape trials in ways which cast doubt on their credibility as victims, based on the 'typical' bodily signs of rape and the standard of how a 'reasonable woman' would respond. Despite several reforms, the Centre for Women's Justice (CWJ) (2020, 2021), which explored how the CJS responds to women who kill abusive men, found that such discourses are still utilized at trial by medical experts to assess the 'reasonableness' of a woman's belief that she is in danger, despite not being trained in issues of violence against women and girls (VAWG). Further, the CWJ (2021) argued that a hierarchy of expertise is evident in such cases whereby psychiatrists are perceived as the most qualified, regardless of the specialism of the medical expert, such as expertise in trauma and VAWG. This operation maintains the elevation of expert knowledge and the relegation of knowledge predicated on experience (a point also highlighted by Tucker in Chapter 4 in this volume).

For us, consequently, these issues are not separate from the ways in which they are spoken about. Questioning the construction of ideas of masculinity and femininity and the ways in which sex, violence and crime are put into discourse (Foucault, 1980; Howe, 2008) is of central importance to the project of feminist criminology. Thinking critically about 'common-sense' ideas around sex and sexuality as they relate to sexual violence is a long-standing feminist concern. Notably, Gavey (2005: 2) highlighted what she terms 'the cultural scaffolding of rape', that is, the everyday, taken for granted, normative forms of heterosexuality. She argues that these normalizing dimensions of contemporary heterosex provide the discursive scaffolding that enables rape. This scaffolding is further supported by the abject failure of the CJS to protect women and deliver justice. In 2019–20, police recorded 55,130 rapes which led to 2,102 prosecutions and 1,439 convictions in England and Wales (Topping and Barr, 2020). These are the lowest ever recorded prosecution and conviction statistics since data on rape has been collected. We are, in 2022, effectively facing the decriminalization of rape.

Poststructuralist feminists have developed these arguments on language, discourse and the construction of sexuality in relation to sexual violence. Alcoff (2018: 3) argues that rape cultures produce a discursive formation in which 'the intelligibility of claims is not by logical argument or evidence, but by frames that set out who can be victimised, who can be accused, which are plausible narratives, and in what contexts rape may be spoken about, even in private spaces'. Discourses, therefore, determine the criteria by which the statement of experiences of sexual violence are interpreted. Feminist work has, however, challenged the normalization of these discourses and shown how these common-sense ideas and claims to truth are, in fact, an exercise of power, reinforcing and regulating the gender order (Bumiller, 1987; Smart, 1989; Lees, 1997; Ussher, 1997). This exercise of power is central to many of the analyses in this collection which document a series of feminist interventions into criminology. For example, some common-sense ideas which have been challenged by feminist thinking and praxis include the victim/offender binary for women (Clarke and Chadwick, 2020; Barr and Hart, Chapter 8, this volume), and the 'discovery' of girls' violence and the enduring fascination with 'new' forms of violence encapsulated in the slogan 'girls gone wild' (Chesney-Lind and Irwin, 2008; Hodgson, Chapter 12, this volume).

## The state and the gendered social order

This collection also seeks to centralize the role of the state and its relationship to a gendered social order, underutilized as a point of analysis in our view.

The state's role in gendered relations has been theorized from different perspectives and, irrespective of the feminist position taken, and the ways in which its varied institutional sites are understood, the state remains a relevant site of analysis for theorizing gender relations and the often-violent maintenance of a hierarchical, gendered social order.

A particularly useful analysis, for us, comes from Connell (1994), who outlined a framework for analysing the interplay of existing power relations in which gender relations are understood as inseparable from the state and its institutions. For Connell, the state is not 'essentially patriarchal or male ... the state is *historically* patriarchal, patriarchal as a matter of concrete social practices' (Connell, 1994: 163, emphasis in original). It represents the institutionalization of power relations persisting over time. Importantly, however, it is not the only institutionalization of power, nor does it hold the monopoly on the use of force to regulate gender relations. As Connell points out, feminist work has highlighted the ways in which gender relations are enforced through violence in the home. It is, therefore, appropriate to view the state as just one part of 'a wider structure of gender relations that embody violence or other means of control' (Connell, 1994: 520). It is through a conceptualization of the gender order that unequal gender relations can be understood at both the micro and macro levels, in terms of their connections and disjunctions. The violence within interpersonal relationships, for example, is, at times, reflected in the operation of state institutions (Richie, 2012; Connell and Pearse, 2015). This is at times direct, in that it is perpetrated by state actors and agents against women, as seen in the murder of Sarah Everard[3] (BBC News, 2021), the handling of the murders of Bibaa Henry and Nicole Smallman[4] (Dodd, 2021), in the range of work carried out by INCITE! (2018) which explores the intersection of gender violence and state violence, and in the information being uncovered by SPYCOPS about the number of women deceived into sexual relationships with undercover police officers (SPYCOPS, 2021).

This violence is also indirect, a result of inaction, negligent policy and practice and a lack of protection for victims of various injustices. This can be seen through the work of INQUEST (2018) on the levels of self-harm and death in women's prisons, also explored by Atkinson, Monk and Sim in this volume (Chapter 10), in the drop in the prosecution of rape to the lowest ever recorded conviction rates, as already discussed in this chapter, and in relation to the asylum system (Canning, Chapter 7, this volume). Whether directly perpetrated by state actors or as an indirect result of state practices, the effect is the extension of interpersonal violence from the family to the institutional violence of the state, its institutions and practices (Richie, 2012; Davis, 2016).

Centralizing the role of the state and its relationship to the coercive maintenance and reproduction of a gendered social order, requires an analysis of the state's response to behaviours in both public and private. As Susan Edwards noted, there is a 'clear existence of a public/private divide in law, which organises and ratifies a different level of response to similar conduct in two terrains, including a different level of police response and priorities' (Edwards, 1989: 4). The Femicide Census report states that in 47 per cent of men's fatal violence against women, men used a sharp instrument as a weapon to kill (Long et al, 2020: 34). That is, 675 women were killed by being (repeatedly) struck by some sort of weapon and these women were seven times more likely to be killed in their own home than any outdoor or public area (Long et al, 2020: 34). The emphasis placed on the use of weapons in public space has shaped the law and order agenda, concentrating on the causes, prevention and punishment of conflict, crime and public, often racialized, disorder (Grimshaw and Ford, 2018; Williams and Clarke, 2018), at the expense of acknowledging and foregrounding weapons as the most frequent method of violence in femicides. What concerns us here, through an intersectional feminist lens, is that issues of private order are edged out of the debate. The maintenance and regulation of public order remains at the heart of the state and the phallocentric legal system's response to issues of criminal justice. This disjuncture is significant for several reasons.

First, this example brings into sharp focus Edwards' (1989) point about differential responses to similar conduct which takes place either in the full glare of public surveillance or the silence of the domesticized sphere. Drawing a state-led distinction here between the public and the private sphere is crucial to reinscribing women's place in the home, and, in turn, their place in the social order. One fundamental way of maintaining this ideology is by underutilizing the criminal law and criminal justice protections for women who are abused by men known to them (Hanmer et al, 1989; Naffine, 2003). Another way is to punish women who are seen to be disorderly, rather than necessarily law-breaking, in public (Chadwick and Little, 1987), an argument developed by Jackson and Monk in Chapter 6 of this collection.

Second, these different responses clearly delineate issues which are considered to be 'law and order issues'. A preoccupation with anti-social behaviour and violence in the public sphere and the state's woeful response to men's violence against women perpetrated predominantly in the private sphere, indicates that only certain forms of aggression are criminalized and discriminates between acceptable (private) and unacceptable (public) forms of violence (Radford, 1989; Naffine, 2003). Sitting outside of the dominant focus of law and order, the institution of the family, a well-established gender regime and one which acts as a collective site for the production of specific gendered behaviours and relations (Connell, 2009; Morris, 2009), is left largely unregulated by criminal law or state intervention (Naffine, 2003). To treat men's violence against women as a serious social harm and to afford women safety and protection in the private order of the family and the home, would serve to undermine the public social order that the state is so keen to uphold. We need to analyse the structural conditions under which certain forms of violence are sanctioned and unpick the proximity of these sanctioned acts to the stabilization of the social order (discussed further by Canning in Chapter 7 of this volume).

However, calls for more serious approaches to men's violence against women come alongside feminist calls for anti-carceral approaches, fewer police and less imprisonment. The issue of VAWG forces us to confront the intricacies and penological contradictions of these complex ideas. As we discuss further in this chapter, these arguments can be made simultaneously, with immediate reform to current systems (see Howe, Chapter 11, this volume) as a necessary part of the move towards more radical structural change towards what Carlen (1990), and many of this book's contributors, refer to as a 'woman [and girl] wise penology'.

## Challenging state power, seeking justice

Given the operation of power through criminal justice and state institutions, some feminists have engaged with the state, its institutions and practices, to different extents, in order to challenge the operation and exercise of patriarchal power. Feminists have been able to achieve reforms to policy and legislation, particularly in relation to sexual violence and violence against women. Notwithstanding this range of reforms, as Ballinger (2009) asserted, such changes have done little, if anything, to reduce the extent of sexual violence. She argues that when the failures of the state to respond to sexual violence are conceptualized as a '"legitimacy deficit"…that the law is faulty and in need of reform', they are removed from 'the structural context of the heteropatriarchal social order which feminists have identified as being responsible for gendered violence in the first place' (Ballinger, 2009: 4). The social context and the power of the law, which make gendered violence routine, Ballinger (2009) argues, remains effectively unchanged.

Lees (1997: 175) also noted the 'profound scepticism' of researching state institutions, particularly the legal system, due to the fact that too much is conceded when the state is engaged with. Rather than an acceptance of the significance of the law, Smart (1989) argues for a resistance to the law, as a system of knowledge which is juridogenic in nature and is enhanced by its extension into new modes of regulation and disciplinary mechanisms, a point picked up by Atkinson in Chapter 5. Ultimately, rather than focusing on reform, the law should be challenged on the grounds that it has the 'power to define and disqualify' (Smart, 1989: 164). Feminism's focus on the power of the law should, therefore, be to redefine law's 'truth' (Foucault, 2000), through the development and articulation of feminist knowledge, a focus which this collection seeks to address. Feminist use of the law and criminal justice institutions, as an avenue for intervention and seeking justice, is explored in Chapters 9 and 11 by Gill and Howe respectively, in relation to sexual abuse against British South Asian women and defences to intimate partner femicide.

It could be argued that through legal and policy reforms, campaigns against violence against women have achieved 'sufficient social validation … [and] won mainstream legitimization' (Richie, 2012: 65). For Richie (2012), however, this validation has been achieved through a softening of the radical politics of anti-violence, grassroots movements. That is a move from identifying sexual violence as a result of gender inequality in both public and private spheres, 'rooted in the politics of patriarchy' (Richie, 2012: 68), to a movement which has been institutionalized and co-opted. Reforms which result from such softened anti-violence politics, moreover, do little for the most marginalized women who often bear the brunt of hostile social policies which stigmatize and compound the impacts of men's violence (Richie, 2012). A feminist conceptualization of justice is therefore required, which not only highlights the organization of the social world as one in which women experience disproportionate levels of violence, but also recognizes that deferring to traditional institutional responses, 'places women on the margins (poor, black, trans, disabled) in danger' (Olufemi, 2020: 111–12).

As such, it is important to state what is meant, in this collection, by 'justice', particularly as we begin to make the case for a feminist criminology which is equipped to contest and dismantle the historically hetero-patriarchal state and the social harms it produces and maintains. It is not the remit of this collection to focus *only* on justice which is state-sanctioned. Indeed, as already noted, and as will be detailed in many of the chapters to follow, the CJS does not offer safety and justice to women and girls. For those who are harmed by misogyny and patriarchal structures, the CJS can be a site of secondary victimization and trauma. Rather than a focus, then, on criminal justice only, we propose a way of moving forward which challenges harm more widely and broadens our perception of justice.

The concept of social harm emerged from a critique of criminology which was developed by Hillyard and colleagues (2004). The authors contended that the discipline of criminology is problematic in its perpetuation of the myth of crime, which has no ontological reality and focuses its downward gaze on (often petty) crimes of the powerless. Criminology's focus, moreover, excludes state and corporate harm, legitimates the expansion of crime control and reinforces hegemonic power relations. Providing a new lens through which to view injustices, the authors argued for a move from the study of crime to the study of harm including: physical harms, financial/economic harms, emotional and psychological harms and cultural safety (for a consolidation and development of this typology of harms see Canning and Tombs, 2021, which adds harms of recognition and autonomy harms). In terms of an ontological basis for a social harm or zemiological approach, Pemberton (2015: 9) defines harms 'as specific events or instances where human flourishing is demonstrably compromised'. This theoretical framework takes into account the wider structural inequalities created by patriarchal, neoliberal, neo-colonial, heteronormative, ableist structures. Feminist studies of social harm both explicitly and implicitly apply these concepts when intersectionality is at the forefront of their investigations.

This does not mean, however, that all feminist studies are concerned with social harm. In particular, 'carceral feminism' which relies *only* on the structures of the carceral state to achieve justice can be critiqued. Phipps (2020: 46) argues that carceral feminism 'pays little or no attention to the people of colour and working-class white people who tend to be the targets of punitive state systems and community retribution'. As Watts (2018) has argued, the carceral shadow of the prison continues into the prisoner re-entry industry, and into carceral devolution in schools, welfare agencies and even supermarkets. As such, carceral feminism can increase women's experiences of harm in a number of ways. From the 1970s onwards, a movement led by Black feminists produced activist organizations which called for solutions to, and analysis of, both interpersonal and state violence. As McNaul (2021) sets out, this led to activist collaboration with the anti-prison movement to provide strategies for addressing violence experienced by women and LGBTQI people which provide safety and accountability. This collaboration continues to influence activist organizations in the US and beyond, for example in the Black Lives Matter movement and in Britain and Ireland, in the response to sexual violence and the violence of austerity as challenged by groups such as Sisters Uncut, Women in Prison, Alliance for Choice and Reclaim the Agenda (McNaul, 2021).

How, then, are just futures envisaged by anti-carceral approaches? Inspired by the work of anti-carceral Black feminists, Marc Lamont-Hill (2020) set out the possibility of anti-carceral futures in a recent examination of the role of policing and protest in the COVID-19 pandemic and the unfolding of the Movement for Black Lives in the US, and around the world. He argues:

> [W]e must ask challenging questions about the sources of the various forms of unsafety and harm we experience. We must also develop proactive measures to mitigate the harm we experience in our neighbourhoods. Investment in mental health, conflict resolution, violence interruption – not to mention food, clothing, shelter, education and living-wage jobs – are the starting point for addressing and preventing the various forms of suffering experienced by the vulnerable. (Lamont-Hill, 2020: 115)

To this, we add calls for properly funded domestic and sexual violence services, which the UN Special Rapporteur on extreme poverty have found 'not fit for purpose' (Alston, 2018: 142), an end to the 'hostile environment', equal access to abortion services across Britain, Ireland and beyond, high-quality childcare, decriminalization of sex work and drug use, and abolishing the politics of, and policies around, austerity in all its forms. McNaul (2021) calls for 'transformative justice' which supports and encourages recovery from interpersonal, cultural and institutional violence, building on the success of intersectional, feminist activism.

In addition to the need for a recognition of harm, beyond the category of crime, a reconceptualization of justice, which centralizes the person who has experienced injustice, and reflects the broad range of intersecting harms experienced by many is vital. Expanding our understanding of justice, beyond a punitive, reactive, carceral framework, means considering approaches which foreground prevention and offer a diversity of options for those who have been harmed. These options should reflect the harms experienced and offer the ability to take control of the process of justice seeking, a point which is imperative for those who have often had their decision-making capacities violated. One way in which this can be conceptualized is through expanding the discourse of justice to reflect the broad range of harms which result from injustices perpetrated at structural, subjective and discursive levels.

Discussing justice for those who have experienced sexual violence, McGlynn and Westmarland (2019: 179) developed the term 'kaleidoscopic justice' whereby justice is not solely understood through a 'linear, dichotomous and incident-based' (McGlynn and Westmarland, 2019: 181) criminal justice conceptualization in which justice is achieved, or not. Instead, kaleidoscopic justice reflects the fact that justice is 'a constantly shifting pattern … is constantly refracted through new experiences or understandings … and is an ever-evolving, nuanced lived experience' (McGlynn and Westmarland, 2019: 179). Justice is, moreover, understood as a collective pursuit and relates to 'consequences, recognition, dignity, voice, prevention and connectedness'.

Given the evidence, documented in this collection and elsewhere, which demonstrates the harms of the CJS, and state institutions more broadly, the principles of kaleidoscopic justice can be used to inform policies and practices which respond to those who have been harmed. McGlynn and Westmarland (2019) do highlight the harms of the CJS, and recognize this is not a suitable option for all, however, in recognition of the need to challenge the operation of state power, and the state's role in the perpetration and perpetuation of a multitude of harms, commitment to radical, transformative change to the operation of state institutions is also crucial. Therefore, beyond reforms to improve the current situation, it is key that these are undertaken alongside a broader commitment to radical, transformative change in society and its institutions.

As McGlynn and Westmarland (2019) and others note, justice ultimately equates to the prevention of harm. The safety and protection of women and girls from harms experienced at multiple levels, in public and private, is the goal. Taken together, the contributions to this collection evidence the need, as Sim (2020) highlights, to challenge dominant discourses of safety and protection and to make the connections between harms experienced by a range of marginalized groups. Overall, it is essential that harm and (in)justice are considered beyond limited, individualized and punitive frameworks in order to challenge the brutal and persistent maintenance of the dominant social order, outlined by Dobash and Dobash (1979) over 40 years ago.

## The gendered spectre of COVID-19

While writing and editing this book, COVID-19 took hold across the world, ushering in a global health pandemic which resulted in deaths on a mass scale, collective trauma and grief, new ways of being and a variety of measures taken by nation states to control and contain the virus, including what has come to be known as 'lockdown' in Britain and Ireland. Although data demonstrates that men die of COVID-19 at a higher rate (Mallapaty, 2020), the other silent killers in this crisis, not documented in the official, government statistics, are rooted in structural inequalities, brought to bear on marginalized groups through political and ideological decisions which pre-date the virus (Cooper and Whyte, 2017). At the same time, several modes of privilege and power have served to shift risk onto others. Women have performed more paid work on the frontline of the pandemic (Summers, 2021). The structural conditions and operation of systemic racism have also resulted in a disproportionate number of Black and Minority Ethnic people dying or becoming seriously ill from COVID-19 (Haque et al, 2020). Here, applying an intersectional lens to an analysis of those unduly affected by the disease is vitally important if we also wish to capture the wider implications of unequal power distribution (Haque et al, 2020).

Women have been impacted by the crisis in numerous ways. Existing issues have been exacerbated by COVID-19 and by the restrictions implemented to tackle the spread of the virus. The home is a notoriously unsafe space for many women. Levels of violence against women and girls increased as a result of lockdown measures globally (Sri et al, 2021). In the UK, within the first month of lockdown from March 2020, 16 women and girls were killed, a rate three times higher than the same period in 2019 (Taub and Bradley, 2020). Frontline services have experienced a rising demand for refuge space and support services during the pandemic citing a myriad of issues including an increase in domestic abuse, further restrictions to accessing support, additional barriers to leaving an abusive situation, increased abuse towards children and post-relationship abuse (Davldge, 2020). Black and minoritized women experienced an increase in interpersonal violence exacerbated by the heightened structural discrimination rampant throughout the pandemic (Banga and Roy, 2020). Similarly, the impact of COVID-19 on disabled women calls for a centralization of their experiences, in a landscape where access to health, medical and social care is restricted (Davldge, 2020). The decision not to undertake large-scale early release measures and radically reduce the prison population in the wake of COVID-19 has had devastating and deadly impact across the CJS (INQUEST, 2021). Short scrutiny visits by the Prisons Inspectorate (HM Chief Inspector of Prisons, 2020) highlighted the catastrophic impact of lockdown measures on the women's prison estate including reduced time out of cells, suspension of education, withdrawal of a range of interventions including reduced mental health support, suspension of family visits, and delays to the rollout of virtual visiting, which meant some women had not seen their children for months. These have no doubt contributed to the increase on the already high levels of self-harm in women's prisons with INQUEST (2021) noting a 13 per cent increase in the year to December 2020 on the previous year, and further increases in the first quarter of 2021.

The disproportionate impact of COVID-19 has also seeped through into other aspects of home and work life. Women are more likely to have taken on the home schooling of their children; have been dealt an unequal distribution of parenting responsibilities (Adams-Prassl et al, 2020); considered leaving or have left their work outside of the home (Topping, 2020); and faced redundancy and risk to employment going forward (Topping, 2021). This has been noted in academia with women publishing far less in lockdown than their male counterparts (Andersen et al, 2020). Certainly, as an all-woman editorial team we have faced our own challenges in completing this book. Deadlines passed as we worked, studied and parented at home (and finished a PhD in isolation!), separated from family, friends, colleagues and each other and grappling with the profound changes to our lives as feminist academics. The reactivation of prescribed gender roles in the home during lockdown deserves attention, and most certainly lockdown conditions had an impact on the longevity of writing this collection, for us, and many of the contributing authors. The chapters that make up this collection, consequently, span a three-year period (2019–21), an unavoidable outcome of being thrown into a global health crisis and one that deserves documenting for posterity reasons if nothing else.

Moving forward, the pandemic has exacerbated gender inequalities in almost all senses, rolling back gains made through feminist praxis and activism in recent years. Long-term consequences of the pandemic are estimated to effect women disproportionately in a range of areas, including employment, wage earnings, the gender pay gap, employment rights, maternity discrimination, childcare accessibility, and victimization (Topping, 2020). As such, the material and symbolic effects of COVID-19 are ripe for feminist analysis.

It is our assertion that the conditions under which we have had to live and work during the pandemic will undoubtedly shape and revise the feminist tools (Ahmed, 2017) with which we can contest and challenge the state's gendered strategy of discipline, punishment and control. While we do not have the space to sufficiently consider what a feminist criminology will look like in the age of COVID-19, and many of the contributions to this collection pre-date the pandemic, the prospect of our lives being radically changed on a number of different levels does raise significant questions for feminist theory and practice. We hope that feminists, including those who work with questions of injustice with the central aim of holding the state to account, can continue to produce ways of knowing that enable us to move forward in this new era, and that the terrain that we outline here will be useful in this period of adaptation. Despite the uncertain political, social and economic landscape left by the onslaught of COVID-19, this new decade is an energetic and creative time for feminist thought and praxis across the social sciences.

## Structure of the collection

This book is divided into three parts. This introduction sits alongside Chapter 2 (Anette Ballinger) and, taken together, these chapters discuss the continuities across contemporary and long-standing concerns around the brutal exercise of patriarchal state power and injustice. Ballinger revisits her pertinent question from her seminal piece 'Gender, power and the state: Same as it ever was?' (2009). The chapter foregrounds an understanding of all knowledge as politically situated and interrogates how regulatory state apparatuses across Britain and Ireland contribute to experiences of gendered injustice. Drawing upon arguments which seek to explain the state's material and ideological interventions into maintaining and reproducing a hetero-patriarchal social order, these two chapters contribute towards our aim to extend critical, feminist, intersectional analysis through the concepts of feminist epistemology and feminist praxis, illustrating their usefulness as theoretical, methodological and political models for the 21st century.

The second part of the book explores the relationship between state practice and feminist praxis. The third part presents a critical analysis of the role of the CJS in patriarchal structures of domination and subjugation and their relationship with feminist praxis. In both parts, the authors all support the arguments for intersectional feminist justice, based on the myriad of case studies and theoretical perspectives examined. Justice in all cases is interrogated from a feminist perspective. Yet, as is to be expected in an edited collection, there is no one-size-fits-all solution offered to the multitude of gendered harms examined. In a number of chapters, the harms of the CJS itself are expounded upon, for example Jackson and Monk in Chapter 6 examine police as both perpetrators of violence and ineffective protectors. Howe (in Chapter 11) considers the (mostly) historical injustices perpetuated by the provocation defence of infidelity in the context of femicide. Hodgson and Barr and Hart (Chapters 12 and 8) respectively examine the harms faced by criminalized girls and women. Self-harm and the deaths of women in prison are critically examined by Atkinson, Monk and Sim in Chapter 10. In both Gill and McDaid and Nelis' chapters (9 and 3) the neglect of attention by the state to harms experienced by certain groups of women – British South Asian Women experiencing sexual abuse and Irish women seeking abortions, including in the six counties of Northern Ireland, is critiqued. Similarly, the neglect of state attention to the gendered aspects of child sexual abuse is examined by Tucker in Chapter 4. Harm producing aspects of state institutions are examined in Chapter 5, in Atkinson's exploration of sexual violence against women university students and the 'truth' that is constructed about this violence. Canning also explores intersectional experiences of harm in Chapter 7, highlighting the myriad forms of patriarchal and racist harms experienced by women (often survivors of sexual violence) seeking asylum in the North West of England.

Again, as would be expected from a diverse range of feminist researchers, there are a variety of theoretical, methodological and activist implications for achieving justice. Some of the chapters take an explicitly anti-carceral or abolitionist approach to achieving gendered justice. Barr and Hart, for example, examine the theoretical and practical implications of developing a feminist desistance which is intersectional and anti-carceral in nature. Hodgson proposes the development of a 'girl-wise penology' which directly challenges the harms of the carceral state particularly faced by criminal justice involved girls. Atkinson, Monk and Sim also return to Pat Carlen's (1990) call for a 'woman wise penology' built on an 'open-ended feminist jurisprudence' as key steps leading eventually to 'the virtual abolition of women's imprisonment' (Carlen, 1990: 9 cited in Atkinson, Monk and Sim, Chapter 10, this volume).

A number of other chapters also situate justice beyond the realms of the CJS, in particular noting how state institutions, which appear to have reformed and focused on justice, must be continuously challenged from an avowedly feminist perspective. Canning presents a six-point proposal for those working on women's right to asylum, which includes a recognition of the asylum system as something which is not broken but is working as it is intended to, in a harmful way. McDaid and Nelis note that decriminalization of abortion in Ireland has not automatically meant comprehensive provision of abortion access, and, they argue, attention must be paid, and challenge must be given, to the continued denial of bodily autonomy rights. Tucker highlights how intersectional feminist interventions into child sexual abuse have been marginalized and subjugated by official discourse despite heightened public awareness of the issue. Atkinson points to the institutional failings of universities in responding to sexual violence and outlines a framework, based on feminist praxis, for placing victim- and survivor-led responses at the centre of interventions. Jackson and Monk simply call for policing to always be considered as a feminist issue.

Gill examines the potential of reform to policing to encourage the reporting of sexual abuse among South Asian women. What is needed, Gill contends, is a 'multi-layered, intersectional and integrated approach' to understanding how social and cultural difference affects gendered violence, and how it is responded to by the police, in relation to Black and racially minoritized women. Howe celebrates the success of feminist interventions to reform the legal system by ending provocation defences of infidelity for wife-killers. As she persuasively argues, this must surely count as a resounding success for a feminist reform movement determined to stop men getting away with murder. In both chapters, the need for immediate intersectional reform is clear in the absence of community justice alternatives. Moderate tools can nonetheless achieve radical aims. As Bree Carlton (2018) has maintained, anti-carceral feminist approaches to justice can be informed by feminist reforms, even to the CJS. Carlton (2018) rejects the simplistic dualism of reform and abolition, particularly in the seeking, demanding and implementing of feminist justice. These chapters have at their heart a resistance to gendered violence, whether this violence is interpersonal, symbolic or is perpetrated by the state. On this note, 'reformist strategies … within a broader vision striving for social and structural change rather than just penal change is the only way forward' (Carlton, 2018: 302). This argument is reflected across the chapters in this collection which call for immediate feminist intervention to radically change the socially harmful systems of patriarchal power at all levels of a gender divided society.

Ultimately, in the 21st century, against the current tumultuous economic, political, ideological and cultural backdrop, and the desperate and traumatic impact of this backdrop on women and girls across a range of different social arenas, the contributions to this collection explore contemporary research areas and consider new directions in feminist research, theory, policy and practice in order to present a feminist criminology for this century. It seeks, in its own way, to contribute to a socially just and safe world for women and girls.

### Notes

[1]  The chapter title is paraphrased from Susan Brownmiller's classic text *Against Our Will* (1975: 454).

[2] The chapters in this collection utilize varying terminology to denote ethnicity and 'race'. While we, as editors, utilize the term Black and racially minoritized women where relevant, we also reproduce the original terminology used in sources when this is what we are directly referring to and when data has been collected through use of this terminology. Other contributors use different language which reflects, as specifically as possible, the ethnicity, 'race' and processes of minoritization imposed on the people being referred to.

[3] The case is explained further by Jackson and Monk, Chapter 6 in this collection.

[4] The Metropolitan Police failed the family of Bibaa Henry and Nicole Smallman when they did not follow their missing person's policies. Two Metropolitan Police officers are also facing criminal charges over taking photos at the scene where the sisters' bodies were found murdered. See Dodd (2021) for more details.

## References

Adams-Prassl, A., Boneva, T., Golin, M. and Rauh, C. (2020) *Inequality in the Impact of the Coronavirus Shock: Evidence from Real Time Surveys*, Bonn: IZA Institute of Labor Economics.

Ahmed, S. (2017) *Living a Feminist Life*, Durham, NC and London: Duke University Press.

Alcoff, L.M. (2018) *Rape and Resistance*, Cambridge: Polity Press.

Alston, P. (2018) *Statement on Visit to the United Kingdom, by Professor Philip Alston, United Nations Special Rapporteur on Extreme Poverty and Human Rights*, available at: https://www.ohchr.org/EN/NewsEvents/Pages/Disp layNews.aspx?NewsID=23881&LangID=E [accessed 27 December 2018].

Andersen, J.P., Nielsen, M.W., Simone, N.L., Lewiss, R.E. and Jagsi, R. (2020) 'COVID-19 medical papers have fewer women first authors than expected', *eLife*, 9: e58807.

Ballinger, A. (2009) 'Gender, power and the state: Same as it ever was?' in R. Coleman, J. Sim, S. Tombs and D. Whyte (eds) *State, Power, Crime*, London: SAGE, pp 20–3.

Banga, B. and Roy, S. (2020) *The Impact of the Dual Pandemics: Violence against Women and Girls and COVID-19 on Black and Minoritised Women and Girls*, London: Imkaan.

BBC News (2021) 'Sarah Everard: Met PC Wayne Couzens charged with murder', *BBC News*, [online] 13 March, available at: https://www.bbc.co.uk/news/uk-england-london-56331948 [accessed 4 May 2021].

Bumiller, K. (1987) 'Rape as a legal symbol: An essay on sexual violence and racism', *University of Miami Law Review*, 42(1): 75–91.

Burgess-Proctor, A. (2006) 'Intersections of race, class, gender, and crime: Future directions for feminist criminology', *Feminist Criminology*, 1(1): 27–47.

Canning, V. and Tombs, S. (2021) *From Social Harm to Zemiology*, London: Taylor & Francis.

Carlen, P. (1983) *Women's Imprisonment: A Study in Social Control*, London: Routledge and Kegan Paul.

Carlen, P. (1990) *Alternatives to Women's Imprisonment*, Milton Keynes: Open University Press.

Carlen, P. (1998) *Sledgehammer: Women's Imprisonment at the Millennium*, London: Palgrave Macmillan.

Carlton, B. (2018) 'Penal reform, anti-carceral feminist campaigns and the politics of change in women's prisons, Victoria, Australia', *Punishment & Society*, 20(3): 283–307.

Carrington, K. (2018) 'Feminist criminologies' in P. Carlen and L.A. França (eds) *Alternative Criminologies*, Abingdon: Routledge, pp 110–24.

Centre for Women's Justice (2020) 'Evidence of CPS failure on rape', [online] available at: https://www.centreforwomensjustice.org.uk/news/2020/6/29/1pti6p5e19unqglo7wd9mm68d621b7 [accessed 12 August 2021].

Centre for Women's Justice (2021) 'Women's groups deeply disappointed by judges failure to hold CPS accountable on rape prosecutions collapse', [online] available at: https://www.centreforwomensjustice.org.uk/news/2021/3/15/pr-rape-prosecutions-todays-judgment [accessed 4 May 2021].

Chadwick, K. and Little, C. (1987) 'The criminalization of women' in P. Scraton (ed) *Law, Order and the Authoritarian State*, Milton Keynes: Open University Press, pp 355–60.

Chesney-Lind, M. and Irwin, K. (2008) 'Girls gone wild?' in M. Chesney-Lind and K. Irwin (eds) *Beyond Bad Girls: Gender, Violence and Hype*, New York: Routledge, pp 1–10.

Clarke, B. and Chadwick, K. (2020) *Stories of Injustice: The Criminalisation of Women Convicted Under Joint Enterprise Laws*, London: Barrow Cadbury Trust.

Collins, P.H. (2000) *Black Feminist Thought: Knowledge, Consciousness, and the Politics of Empowerment* (second edition), London: Unwin Hyman.

Connell, R. (1994) 'The state, gender and sexual politics' in H.L. Radtke and J. Stam (eds) *Power/Gender: Social Relations in Theory and Practice*, London: SAGE, pp 136–73.

Connell, R. (2009) *Gender*, Cambridge: Polity Press.

Connell, R. and Pearse, R. (2015) *Gender: In World Perspective*, Cambridge: Polity Press.

Cooper, V. and Whyte, D. (2017) *The Violence of Austerity*, London: Pluto Press.

Crenshaw, K. (1991) 'Mapping the margins: Intersectionality, identity politics, and violence against women of color', *Stanford Law Review*, 43(6): 1241–99.

Daly, K. (2010) 'Feminist perspectives in criminology: A review with Gen Y in mind' in E. McLaughlin and T. Newburn (eds) *The SAGE Handbook of Criminological Theory*, London: SAGE, pp 225–46.

Daly, K. and Stephens, D.J. (1995) 'The "dark figure" of criminology: Towards a Black and multi-ethnic feminist agenda for theory and research' in N. Hahn Rafter and F. Heidensohn (eds) *International Feminist Perspectives in Criminology: Engendering a Discipline*, Philadelphia: Open University Press, pp 189–215.

Davis, A.Y. (1983) *Women, Race and Class*, New York: Vintage Books.

Davis, A.Y. (2016) *Freedom is a Constant Struggle*, Chicago: Haymarket Books.

Davldge, S. (2020) *A Perfect Storm: The Impact of the COVID-19 Pandemic on Domestic Abuse Survivors and the Services Supporting Them*, Bristol: Women's Aid Federation of England.

Dobash, R.E. and Dobash, R.P. (1979) *Violence Against Wives: A Case against the Patriarchy*, New York: Free Press.

Dodd, V. (2021) 'Metropolitan police failed family of murdered sisters, watchdog finds', *The Guardian*, [online] 25 October, available at: https://www.theguardian.com/uk-news/2021/oct/25/metropolitan-police-to-apologise-to-family-of-murdered-sisters [accessed 25 October 2021].

Edwards, S.M. (1989) *Policing 'Domestic' Violence: Women, the Law and the State*, London: SAGE.

Foucault, M. (1977) *Discipline and Punish: The Birth of the Modern Prison*, New York: Pantheon Books.

Foucault, M. (1980) *Power/ Knowledge: Selected Interviews and Other Writings 1972–1977*, edited by C. Gordon, New York: Penguin Books.

Foucault, M. (2000) 'Truth and power' in D. Faubion (ed) *Michel Foucault: Essential Works of Foucault 1954–1984* (volume 3), London: Penguin Books, pp 111–33.

Gavey, N. (2005) *Just Sex: The Cultural Scaffolding of Rape*, East Sussex: Routledge.

Gavey, N. (2019) 'Men's violence against women: The blind spots in the Grace Millane trial', *The Spinoff*, [online] 26 November, available at: https://thespinoff.co.nz/society/26-11-2019/mens-violence-against-women-the-blind-spots-in-the-grace-millane-trial/ [accessed 11 August 2021].

Grimshaw, R. and Ford, M. (2018) *Young People, Violence and Knives: Revisiting the Evidence and Policy Discussions*, London: Centre for Crime and Justice Studies.

Hanmer, J., Radford, J. and Stanko, E. (eds) (1989) *Women, Policing, and Male Violence: International Perspectives*, London: Routledge.

Haque, Z., Becares, L. and Treloar, N. (2020) *Over-Exposed and Under-Protected: The Devastating Impact of COVID-19 on Black and Minority Ethnic Communities in Great Britain*, London: Runnymede Trust.

Harte, A. (2019) 'A man tried to choke me during sex without warning', *BBC*, [online] 28 November, available at: https://www.bbc.co.uk/news/uk-50546184 [accessed 3 June 2021].

Hillyard, P., Pantazis, C., Tombs, S. and Gordon, D. (2004) *Beyond Criminology: Taking Harm Seriously*, London: Pluto Press.

HM Chief Inspector of Prisons (2020) *Report on Short Scrutiny Visits to Prisons Holding Women*, available at: https://www.justiceinspectorates.gov.uk/hmi prisons/wp-content/uploads/sites/4/2020/06/Womens-prisons-SSV2020. pdf [accessed 4 April 2022].

hooks, b. (1992) *Black Looks: Race and Representation*, Boston: South End Press.

Howe, A. (2008) *Sex, Violence and Crime: Foucault and the 'Man' Question*, Abingdon: Routledge-Cavendish.

INCITE! (2018) *Law Enforcement Violence against Women of Color and Trans People of Color: A Critical Intersection of Gender Violence and State Violence*, Washington, DC: INCITE! [online] available at: https://incite-national. org/wp-content/uploads/2018/08/TOOLKIT-FINAL.pdf [accessed 6 April 2021].

INQUEST (2018) *Still Dying on the Inside: Examining Women's Deaths in Prison*, London: Inquest.

INQUEST (2021) 'INQUEST responds to record number of deaths in prison', [online] 29 April, available at: https://www.inquest.org.uk/ inquest-responds-to-record-number-of-deaths-in-prison [accessed 21 July 2021].

Kelly, L. (1988) *Surviving Sexual Violence*, Minneapolis: University of Minnesota Press.

King, D.K. (1988) 'Multiple jeopardy, multiple consciousness: The context of a black feminist ideology', *Signs*, 14(1): 42–72.

Lamont-Hill, M. (2020) *We Still Here: Pandemic, Policing, Protest, and Possibility*, Chicago: Haymarket Books.

Lees, S. (1997) *Ruling Passions: Sexual Violence, Reputation and the Law*, Buckingham: Open University Press.

Levy, A. (2005) *Female Chauvinist Pigs: Women and the Rise of Raunch Culture*, New York: Free Press.

Long, J., Wertens, E., Harper, K., Brennan, D., Harvey, H., Allen, R. and Elliot, K. (2020) *Femicide Census: UK Femicides 2009–2018*, [online] available at: https://www.femicidecensus.org/wp-content/uploads/2020/ 11/Femicide-Census-10-year-report.pdf [accessed 11 August 2021].

Mallapaty, S. (2020) 'The coronavirus is most deadly if you are older and male: New data reveal the risks', *Nature*, [online] available at: https:// www.nature.com/articles/d41586-020-02483-2 [accessed 19 July 2021].

McGlynn, C. and Westmarland, N. (2019) 'Kaleidoscopic justice: Sexual violence and victim-survivors' perceptions of justice', *Social and Legal Studies*, 28(2): 179–201.

McNaul, G. (2021) 'Contextualising violence: An anti-carceral feminist approach' in R. Killean, E. Dowds and A.M. McAlinden (eds) *Sexual Violence on Trial: Local and Comparative Perspectives*, London: Routledge, pp 213–28.

Mohanty, C. (1988) 'Under western eyes: Feminist scholarship and colonial discourses', *Feminist Review*, 30: 61–88.

Monk, H. and Sim, J. (2017) *Women, Crime and Criminology: A Celebration*, London: EG Press and Centre for the Study of Crime, Criminalisation and Social Exclusion.

Morris, A. (2009) 'Gendered dynamics of abuse and violence in families: Considering the abusive household gender regime', *Child Abuse Review*, 18(6): 414–27.

Naffine, N. (2003) 'The "man question" of crime, criminology and criminal law', *Criminal Justice Matters*, 53(1): 10–11.

Olufemi, L. (2020) *Feminism Interrupted: Disrupting Power*, London: Pluto Press.

Paik, L. (2017) 'Critical perspectives on intersectionality and criminology: Introduction', *Theoretical Criminology*, 21(1): 4–10.

Parmar, A. (2017) 'Intersectionality, British criminology and race: Are we there yet?', *Theoretical Criminology*, 21(1): 35–45.

Pemberton, S. (2015) *Harmful Societies: Understanding Social Harm*, Bristol: Policy Press.

Phipps, A. (2019) 'The fight against sexual violence', *Soundings: A Journal of Politics and Culture*, 71: 62–74.

Phipps, A. (2020) *Me Not You: The Trouble with Mainstream Feminism*, Manchester: Manchester University Press.

Potter, H. (2013) 'Intersectional criminology: Interrogating identity and power in criminological research and theory', *Critical Criminology*, 21(3): 305–18.

Potter, H. (2015) *Intersectionality and Criminology: Disrupting and Revolutionizing Studies of Crime*, London: Routledge.

Radford, J. (1989) 'Women and policing: Contradictions old and new' in J. Hanmer, J. Radford and E. Stanko (eds) *Women, Policing, and Male Violence: International Perspectives*, London: Routledge, pp 13–45.

Rice, M. (1990) 'Challenging orthodoxies in feminist theory: A black feminist critique' in L. Gelsthorpe, and A. Morris (eds) *Feminist Perspectives in Criminology*, Buckinghamshire: Open University Press, pp 57–69.

Richie, B.E. (1996) *Compelled to Crime: The Gender Entrapment of Battered Black Women*, New York: Routledge.

Richie, B.E. (2005) 'A black feminist reflection on the antiviolence movement' in N.J. Sokoloff and C. Pratt (eds) *Domestic Violence at the Margins: Readings on Race, Class, Gender, and Culture*, New Brunswick: Rutgers University Press, pp 50–5.

Richie, B.E. (2012) *Arrested Justice: Black Women, Violence and America's Prison Nation*, New York: New York University Press.

Sim, J. (2020) ' "Help me please": Death and self-harm in male prisons in England and Wales' in M. Coyle and D. Scott (eds) *The Routledge International Handbook of Penal Abolition*, Abingdon: Routledge, pp 119–30.

Smart, C. (1976) *Women, Crime and Criminology: A Feminist Critique*, London: RKP.

Smart, C. (1989) *Feminism and the Power of Law*, London: Routledge.

Smart, C. (1995) *Law, Crime and Sexuality: Essays in Feminism*, London: SAGE.

Spivak, G. (1990) 'Criticism, feminism and the institution' in S. Harasym (ed) *The Post-Colonial Critic*, New York: Routledge, pp 1–16.

SPYCOPS (2021) 'SPYCOPS: The story', [online] available at: https://www.spycops.co.uk/the-story/ [accessed 4 May 2021].

Sri, A.S., Das, P., Gnanapragasam, S. and Persaud, A. (2021) 'COVID-19 and the violence against women and girls: "The shadow pandemic"', *International Journal of Social Psychiatry*, 67(8): 971–3.

Stanley, L. (1990) 'Feminist praxis and the academic mode of production: An editorial introduction' in L. Stanley (ed) *Feminist Praxis: Research Theory and Epistemology in Feminist Sociology*, London: Routledge, pp 3–19.

Summers, H. (2021) 'UK government "failed to consider gender" in its response to Covid pandemic', *The Guardian*, [online] 8 May, available at: https://www.theguardian.com/world/2021/may/08/uk-government-failed-to-consider-gender-in-its-response-to-covid-pandemic [accessed 3 June 2021].

Taub, A. and Bradley, J. (2020) 'As domestic abuse rises, UK failings leave victims in peril', *New York Times*, [online] 21 July, available at: https://www.nytimes.com/interactive/2020/07/02/world/europe/uk-coronavirus-domestic-abuse.html [accessed 22 July 2021].

Thiara, R.K. and Gill, A.K. (2010) 'Understanding violence against South Asian women: What it means for practice' in R.K. Thiara and A.K. Gill (eds) *Violence Against Women in South Asian Communities: Issues for Policy and Practice*, London: Jessica Kingsley Publishers, pp 29–54.

Topping, A. (2020) 'COVID-19 crisis could set women back decades, experts fear', *The Guardian*, [online] 3 June, available at: https://www.theguardian.com/world/2020/may/29/covid-19-crisis-could-set-women-back-decades-experts-fear [accessed 3 June 2021].

Topping, A. (2021) 'Women face significant jobs risk during Covid pandemic, UK analysis finds', *The Guardian*, [online] 4 May, available at: https://www.theguardian.com/world/2021/may/04/women-jobs-risk-covid-pandemic-uk-analysis [accessed 4 May 2021].

Topping, A. and Barr, C. (2020) 'Prosecution service under fire over record low rape convictions', *The Guardian*, [online] 30 July, available at: https://www.theguardian.com/society/2020/jul/30/prosecution-service-under-fire-over-record-low-convictions [accessed 27 July 2021].

Ussher, J. (1997) *Fantasies of Femininity: Reframing the Boundaries of Sex*, London: Penguin.

Watts, J. (2018) 'No wonder people on benefits live in fear: Supermarkets spy on them now', *The Guardian*, [online] 31 May, available at: https://www.theguardian.com/commentisfree/2018/may/31/benefits-claimants-fear-supermarkets-spy-poor-disabled [accessed 29 April 2021].

We Can't Consent To This (2020) *Consent Defences and the Criminal Justice System*, [online] available at: https://static1.squarespace.com/static/5c49b798e749409bfb9b6ef2/t/5ee12c4d1cdc3e7c573e43a6/1591815261033/WCCTT+Criminal+Justice+System+and+Consent+Defences.pdf [accessed 13 April 2021].

Whalley, E. and Hackett, C. (2017) 'Carceral feminisms: The abolitionist project and undoing dominant feminisms', *Contemporary Justice Review*, 20(4): 456–73.

Williams, P. and Clarke, B. (2018) 'The black criminal other as an object of social control', *Social Sciences*, 7(11): 234–67.

Yuval-Davis, N. (2006) 'Intersectionality and feminist politics', *European Journal of Women's Studies*, 13(3): 193–209.

2

# Denying Violence against Women a Future:[1] Feminist Epistemology and the Struggle for Social Justice

*Anette Ballinger*

## Introduction

In 2009, during an assessment of the progress made in eliminating violence against women over the past three decades and achieving social and financial equality with men, I argued that 'the clock had stopped' (Ballinger, 2009: 21). This argument was based on the findings of feminist activist groups and organizations, as well as statistics published in various official and non-governmental organization reports. For example, in 2007, the Fawcett Society estimated that 'at the present rate of change, it will take 140 years before women achieve equal pay' (*Guardian*, 14 June 2007, in Ballinger, 2009: 21). That year also saw the publication of the *Equalities Review Report* which pointed to the existence of 'an array of "entrenched" inequalities' so extensive that 'in some areas "we have stopped the clock"'; in others, 'it is starting to turn backwards' (in Ballinger, 2009: 21).

In terms of violence against women during the first decade of the 21st century, it was estimated that 50,000 rapes occurred annually in Britain, while the conviction rate for reported cases stood at 5.3 per cent (*New Statesman*, in Ballinger, 2009: 21). On average, two women were killed a week 'by a current or former partner', while 'domestic violence was the biggest cause of death and disability for all women under the age of 44' (Council of Europe, 2006, in Ballinger, 2009: 21).

To place these statistics within a wider context, while the figure for domestic violence-related female deaths had remained unaltered for several decades, cases of reported rape had increased by 165 per cent during the 1990s (Itzin, 2000: 37). Thus, during an era where women had *appeared* to gain unprecedented levels of personal and economic freedom and formal equality – reinforced by the Gender Equality Duty legislation in 2007 – violence against women either remained static, or continued to increase.

As stated, a key theme in my publication 'Same as it ever was?' – where the statistics were brought together and published at the end of the first decade of the 21st century – was to assess what progress had been made since the 1970s, in creating substantive, as well as formal equality between women and men, and thus, ensuring social justice for all. Instead, the statistics provided a small sample of a much larger dataset which confirmed that the clock had indeed stopped, and in some cases, started 'to turn backwards' – not only in terms of equal pay – but also with regard to eliminating violence against women in the UK.

As we enter the third decade of the 21st century, feminist scholars are therefore justified in asking: what progress, if any, has been made during this last decade, in terms of reducing violence against women and creating social justice for all? Living without fear of physical attack and feeling confident that justice will be achieved for victim-survivors of gendered violence when it does occur, form two crucial aspects of substantive as well as legal justice. An assessment of the statistical evidence on these topics with regard to the second decade of this century is therefore essential.

Statistics published in 2019 reveal there has been a 'collapse in rape cases that end up in court [with] only one in 65 rape cases reported to the police result[ing] in suspects being summonsed or charged' (Bowcott and Barr, 2019a). This demonstrates a substantial drop since 2015–16 when 14 per cent 'of cases led to a suspect being charged or summonsed', compared to 1.5 per cent today (Bowcott and Barr, 2019a: 1). Furthermore, estimated cases of rape are now 97,000 annually, an increase of almost 100 per cent since 2009, with 'a conviction less likely than a decade ago' (Bowcott and Barr, 2019a: 1), an observation which has led Hitchen to comment that 'of every 200 cases of rape reported to the police, only three will actually be prosecuted and go to trial. If nothing changes we can argue that rape has effectively been decriminalised' (cited in Bowcott and Barr, 2019a: 6). Data emerging from the Prime Minister's Implementation Unit[2] indicate that between 2014 and 2018 'recorded rape increased by 173 per cent, while police referred 19 per cent fewer cases for charging decisions, and CPS decisions to prosecute tumbled by 44 per cent in the same period' (Bowcott and Barr, 2019b).

A similar picture emerges with regard to recently self-reported statistics concerned with domestic violence. The Crime Survey of England and Wales (CSEW) indicates that:

7.9 per cent (1.3 million) of women experienced some form of domestic abuse in the year ending March 2018, and an estimated 28.9

per cent (4.8 million) of women aged 16 to 59 years have experienced some form of domestic abuse. ... On average the police in England and Wales receive over 100 calls relating to domestic abuse every hour. (HMIC, 2015, in Domestic Abuse Bill 2017–19, 2019)

In total, the police recorded 599,549 domestic abuse-related crimes in the year ending March 2018, an increase of 23 per cent from the previous year, according to the Office for National Statistics (ONS) (in Domestic Abuse Bill 2017–19, 2019).

While increases in recorded rape and domestic violence may be partly due to an increased willingness to report, this should be seen within the context that both crimes are notoriously 'hidden' in nature and, as such, remain hugely under-reported.[3] The ONS observed that 'over recent years there has been little change in the prevalence of domestic abuse' (in Domestic Abuse Bill 2017–19, 2019). Davina James-Hanman – a consultant on violence against women, who has authored over 30 domestic homicide reviews in as many years – disagrees. She observes that in 2018, 173 people were killed through domestic violence, 'the highest number for five years', and that those killed by partners or ex-partners are currently averaging three a week, 73 per cent of whom are women (James-Hanman, in Usborne, 2019: 4).

In sum, as was the case a decade ago, there is extensive evidence currently to indicate that the clock has indeed stopped, or, in some cases, is running backwards, when it comes to protecting women from male violence and moving towards achieving gender equality. How can this be? After all, neither politicians nor the criminal justice system have been impervious to issues around violence against women. On the contrary, as had been the case prior to 2009, an array of proposals, initiatives and legislative measures have been introduced during the past decade. A recent example is that of the Domestic Abuse Bill, published in draft form in January 2019, which proposes to widen the definition of domestic violence, to include economic abuse. It will also reform the nature of protection orders into Domestic Abuse Protection Orders, the intention being to improve the process involved in obtaining them (Duggan, 2019). At a global level, 'the UK has become the *biggest* government funder of projects to prevent violence against women and girls ... with the launch of a seven-year project targeting countries with some of the worst abuse' (Ford, 2019: 18, emphasis added).

Thus, the question remains: why is it that despite a willingness of consecutive governments to implement measures designed to increase women's safety, progress in protecting women from male violence has been virtually nonexistent? Put another way, why is it, that despite considerable progress in obtaining legal equality over the last half a century, progress in ensuring women's safety – an essential aspect of *substantive* equality, and therefore, also an essential aspect of women's *lived* realities – has failed to materialize?

To answer this question it is necessary to examine the nature and operation of the state itself and within that, the legal system which forms a crucial aspect of the state, since both ultimately are responsible for determining how women's subordination is addressed, whether in financial, legal or social terms. Thus, in the following section I provide a brief outline of the contribution made by feminist scholars over the past 50 years, with specific focus on a feminist analysis of the criminal justice system, as well as of the state itself within which it operates. It will become apparent that this contribution rests firmly on an interpretive underpinning of feminist epistemology, because, as I shall demonstrate, only this particular theory of knowledge has the capacity to offer an adequate analysis of the continuing failure of legal reforms to reduce statistics such as those outlined. I therefore begin by tracing the history and development of feminist epistemology itself. This is followed by an acknowledgement of the fundamental impact feminist theory has had on the study of gender, as well as a review of the symbiotic relationship which exists between epistemology and theory, for it is largely as a result of the work of second-wave feminists in developing these two analytical tools that we have a wealth of statistics available to us, as exemplified.

To illustrate the continuing importance of this symbiotic relationship in the 21st century, I apply themes and perspectives from the previous sections to the case of Fri Martin, who in 2015 received a life sentence after being found guilty of murdering her abusive partner. This case will be analysed to illustrate that feminist epistemology and theory have not only been successful in uncovering the deplorable level of female victimization taking place within the private sphere; it has also addressed the fate of those women who eventually retaliate against such victimization. As I shall demonstrate, here too law remains phallocentric in its treatment of women, due to its failure to adequately consider the material circumstances leading up to such retaliation, particularly the brutal exercise of patriarchal power.

The final section explores the impact that modern technology and social media have had – not only in normalizing pornography and sexualizing violence against women – but also in generating new forms of gendered violence and social control of women in the 21st century.

## Creating knowledge from below: a brief history of the feminist challenge to traditional knowledge production

> Law's purported neutrality is simply a mask for the 'masculinity' of its judgements.
>
> Mackinnon, cited in Collier (2010: 15)

Following the arrival of second-wave feminism in the early 1970s, the creation of a feminist epistemology can be understood as having gone hand in hand with emerging perspectives of feminist theory, culminating in analysis of the very foundations and principles upon which knowledge – and therefore reality itself – is founded. With the publication of *Breaking Out* in 1983, Stanley and Wise had created a ground-breaking book which systematically challenged the methods employed by traditional positivist researchers and their claim to produce 'objective' knowledge. The authors argued that this type of research was phallocentric in nature – 'neither objective nor value-free' but 'the creation of masculine subjectivity' and 'masculine ideologies' (Stanley and Wise, 1983: 49, 12).

Following this publication, a number of feminist scholars developed specific justificatory strategies within feminist epistemology, all of which have contributed to the establishment of a feminist theory of knowledge that is capable of identifying and challenging power relationships within knowledge production (see, for example, Harding, 1986, 1987, 1990; Smart, 1989; Cain, 1990a, 1990b; Holmwood, 1995).[4] A key aspect of this epistemology was its embracing of 'the politics of naming' (Ballinger, 2016a: 9) which enabled it to create new discourses based not on 'objective research' but on women's lived experiences, a process which, in turn, resulted in the excavation of new knowledge from 'below' – and crucially – from within the private sphere (Ballinger, 2016a: 12; 2011: 112). For example, contemporary terms such as 'domestic violence' entered discourse for the first time as part of a new language created by second-wave feminists, thereby ensuring that, henceforth, it would be visible on 'the public agenda' and, as such, would require a response from state agencies (Ballinger, 2012: 309).

The impact of feminist epistemology on research methods and methodology cannot be overestimated, inspiring as it did, an entire re-evaluation of the nature of knowledge itself, how it is produced and by whom, for what purpose and whose benefit (Ballinger, 2016a: 9). Thus, the establishment of feminist epistemology saw the end of an automatic acceptance of universalizing truth-claims, created by powerful Enlightenment discourses that involved the application of scientific methods for the purpose of reaching an 'objective truth' (Holmwood, 1995: 420). As Foucault has observed: 'Far from being based in reason and rationality, Enlightenment truth production is based on the disqualification of "minor" knowledge "in order to promote centralisation, normalisation and disciplinarisation of dominant knowledges"' (cited in Ballinger, 2016a: 23).

With this in mind, feminist scholars were now able to demonstrate that *all* knowledge is politically situated, and that traditional knowledge producers who fail to acknowledge this have in fact failed to critically interrogate their privileged position, and the impact that position has on their research, as well as the knowledge that flows from it (Harding, 1993, cited in Letherby,

2003: 45). The male 'experience as the benchmark for entitlement' would never again go unchallenged (Munro, 2007: 134); nor would experts be allowed 'to construct themselves as standing outside the social order as a result of their rigorous adherence to "objective" and value-free scientific methods and procedures' (Ballinger, 2016a: 21). Instead, feminist epistemology now offered critical researchers the tools with which to demonstrate that all knowledge is produced from a specific site (Cain, 1990a: 132; 1993: 88). It is therefore incumbent on those engaging in research to acknowledge the politics and values attached to the site from which they speak (Smart, 1989; Cain, 1990a).

In deconstructing official truths and dominant knowledge according to the site from whence it was generated, feminist scholars were now able to identify and challenge the socially constructed nature of state-defined 'truths' from their perspective. This process exposed the power inequality between those in privileged positions who construct official discourse and those who are members of subordinate groups whose voices hitherto had remained silent within the hierarchy of knowledge (Inglis, 2003; Ballinger, 2011: 112). Following this de-construction, new knowledge could be generated by *re*-constructing official discourse, and engaging in theoretical reflection from a feminist standpoint (Cain, 1990b: 6).

The success of feminist epistemology and its processes – from 'the politics of naming' (Ballinger, 2016a: 9) through to excavating subjugated knowledge from women whose lived experiences had hitherto been hidden or ignored – is evident from the colossal body of literature generated since the 1980s, particularly with regard to the nature and extent of violence perpetrated against women and children within the private sphere. The end products of what was now recognized as phallocentric knowledge production also came under scrutiny in other areas, including those of legal truth claims and the gendered nature of law, issues to which this chapter now turns.

## Feminist challenges to the hetero-patriarchal state and phallocentric law

> Once masculinity appears as a specific position, not just the way things are, its judgements will be revealed in process and procedure, as well as adjudication and legislation.
>
> Mackinnon in Collier (1995: 21),
> quoted in Ballinger (2016a: 19)

The creation of a feminist epistemology resulted in a profound challenge to the established hierarchy of knowledge – the apex of which had traditionally been occupied by law and science – two disciplines which had not only positioned themselves as standing outside the social order, but also as 'the judges of normality' (Foucault, 1977: 304). As such, they had carried superior legitimacy due to their claim of being based on the Enlightenment principles of reason, rationality, objectivity and neutrality (Lacey et al, 1990: 152). Now, however, in pointing to this hierarchy of knowledge through a feminist epistemology, critical scholars were able to demonstrate that women's voices – historically and contemporaneously – were, in many ways, at the bottom of this hierarchy. This is because within phallocentric knowledge production, 'representations of truth are inextricably intertwined with prevailing sets of power relations' (Gilligan, 2004: 20). In other words, within a male-dominated law and judiciary 'male definitions and understanding of human behaviour [can be] claimed as universal' (O'Donovan, 1993: 428). Consequently, throughout history, women's knowledge – their 'truths' – have been subjugated, disqualified or 'muted' altogether within a culture based on the values of hetero-patriarchy (Worrall, 1990: 21). These values were supported by a range of state institutions which, although beset by contradictions, ultimately reinforced and reproduced them.

Having thus observed that 'the authority to identify "empirical truths" and to interpret testable "facts" is dependent on existent power relations within given social contexts' (Faith, 1993, cited in Ballinger, 2016a: 2), feminist scholars were able to demonstrate that knowledge produced by powerful groups such as state agencies or scientific communities, is socially constructed in much the same manner as other forms of knowledge. With this in mind, they turned their critical focus towards subjugated knowledge generated within the private sphere. Traditionally considered to be the space for women and children, the private sphere had been largely ignored as an area of interest for either research or legislation. Now, however, armed with a feminist epistemology as a tool for knowledge production, scholars and activists focused on excavating knowledge from 'below' by opening up a site through which hitherto muted voices could be heard and experiences documented. By listening to accounts of women's lived experiences and taking their voices seriously, a large body of hitherto subjugated knowledge was excavated, exposing the sheer level of violence against women and children taking place within the private sphere (see, for example, Dobash and Dobash, 1979; Wilson, 1983; Browne, 1987; Hanmer and Maynard, 1987; Edwards, 1989). In short, feminist epistemology had 'named' the home as the most dangerous place for women and children (Dobash and Dobash, 1979: 7; Edwards, 1989: 159), thereby ensuring crime occurring within the private sphere was put into discourse for public analysis.

Running in tandem with this excavation, ground-breaking feminist theory was developed with which to analyse women's subordinate position within the social order, which lay at the heart of their victimization, as well as their experiences of criminal procedures and law, following their attempts to gain justice through the legal system. Carol Smart identified law and its legal system as gendered in nature and noted the way in which law and masculinity frequently overlapped (1989: 86). This is because 'law is not a free-floating entity, it is grounded in patriarchy as well as class and ethnic divisions' (1989: 86, 88). Meanwhile, Connell pointed to the symbiotic relationship between the state and hetero-patriarchy (1994), explaining how – in its effort to maintain a gendered social order – the state is 'an active player in gender politics … ["doing gender"] through procedures and self-defined objective structures' (Connell in Ballinger, 2009: 22–3). Applying this analysis to rape trials, Connell argued:

> The courts are not patriarchal because they are improperly biased against women, rather they are patriarchal through the way the whole structure of rape law operates. The more objective they are in procedure, the more effectively patriarchal they are. The norm of 'legal objectivity' has thus become an institution of men's interests. (Connell, 1994: 145)

Analyses such as those by Smart and Connell go to the very heart of feminist epistemology, since, starting from the historical fact that law itself was formulated during an era where women were the property of men and therefore had no legal status (Burton, 2001: 254), they are able to reveal that the legal system 'has been constructed from a male perspective, according to male standards, so that it either excludes, devalues or distorts women's experiences and motivations' (Fox, 1995: 171).

Utilizing feminist epistemology and theory to de-construct the operation of law and the legal system thus reveals that its emphasis on 'legal objectivity' is *precisely* what makes it gendered since it ignores the structurally inferior position of women within a hetero-patriarchal social order. Consequently, however 'objective' the law is, and however many reforms are implemented, neither aspect will change or eliminate 'the wider social relationships and material realities which condition men's sexual violence and women's sexual victimisation. In short, the power of law remains unchallenged, as does the social context that makes sexual violation routine' (Phoenix and Oerton, 2005: 39).

This analysis provides a concrete example of the importance of the feminist-inspired praxis and processes described earlier – de-construction, re-construction and reflective theorizing – because it can explain why numerous efforts by law – and the state more generally – to combat violence against women have failed, as indicated by the statistics. The combination of feminist epistemology and theory has *de*-constructed phallocentric knowledge, *re*-constructed the new knowledge emerging from that de-construction, and reflected theoretically from a feminist perspective, as to the meaning of that new knowledge. In so doing, it has been able to conclude that 'feminism should not become seduced by law – new laws will not necessarily make things better' (Smart, 1989: 160). On the contrary, new legislation *increases* the power of the 'legal forum by confirming that it is the most appropriate body to initiate change and reform' (Ballinger, 2012: 464). It therefore follows that it is the power of law itself which should be the focus of a feminist challenge because real political and revolutionary gains – rather than piecemeal reform to existing structures, which have been the norm over the last two centuries – will only be achieved when a feminist strategy of de-centring 'law's power to define and disqualify' has been completed and in its place, 'the legitimacy of feminist knowledge' established (Smart, 1989: 165).

In sum, this analysis demonstrates how the state is able to maintain the social order by 'doing gender' through the 'procedures and self-defined objective structures' described earlier, since 'legal reform, without a fundamental overhaul of the interpretative background, amounts to little more than tinkering with the edges of systematic and structural injustice' (Jackson, cited in Chan, 2001: 169). Thus, 'doing gender' in this manner can explain not only why a myriad of reforms to the legal system have failed to protect women from male violence – as indicated by the statistics in the introduction – but also why numerous legislative changes introduced in recent decades – designed to deliver justice for retaliating women through considering the abuse they had suffered prior to killing their abusers – have failed, as I indicate in the following section.

## A case of 'regressive modernisation'⁵? The (non-) impact of reform

Despite the success by feminist scholars and activists in uncovering the nature and extent of violence occurring within the private sphere over the past four decades, and arguably, as a direct result of the refusal by the state to engage in 'a fundamental overhaul of the interpretative background' (Jackson, cited in Chan, 2001: 169), it has so far proved impossible to eliminate stereotypical images around women who eventually retaliate by killing their abusive partner. From Ruth Ellis, the last woman to be executed in England and Wales in 1955,⁶ to Sara Thornton in 1990 (Nadel, 1993) and Sally Challen in 2010 (EWCA Crim 916 No. 201605604 B2), the discourses of the cold, calculating, vengeful and/or jealous woman who kills an apparently defenceless male partner are instantly recognizable.⁷ Hence, one of the most intensely fought feminist battles in recent decades is arguably the campaign to have the specific *gendered* circumstances recognized that lead up to women's retaliation against an abusive partner. Numerous legislative changes have taken place since the 1990s, designed to address the fact that abused women who eventually kill their abusers frequently do so to save their own lives, unlike men who are more likely to kill their partners following escalating violence against them (Edwards, 1996: 372).

One example of such legislation is the introduction of Battered Woman Syndrome (BWS) as a partial defence which was originally designed to assist women in demonstrating that their action had been 'reasonable given the circumstances' (Morrissey, 2003: 73). However, it was quickly appropriated as support for a defence of diminished responsibility (Worrall, 2002: 57). As such it can be understood as having replaced one stereotype with another: undermining the image of the vengeful, jealous woman by reinforcing traditional discourses around women's unstable minds, lack of agency and tendencies towards mental fragility and illness. This was the case during the 1990s, when high-profile cases such as those of Sara Thornton,[8] Emma Humphrys[9] and Kiranjit Ahluwalia[10] all had to base their appeals on 'abnormality of the mind' type defences (Ballinger, 1996: 27–8), rather than provocation or self-defence, and it remains the case in the 21st century, as illustrated in the case study in the next section.

A second example is the defence of 'loss of control' introduced in an attempt to address the issue of 'immediacy' – a concept which 'has engaged feminist and legal scholarship' since the 1970s (Edwards, 2010: 226). Here, too, the legal system has repeatedly proved willing to introduce various changes in an attempt to take account of the fact that abused women do not necessarily kill in accordance with the masculine norm – 'in the heat of the moment' – a fact which should not automatically translate into pre-meditation. Thus, 2009[11] saw the removal of the 'immediacy principle' with the introduction of the 'loss of control' defence. Again, however, its intended purpose has been diluted for as Edwards has observed, 'a lapse of time will nevertheless be taken into consideration as background circumstances' thus weakening this defence considerably (Edwards, 2010: 226).

In 2015 the defence of 'coercive control' was introduced in an attempt to take account of a wider range of behaviour over and above physical violence, and thus provide 'a deeper understanding of abuse' (Challen, 2019: 43). The case of Sally Challen, who killed her husband Richard in 2010, highlights the type of behaviour that qualifies as 'coercive control'. According to Sally's son, David:

> He bullied and humiliated her, isolated her from her friends and family, controlled who she could socialise with, controlled her money, restricted her movement and created a culture of fear and dependency. … While he forced strict restrictions on her behaviour, he would have numerous affairs and visit brothels. If she challenged him, he would gaslight her, make her question her sanity and seek to control us as sons to believe our mother was mad. (Challen, 2019: 43)

The case took place five years prior to the 'coercive control' defence coming into effect, and Sally was given a life sentence for murder. In February 2019 her conviction was quashed in what was described as a 'landmark case' which recognized 'the true severity of coercive control' (Hill and Weaver, 2019: 5). While this outcome is to be welcomed, it is nevertheless a fact that, as was the case with BWS which was appropriated to support a defence of diminished responsibility, so the appeal court was told that Sally suffered from 'two mental disorders at the time of the killing, and that her condition was likely to have been made worse by her husband's coercive control' (Hill and Weaver, 2019: 5). In other words, as was the case in the 20th century – so it is in the 21st century – retaliation following long-term abuse cannot be deemed reasonable behaviour by a sane or 'normal' woman, a point which is further confirmed by the case study that follows.

## The case of Fri Martin

As noted by Elmhirst, there are important differences between Sally Challen and Fri Martin, 'age, race, class and geography', for example (Elmhirst, 2019: 11). Nonetheless, despite the fact that Fri's partner Kyle had also committed physical violence as well as rape and extreme forms of controlling behaviour against her for several years, the two cases are identical in one area – the punishment received after having killed their abusive partners, for Fri was also given a life sentence in 2015, after having stabbed Kyle. On the night of the stabbing, she had been visiting a friend, and while there, received text messages from Kyle 'every 15 seconds or so. In ten minutes, he had sent nearly 30 … this always happened when she was out without him. … Even when she was just round the corner with a friend, he'd barrage her with messages, then show up at the door to take her home'. Like his behaviour, the messages were offensive and violent in nature: 'lil slag stay out get shagged or raped' (Elmhirst, 2019: 9).

Specific incidents of violence included punching Fri in the stomach while she was expecting their first child. Examples of his provocative behaviour included making another woman pregnant, also while Fri was pregnant. Over and above Kyle's cheating and violent behaviour, Fri 'felt she couldn't do anything without his permission' and noted that he was jealous and obsessed – 'convinced she was sleeping with his friends', to the point where he was picking her up from college 'so she wouldn't walk past any men on the way back'. On several occasions he 'raped her. He'd pin her down, spit on her and mock her body'. Immediately before the stabbing, Kyle had smashed her phone, grabbed her by the neck and pressed his thumbs against her throat, causing injuries verified by a medical examiner (Elmhirst, 2019: 10).

The stabbing was reported in a very different language by the *Daily Mirror*, thereby emphasizing the feminist epistemological point that 'truth' is socially constructed through language, according to the site from which the knowledge producer speaks:

> Boozed-up Farieissia[12] Martin arrived home at 4.30am after drinking half a bottle of brandy during a night out with pals. But the 22-year-old *argued* with boyfriend Kyle Farrell, 21, who had been *looking after* their two children, when she returned as he accused her *of seeing other men*. He requested to see her phone, but then Martin grabbed a kitchen knife and plunged it into the chest of Farrell. (Harris, 2015, emphasis added)

The defence focused on self-defence and loss of control. The jury disagreed and found her guilty of murder after 90 minutes of deliberation (Elmhirst, 2019: 11).[13] Neither self-defence nor the partial 'loss of control' defence worked for Fri, because 'all trials require performance' and Fri failed to perform according to either public or legal expectations (Elmhirst, 2019: 11, see also Carlen, 1976).[14] This failure to perform according to expectations is a common feature in trials involving retaliating women who have suffered long-term abuse and can be traced back several decades. For example, the very same observation was made with regard to Ruth Ellis in 1955, when she stood trial for killing her abusive partner, David Blakely, and was considered to have made an important contribution towards ensuring the death sentence was carried out.[15] It remains a regular occurrence to the present day and is associated with the mental state resulting from this type of victimization (Walker, 1989, in Edwards, 2010: 169–70). As such, this chasm between public/legal expectation and lived experience provides a stark example of the power difference between those in a position to construct dominant phallocentric knowledge destined to become official discourse, versus subordinate knowledge generated from women's lived experience destined to become knowledge from 'below'. In Fri's case, although she had revealed the abuse to close friends, she had not told her own family (Elmhirst, 2019: 11). Again this is not untypical in cases of abused women, who may have internalized it, and who may be made to feel partly to blame or ashamed. When Fri took the stand she appeared to be still in shock – looking 'terrified' and 'sobb[ing]' – rather than 'perform[ing]' according to courtroom expectations. No psychiatric evaluation had taken place as she was deemed to be 'sane' and 'rational' (Elmhirst, 2019: 11).

Years later, in preparation for her appeal, a psychiatrist found that 'only after repeated visits and the encouragement of a support worker in prison was Fri able to talk openly about the abuse she had experienced' (Elmhirst, 2019: 11). In short, the journey from victim to survivor of abuse may be a slow process that does not necessarily conform to dominant discourses about how a victim should 'behave'.

At the time of writing (2021) her appeal is being fought on the grounds that at the time of the killing she had been suffering 'traumatic amnesia and mild depressive disorder'. The 'trigger' was Kyle putting his hands around her throat, and hence, the partial defence of diminished responsibility and loss of control could now be deployed (Elmhirst, 2019: 11).

The fact that a trigger must be still be evident which accords with the masculine norm, and that women must continue to rely on new evidence deeming them to be mentally ill at the time of their retaliation, demonstrates that feminist epistemology has much work to do – through no fault of its own – before 'the legitimacy of feminist knowledge' (Smart, 1989: 165) enters dominant legal discourse: '[W]e are still a long way from recognising the retaliation of an abused women is a desperate bid to escape, rather than an act of murderous insanity' (Elmhirst, 2019: 11). In short, feminist epistemology is still fighting to have its different starting point formally accepted in law. That is to say, rather than defining domestic abuse as a 'series of individual violent episodes', it can be understood as 'long-term liberty deprivation', and 'rather than measuring women's suffering in broken bones', being controlled coercively 'is better understood as living under a tyrannical regime' (Elmhirst, 2019: 11). In Fri's case, victimization could be measured according to both, for she had had long-term experience of physical violence *and* living under a tyrannical regime. The fact that she was nonetheless given a life sentence for her bid to escape further violence, demonstrates that court procedures continue to operate according to masculine judgements and subject positions. As such, it also illustrates why achieving formal equality has had little or no impact on creating substantive equality, for this achievement has not resulted in the creation of 'new *subject* positions for retaliating women' (Ballinger, 2012: 457, emphasis in original). Instead, it confirms that legal changes merely introduce reform to existing subject positions – they do *not* address women's subordinate position within a deeply unequal gender order where the problem of domestic violence itself is rooted and normalized (Ballinger, 2012: 457). Thus, whether a retaliating woman relies on BWS, 'slow burn provocation' or 'coercive control' – all recognized in law – her 'state of mind must still culminate in a qualifying trigger according to the masculine norm' (Munro, 2007: 134; Ballinger, 2012: 455). This is unsurprising because, as observed by Hanmer et al (cited in Kantola, 2005: 85), it is not possible to treat 'men's violence as a serious crime without undermining the social order'.

To elaborate, a key component of the hetero-patriarchal social order is the law, hence, a reliance on law to remedy a problem it itself has created – the disqualification of women's own accounts and lived experiences – allows its power as 'a system of knowledge' with a monopoly on 'the definition of events' to remain unchallenged (Smart, 1989: 86, 162). Again we note the continuing importance of feminist epistemology, because only when the struggle to eliminate 'law's power to define and disqualify' has been won, and 'the legitimacy of feminist knowledge' put in its place (Smart, 1989: 165), will male violence and women's responses to it be understood from the experiential site of the victim. 'Without such de-centring, law's superior position at the apex of the hierarchy of truth production will be maintained and the continuity' of a phallocentric legal system assured (Ballinger, 2016a: 464). Within this context, legal reform and new legislation – seemingly sympathetic to victims of male violence – can be understood as preserving and *strengthening* the gendered social order, because without such concessions to the plight of abused women, a crisis of legitimacy may occur, as was the case during the 1990s, when the state came under increasing pressure to take concerns about sexual violence more seriously due to issues such as reporting and attrition rates, and – according to Phoenix and Oerton (2005: 32) – responded by introducing the Sexual Offences Act 2003.

## Technological misogyny: on the road to Gilead[16]?

> There is no secret abuser's handbook. It's called mainstream culture.
>
> James-Hanman, in Usborne (2019: 4)

> Misogyny has become so mainstream that men are seriously asking juries to believe 'she asked for it', even when what she supposedly 'asked' for has ended in death.
>
> (Smith, 2019b: 3)

The Fri Martin case confirms that despite numerous legislative changes over recent decades with regard to domestic abuse, the insistence by the legal system on focusing on individual cases, rather than the social and structural context within which violence against women occurs, has remained unchanged. It is the individual retaliator's mental state that 'caused' her to kill her abuser – not the violent and misogynist culture within which both male abuse and victim-blaming are, not only normalized, but also condoned by media discourses and state practices.

Conversely, when it comes to explaining the reasons for the increase in rape complaints and the decrease in prosecutions and convictions of this crime – currently deemed to be the lowest since records began (Bowcott and Barr, 2019a: 1; Smith, 2019b) – a similar picture emerges. Various legislative changes have been introduced in recent decades in an attempt to reassure complainants that victim-blaming has been eliminated. For example, legislation was implemented in 1999 to prevent the complainant's sexual history being revealed or discussed within the courtroom (Youth Justice and Criminal Evidence Act 1999). Despite this, '[t]he culture of suspicion is now so deep-rooted that police forces are subjecting complainants to a massive invasion of privacy, demanding that they hand over mobile phones and school, college and medical records that predate the alleged attack by decades' (Smith, 2019a). Indeed, these types of background checks on the complainant are now routinely offered as the explanation, not only for the reduction in prosecutions, but also for the delay in processing rape complaints (Barr, 2019: 6). Victim-blaming and disbelief have always been associated with rape complaints[17] and the introduction of legislation, supposedly to enhance the complainant's experience of the legal system and ensure a higher number of convictions, has instead *increased* the intensity of scrutiny of the complainant and *decreased*, not only the number of prosecutions but also the number of convictions.

Victim-blaming and victim-scrutiny reached an arguably new level of misogyny, following the murder of Grace Millane in December 2018. As such, this case offers yet further evidence of the clock 'turning backwards' when it comes to violence against women, with the circumstances of the murder reported 'in a manner that should no longer be acceptable' (Richards, 2019: 15). Following the defendant's claim that her death had been accidental after a 'rough sex' game going wrong, 'the trial focused almost exclusively on details of her sexual preferences, previous partners, and alleged proclivity for BDSM' (Richards, 2019: 15). The media followed with headlines such as 'Grace liked to be choked and joined bondage sites' (Taylor, 2019: 19). She was accused of being 'naïve' about dating websites, and of enjoying being 'choked' during sex (Taylor, 2019: 19). Such accusations ensured responsibility was shifted 'away from the murderer and onto the victim' (Moore, 2019: 4), thereby confirming Edwards' observation in 1987 that women are routinely accused of 'provoking their own demise', is as relevant in the 21st century, as it was in the previous century (Edwards, 1987). Moreover, Grace's case exemplifies 'what appears to be a growing legal trend for "rough sex" being used as part of a defence plea'[18] (Ellen, 2019: 53).[19]

This extreme form of victim-blaming was made possible, once again, by focusing on the circumstances of an individual murder, rather than the wider structure of 'hard-core pornography' available online, which 'has doubtless popularised rough sex' watched mainly by men, in turn, putting pressure on women to give their consent to this type of activity (Ellen, 2019: 53). Claiming that victims consented to their own death can be understood as the 'logical endpoint' of a long history of murdered women being accused of having 'brought it on themselves' (Moore, 2019: 4). It has no status in law, yet 'it has resulted in a lesser charge, lighter sentence, or acquittals in 45 per cent of cases' (Mackenzie, in Moore, 2019: 4). As such, it provides another example of phallocentric law retaining its position within the legal system. At the time of writing the MP Harriet Harman' is introducing two amendments to the Domestic Abuse Bill discussed earlier – 'designed to reinforce that consent can be no defence to death' (Moore, 2019: 5). Harman poignantly notes: 'Changing the law is the easy bit. ... The hard part is making sure it works in practice' (in Moore, 2019: 5).

The cases of Fri Martin and Grace Millane provide examples of how technological developments in the 21st century have also brought new opportunities for surveillance of, and violence against, women. In Fri's case, it took the form of a constant bombardment of text messages, which, in any other circumstances, would be considered harassment. In the case of Grace, widely available online 'hardcore pornography' has contributed to the normalization of rough sex, in turn playing a role in normalizing the sexualization of violence against women within a 'creeping pornification of our culture' (Walter, 2010: 117). In addition, dating sites have provided new avenues for facilitating access to victims brought up with the internet where 'real contempt for women characterises so much pornography' and 'male domination' is commonly presented as 'mutual pleasure' (Walter, 2010: 114, 115). At a different level, James-Hanman, in her job as a consultant on violence against women, has observed: 'Abusers now use video calling so they can see which room their partners are in, and put satellite trackers in their cars' (in Usborne, 2019: 4).

While this chapter has concentrated on violence against women within the private sphere for the reasons explained, it is important to emphasize that women with a public profile remain vulnerable too. Since 2016, one female MP has been murdered, one has 'had an actual plot to murder her' averted, one 'has seen a total of six different people convicted for threats to her and her family' (Wollaston, in Perraudin and Murphy, 2019: 9). Technology also plays a part in violence against women in the public eye with online threats, abuse, aggression and intimidation having been one of 'the most insidious effects of the toxic Brexit debate', to the point where a number of female MPs have chosen to stand down from parliament (Reed, in Perraudin and Murphy, 2019: 8), prompting former US presidential candidate Hillary Clinton to comment: 'If people are intimidated out of running for office in a democracy because of these hate-mongers ... that is the path [to] authoritarianism, that is the path [to] fascism' (Addley, 2019: 23).

## Conclusion

I introduced this chapter by quoting from the *Equalities Review Report* published in 2007, which observed that with regard to gender equality and elimination of violence against women, we have not just 'stopped the clock' – in some cases – 'it is starting to turn backwards'. Twelve years later, speaking of the hostility and abuse endured by female MPs, Sam Smethers of the Fawcett Society noted: 'We have to confront the fact that our toxic politics drives good women MPs away – we are going backwards' (in Perraudin and Murphy, 2019: 8). More generally, McNay has observed that feminists tend to be cautious when it comes to asserting that gender relations are being transformed because frequently 'the emergence of new forms of autonomy coincides with new forms of ... subordination' (McNay, 2004: 174).

Yet, it can also be argued that with new forms of subordination come new forms of resistance, as evidenced from recently established campaign groups in response to new challenges faced by feminist activists and scholars who continue to fight for substantive equality for, and the elimination of, violence against women. Examples include We Can't Consent to This, which campaigns against the 'rough sex' defence. It has already been successful in uncovering 59 cases similar to that of Grace Millane, thereby making them 'visible' by ensuring they reach the public agenda in keeping with earlier feminist work described previously (Moore, 2019: 4). Meanwhile, established campaign groups such as Justice for Women continue to support women like Fri Martin by utilizing existing law in their fight to have murder verdicts overturned, and have already been successful in their application of the 'coercive control' partial defence in the 'landmark' case outlined here.

That said, the fact that campaign groups such as Justice for Women (and many others), still need to exist two decades into the 21st century, is arguably, in itself, evidence of the state's systematic failure to protect women from male violence. Furthermore, 'feminist epistemology' is not necessarily conceptualized in such direct terms or language in the 21st century. Yet, it is nevertheless the case that the mere existence of this feminist theory of knowledge has prevented – and *continues* to prevent – male hegemony from achieving full domination. Thus, its insistence that 'if you really want to understand male violence, you need to listen to women' (Smith, 2019a: 3), has ensured that its impact, value and contribution remain as vital and important today as at the time of its inception, nearly half a century ago.

## Notes

[1] The chapter title is paraphrased from Susan Brownmiller's classic text *Against Our Will* (1975: 454).

[2] Based in the Cabinet Office.

[3] For example, according to CSEW data for the year ending March 2018, only 18 per cent of women who had experienced partner abuse in the last 12 months reported the abuse to the police (Domestic Abuse Bill 2017–19).

[4] For an overview of justificatory strategies within feminist epistemology see Letherby (2003).

[5] Hall (1988: 2).

[6] For a full account of the Ruth Ellis case, see Ballinger (2000; see also 2000, 2012, 2016b).

[7] For an in-depth analysis of the impact the social construction of femininity may have on female defendants, see Ballinger (2000).

[8] For a full account of the Sara Thornton case, see Nadel (1993).

[9] For a full account of the Emma Humphrys case, see Bindel and Wistrich (2003).

[10] For a full account of the Kiranjit Ahluwalia case, see Ahluwalia and Gupta (1997).

[11] The Coroners and Justice Act 2009 s 56.

[12] Farieissia was, and is always known as, 'Fri'.

13   The *Daily Mirror* reported that the jury deliberated for four hours (June 2015). The campaign group Justice for Women, however, confirms that the jury deliberated for 'one hour and a half'.

14   Carlen writes: 'the ideal of adversary justice is subjugated to an organisational efficiency in whose service body-movement and body-representation are carefully circumscribed and regulated, bewilderment and embarrassment openly fostered and aggravated, uncertainty coolly observed and manipulated' (1976: 20).

15   See Ballinger (2000) for a full account of this case.

16   Atwood (1996).

17   Even when cases go to trial the complainant may be met with suspicion and disbelief by judges. See Swerling (2020) for example.

18   'Up by 90 per cent over the past decade, according to one estimate. The website *We Can't Consent to This* has found that of the 59 women it has identified, who were killed in so-called "consensual" violence in the UK, this defence was successful in almost half of the 18 cases that came to trial in the past five years, leading to a lesser verdict of manslaughter or an acquittal' (Moore, 2019: 4; Smith 2019a).

19   See, for example, Rubenhold's (2019) account of the victims of Jack the Ripper in her book *The Five*. See also Edwards (1987).

## References

Addley, E. (2019) 'Internet abuse of MPs is path to fascism: Clinton', *The Guardian*, 14 November, p 23.

Ahluwalia, K. and Gupta, R. (1997) *Circle of Light: The Autobiography of Kiranjit Ahluwalia*, London: HarperCollins.

Atwood, M. (1996) *The Handmaid's Tale*, London: Vintage.

Ballinger, A. (1996) 'The guilt of the innocent and the innocence of the guilty' in A. Myers and S. Wight (eds) *No Angels*, London: Pandora, pp 1–28.

Ballinger, A. (2000) *Dead Woman Walking*, Aldershot: Ashgate.

Ballinger, A. (2009) 'Gender, power and the state: Same as it ever was?' in R. Coleman, J. Sim, S. Tombs and D. Whyte (eds) *State, Power, Crime*, London: SAGE, pp 20–34.

Ballinger, A. (2011) 'Feminist research, state power and executed women: The case of Louie Calvert' in S. Farrell, M. Hough, S. Maruna and R. Sparks (eds) *Escape Routes: Contemporary Perspectives on Life after Punishment*, Abingdon: GlassHouse, pp 107–33.

Ballinger, A. (2012) 'A muted voice from the past: The "silent silencing" of Ruth Ellis', *Social & Legal Studies*, 21(4:) 445–67.

Ballinger, A. (2016a) *Gender, Truth, and State Power: Capitalising on Punishment*, Abingdon: Routledge.

Ballinger, A. (2016b) 'A question of provocation or responsibility? Revisiting the case of Ruth Ellis and David Blakely' in K. Fitz-Gibbon and S. Walklate (eds) *Homicide, Gender and Responsibility: An International Perspective*, Abingdon: Routledge, pp 15–35.

Barr, C. (2019) 'Police "failed to ask basic questions"', *The Guardian*, 27 July, p 6.

Bindel, J. and Wistrich, H. (2003) *The Map of My Life: The Story of Emma Humphrys*, London: Astraia.

Bowcott, O. and Barr, C. (2019a) 'Revealed: Collapse in rape cases that end up in court', *The Guardian*, 27 July, pp 1, 6.

Bowcott, O. and Barr, C. (2019b) 'Half of rape victims drop out of cases even after suspect is identified', *The Guardian*, [online] 10 November, available at: https://www.theguardian.com/society/2019/nov/10/half-of-victims-drop-out-of-cases-even-after-suspect-is-identified [accessed 5 April 2022].

Browne, A. (1987) *When Battered Women Kill*, New York: Macmillan Free Press.

Brownmiller, S. (1975) *Against Our Will: Men, Women and Rape*, Toronto: Banton Books.

Burton, M. (2001) 'Intimate homicide and the provocation defence: Endangering women? R. v Smith', *Feminist Legal Studies*, 9: 247–58.

Cain, M. (1990a) 'Realist philosophy and standpoint epistemologies or feminist criminology as a successor science' in L. Gelsthorpe and A. Morris (eds) *Feminist Perspectives in Criminology*, Milton Keynes: Open University Press, pp 124–40.

Cain, M. (1990b) 'Towards transgression: New directions in feminist criminology', *International Journal of the Sociology of Law*, 18(1): 1–18.

Cain, M. (1993) 'Foucault, feminism and feeling: What Foucault can and cannot contribute to feminist epistemology' in C. Ramazanoglu (ed) *Up Against Foucault*, London: Routledge, pp 73–96.

Carlen, P. (1976) *Magistrates' Justice*, London: Martin Robertson.

Challen, D. (2019) 'Why are women like my mother still branded as cold killers?', *The Observer*, 9 June, p 43.

Chan, W. (2001) *Women, Murder and Justice*, Basingstoke: Palgrave.

Collier, R. (1995) *Masculinity, Law and the Family*, London: Routledge.

Collier, R. (2010) *Men, Law and Gender: Rethinking the 'Man' of Law*, London: Routledge.

Connell, R.W. (1994) 'The state, gender and sexual politics: Theory and appraisal' in H.L. Radtke and H.J. Stam (eds) *Power/Gender*, London: SAGE, pp 136–73.

Dobash, R. and Dobash, R (1979) *Violence Against Wives*, Shepton Mallet: Open Books.

Domestic Abuse Bill 2017–19 (2019) *House of Commons Library* [online] 30 July, available at: https://commonslibrary.parliament.uk/home-affairs/crime/will-this-be-the-parliament-to-enact-a-domestic-abuse-bill/? see also: https://www.gov.uk/government/publications/domestic-abuse-bill-2019-factsheets [accessed 14 September 2021].

Duggan, M. (2019) 'Domestic Abuse Bill: Proposed changes to protect victims explained', *The Conversation*, [online] 12 August, available at: https://theconversation.com/domestic-abuse-bill-proposed-changes-to-protect-victims-explained-110258 [accessed 14 September 2021].

Edwards, S. (1987) '"Provoking her own demise": From common assault to homicide' in J. Hanmer and M. Maynard (eds) *Women, Violence and Social Control*, London: Macmillan, pp 152–68.

Edwards, S. (1989) *Policing Domestic Violence*, London: SAGE.

Edwards, S. (1996) *Sex and Gender in the Legal Process*, London: Blackstone Press.

Edwards, S. (2010) 'Anger and fear as justifiable preludes for loss of self-control', *Journal of Criminal Law*, 74(3): 223–41.

Ellen, B. (2019) 'The "rough sex" defence plea is growing, it's a shocking trend', *The Observer*, 17 November, p 53.

Elmhirst, S. (2019) 'The long read', *The Guardian*, 31 October, pp 9–11.

Ford, L. (2019) 'Britain takes global lead on violence against women and girls', *The Guardian*, 2 November, p 18.

Foucault, M. (1977) *Discipline and Punish*, Harmondsworth: Peregrine Books.

Fox, M. (1995) 'Legal responses to battered women who kill' in J. Bridgeman and S. Millns (eds) *Law and Body Politics*, Aldershot: Dartmouth, pp 171–200.

Gilligan, G. (2004) 'Official inquiry, truth and criminal justice' in G. Gilligan and J. Pratt (eds) *Crime, Truth and Justice: Official Inquiry, Discourse, Knowledge*, Cullompton: Willan, pp 11–25.

Hall, S. (1988) *The Hard Road to Renewal*, London: Verso.

Hanmer, J. and Maynard, M. (eds) (1987) *Women, Violence and Social Control*, London: Macmillan.

Harding, S. (1986) *The Science Question in Feminism*, New York: Cornell University Press.

Harding, S. (1987) 'Introduction: Is there a feminist method?' and 'Conclusion: Epistemological Questions' in S. Harding (ed) *Feminism and Methodology*, Milton Keynes: Open University Press, pp 1–14 and pp 181–90.

Harding, S. (1990) 'Feminism, science, and the anti-enlightenment critiques' in L.J. Nicholson (ed) *Feminism/Postmodernism*, London: Routledge, pp 83–106.

Harding, S. (1993) 'Rethinking standpoint epistemology: "What is strong objectivity?"' in L. Alcoff and E. Potter (eds) *Feminist Epistemologies*, New York: Routledge, pp 49–82.

Harris, J. (2015) 'Farieissia Martin: Mum jailed for stabbing footballer boyfriend to death following late-night row', *Daily Mirror*, 9 June.

Hill, A. and Weaver, M. (2019) 'Woman who killed abusive husband is freed after judge rules out a retrial', *The Guardian*, 8 June, p 5.

Holmwood, J. (1995) 'Feminism and epistemology: What kind of successor science?', *Sociology*, 29(3): 411–28.

Inglis, T. (2003) *Truth, Power and Lies*, Dublin: University College Dublin Press.

Itzin, C. (2000) 'Gendering domestic violence: The influence of feminism on policy and practice' in J. Hanmer, C. Itzin, S. Quaid and D. Wigglesworth (eds) *Home Truths about Domestic Violence*, London: Routledge, pp 372–96.

Kantola, J. (2005) *Feminists Theorise the State*, Basingstoke: Palgrave.

Lacey, N., Wells, C. and Meure, D. (1990) *Reconstructing Criminal Law*, London: Weidenfeld Paperbacks.

Letherby, G. (2003) *Feminist Research in Theory and Practice*, Milton Keynes: Open University Press.

McNay, L. (2004) 'Situated intersubjectivity' in B. Marshall and A. Witz (eds) *Engendering the Social: Feminist Encounters with Sociological Theory*, Maidenhead: Open University Press, pp 171–86.

Moore, A. (2019) 'There's a new level of anger', *The Guardian*, 26 November, pp 4–5.

Morrissey, B. (2003) *When Women Kill*, London: Routledge.

Munro, V. (2007) *Law and Politics at the Perimeter*, Oxford: Hart Publishing.

Nadel, J. (1993) *Sara Thornton: The Story of a Woman who Killed*, London: Gollancz.

O'Donovan, K. (1993) 'Law's knowledge: The judge, the expert, the battered woman and her syndrome', *Journal of Law and Society*, 20(4): 427–37.

Perraudin, F. and Murphy, S. (2019) 'Female MPs: Alarm at number quitting over hostility and abuse', *The Guardian*, 1 November, pp 8–9.

Phoenix, J. and Oerton, S. (2005) *Illicit and Illegal: Sex, Regulation and Social Control*, Cullompton: Willan.

Richards, D. (2019) 'Grace Millane's trial exposes a dark trend in media coverage of violence against women', *The Conversation*, [online] 26 November, available at: https://theconversation.com/grace-millanes-trial-exposes-a-dark-trend-in-media-coverage-of-violence-against-women-127 733 [accessed 14 September 2021].

Rubenhold, H. (2019) *The Five: The Untold Stories of the Women Killed by Jack the Ripper*, London: Doubleday.

Smart, C. (1989) *Feminism and the Power of Law*, London: Routledge.

Smith, J. (2019a) 'To understand violent men, ask the women who know', *The Guardian*, 1 August.

Smith, J. (2019b) 'The "rough sex" defence is indefensible', *The Guardian*, 23 November.

Stanley, L. and Wise, S. (1983) *Breaking Out: Feminist Ontology and Epistemology*, London: Routledge.

Swerling, G. (2020) 'Female judge criticises male colleague who told woman she wasn't raped as she didn't fight back', *The Telegraph*, 22 January.

Taylor, J. (2019) 'Grace "liked to be choked and joined bondage sites"', *Metro*, 20 November.

Usborne, S. (2019) 'There's no secret abuser's handbook: It's called mainstream culture', *The Guardian*, 10 October, pp 4–5.

Walter, N. (2010) *Living Dolls: The Return of Sexism*, London: Virago.

Wilson, E. (1983) *What is to be Done about Violence Against Women?* Harmondsworth: Penguin Books.

Worrall, A. (1990) *Offending Women*, London: Routledge.

Worrall, A. (2002) 'Rendering women punishable: The making of a penal crisis' in P. Carlen (ed) *Women and Punishment*, Cullompton: Willan, pp 47–66.

## PART II

# State Practice and Feminist Praxis

# 3

# State (In)action and Feminist Resistance to the Denial of Abortion Rights in Northern Ireland

*Maev McDaid and Brian Christopher Nelis*

## Introduction

The island of Ireland has become a focus for the study of state (in)action across its two legal jurisdictions in recent years. This is owing to the significant constitutional change both in the Republic of Ireland, governed by Rialtas na hÉireann, and in Northern Ireland governed by Stormont's Northern Ireland Executive and its Legislative Assembly, and by Westminster. These jurisdictions were created in 1921 after the British state partitioned the island. While the struggle for reproductive justice has been ongoing for decades, there has often been little attention paid to this outside of Ireland. State inaction on the island is the result of the historically conservative nature of its institutions discussed later in the chapter, while other European countries had been much quicker to modernize. Despite being a part of the United Kingdom, Northern Ireland's exceptional status within this context has further contributed to the retention of antiquated law that in the other regions had been significantly changed by the Abortion Act of 1967.

The conservative approach to bodily autonomy is exemplified by the specific provisions relating to abortion in the Offences Against the Person Act (1861), which was passed by the Imperial British Parliament and remained in force for over 140 years. So although there are two different states on the island of Ireland, feminist responses found common cause because they opposed the shared foundation of legal principles found in that surviving legislation, namely that abortion is criminally unlawful and punishable by incarceration. Sections 58 and 59 of the Offences Against the Person Act (1861), remained the basis of the law in the Republic of Ireland until 2018 and remained the law in Northern Ireland until 2019 and stated the following:

> 58. Every woman, being with child, who, with intent to procure her own miscarriage, shall unlawfully administer to herself any poison or other noxious thing, or shall unlawfully use any instrument or other means whatsoever with the like intent, and whosoever, with intent to procure the miscarriage of any woman, whether she be or be not with child, shall unlawfully administer to her or cause to be taken by her any poison or other noxious thing, or shall unlawfully use any instrument or other means whatsoever with the like intent, shall be guilty of felony, and being convicted thereof shall be liable ... to be kept in penal servitude for life.
>
> 59. Whosoever shall unlawfully supply or procure any poison or other noxious thing, or any instrument or thing whatsoever, knowing that the same is intended to be unlawfully used or employed with intent to procure the miscarriage of any woman, whether she be or be not with child, shall be guilty of a misdemeanour, and being convicted thereof shall be liable ... to be kept in penal servitude.

The 8th Amendment to the Constitution of the Republic of Ireland, added in 1983, was not just a reiteration of this principle of law. It rendered any refinement, evolution and reform of the law practically impossible: 'The State acknowledges the right to life of the unborn and, with due regard to the equal right to life of the mother, guarantees in its laws to respect, and, as far as practicable, by its laws to defend and vindicate that right' (Amendment 8, Bunreacht na hEireann 1983). While this constitutional law applied only in the Republic of Ireland, it emboldened the anti-choice agenda across the island, meaning that resistance has been collaborative too, with solidarity actions across the border, defying the divisions imposed by partition. This chapter will thus look at some of the different aspects contributing to the denial of abortion rights in Ireland, but we focus on the reasons for success after years of frustrating setbacks, as well as the nuances in Northern Ireland. As activists in the campaign for abortion rights for over 15 years, we approach this chapter with our own experiences and welcome the inclusion of activist voices in the development of critical feminist criminology. The specifics of the Northern Ireland context can often be overlooked or misunderstood and greater awareness of the campaign for reproductive justice as an all-Ireland campaign could prove useful for the development of feminist practice in future.

First, we briefly discuss the historical and contemporary contexts that allowed abortion laws to be so restrictive, locating the discussions in the context of state action, inaction or 'non decision-making' as well as 'biopower' in relation to bodily autonomy. Next we consider, in practical terms, how restrictions were overturned by broad campaigns with diverse tactics. Finally, we explore why feminist resistance in Ireland was successful despite the huge barriers facing activists. The Offences Against the Person Act (1861) was repealed in Northern Ireland in October 2019. By 2020, Northern Ireland's abortion laws changed considerably with the passing of the total decriminalization of abortion in the region through Westminster (The Abortion (Northern Ireland) Regulations, 2020). Ironically, this new framework far surpassed the law for the rest of Britain, despite the region having spent 50 years behind. The impact of these changes remain to be seen, for example, at the time of writing in 2021 the provision of abortion has still not been rolled out in the region. The decriminalization of abortion in all 32 counties of Ireland had occurred within a timeframe of two years representing a period of substantial change. We aim to draw together how both states in Ireland went from having some of the strictest abortion laws in the world, to now some of the most liberal in legal terms.

In brief, change in the Republic of Ireland came about from a referendum to repeal the 8th Amendment of the Irish Constitution and abortion was decriminalized in May 2018. The huge success of this campaign gave hope and momentum to those activists in Northern Ireland (Kasstan, 2018). At that time, the devolved institutions of Northern Ireland were suspended, so the campaign to decriminalize abortion was taken across the Irish Sea, to Westminster, where a de facto direct-rule was imposed. British politicians felt intense pressure from Irish feminists and their campaign to decriminalize abortion in the region and ultimately those activists forced the hand of Westminster to change the law. Ironically, the majority of MPs from Northern Ireland sitting in Westminster were the most vocally opposed to any change.

In most other European countries, though not all, abortion has been decriminalized for several decades. Understanding the historical and political reasons for Ireland's difference has been important for informing feminist action and so it is useful to look at the methods by which the state legislated on issues of bodily autonomy and the difficulties in resisting state power in the Irish context. Much has been written about the historical factors that placed strictly conservative Catholic institutions at the heart of the Irish state (Girvin, 1996) as well as civil society. From the outset the Catholic Church has dominated provision in education (Ó Buachalla, 1985), health (McKee, 1986) and social care (Finnegan, 2001) in the Republic of Ireland. In addition to being the centre of Irish spiritual life, the Catholic Church also acted as something of a surrogate state among its congregation in Northern Ireland, as the Protestant state did not provide equally to its citizens (Farrell, 1990). Whereas the Republic of Ireland in its earlier conception as a fledgling 'free state' was reeling from newfound independence and a civil war and turned to the wealth and influence of the Catholic Church for support, precisely at the time when other European countries were secularizing. The Catholic Church also narrowed the parameters of public debate across the two states through a regime of censorship that Keating called the 'Cornerstone of Catholic Ireland' (2004b: 289). Operating through a range of institutions and barring married women from working in them, the Church established an idealized notion of Irish womanhood that promoted domesticity, motherhood, large families and female docility.

This was in stark contrast to the vision of Ireland that looked possible during the revolutionary years of 1913, 1916 and 1921. Women's involvement in the movements for independence, anti-imperialism and socialism were both central and heterogeneous (Luddy 1995). So McDiarmid (2015: 123) emphasizes that 'women created a small zone of feminist comfort within a hostile male military zone' in an account of Irish women's role in the 1916 Easter Rising against British Rule. McDiarmid draws on female creativity, emotion and non-violence, while Hearne (1992) notes the militancy of Cumann na Mban (League of Women) founded in April 1916. Indeed figures like Constance Markievicz became known for a commitment to 'militarism', which was expressed 'in a ringing call to nationalist women to take up arms and revive the independent heroic spirit of ancient Irish women warrior' (Hearne, 1992: 4). This was a far cry from the idealized notions of passive Irish womanhood that would come to dominate in the mid-20th century.

The proclamation of the Irish Republic, read outside the General Post Office in 1916 by the leader of its all-male signatories, Patrick Pearse, gave recognition to women. Up to 300 of the 1,600 participants in the armed element of the rising were women (McAuliffe et al, 2016). In the months and years that followed, it was the male protagonists who became idolized, seen as martyrs for their execution, while the women who went to prison were seldom afforded the same celebration. Elizabeth O'Farrell was actually airbrushed from a famous photograph of the rebel surrender, as the state sought to revise the narrative of who was involved in the uprising (Barry, 2016). Thus there were attempts to reshape popular memory in the interests of the ideology of the new state.

In the years after 1916, the Catholic Church came to support Irish independence, bringing with it a conservative current to the movement that acted as a weight against the more radical traditions of the Labour Party and the Trade Union Congress. The Church was 'unequivocally hostile' to socialist ideas (Purséil, 2008: 178). This is recognized in the official history of the Dáil (Houses of the Oireachtas, 2018) and may have contributed to the decision by the leaders of the labour movement not to contest the 1918 election. This was one way in which women were sidelined from electoral politics as Sinn Féin had fewer women in its ranks with one notable exception. Constance Markievicz, standing for Sinn Féin, was elected to Westminster though never took up her seat in the House of Commons due to the policy of abstentionism. She is rarely named by British historians in their accounts of parliamentary firsts, despite being the first ever woman elected to Westminster from her prison cell in Holloway.

In the years that followed Irish independence in 1921, the feminist movement declined sharply and James Connolly's prediction of a 'carnival of reaction' came to fruition. In both jurisdictions of the partitioned Ireland, after 1922, women were subject to restrictions and regulations that did not apply to men, but while these gradually disappeared after 1970, denial of access to abortion remained. From the mid-1920s, the state became highly active in the policing of women's bodies. This chapter intends to unpick how such circumstances arose and the particular responses that brought about the eventual decriminalization.

## Autonomy, abortion and biopower

This section considers why the state seeks to control bodily autonomy in the first place. We consider some of the motivations for state institutions to regulate pregnant bodies and whether the motivations are immutable or contingent. We also offer some reasons that explain why Ireland's move towards decriminalization has been slow. The conflicting responses to these ideas inform the action taken by those who confront the state, often putting their own bodies in danger of arrest, detention and other mistreatment, and so the answers to such questions are of considerable significance to Irish feminists. There are two prevailing explanations why state actors limit abortion rights: one arising out of the Marxist tradition and the other from radical feminism. MacKinnon, in her landmark text *Towards a Feminist Theory of the State* (1989), broadly outlined the similarities and differences in these viewpoints and how a focus on either class distinctions or social/patriarchal distinctions can fundamentally alter the methods of resistance.

Marxists, drawing on the work of Friedrich Engels (2019/1884), have tended to emphasize the centrality of sexual reproduction in regenerating labour-power; its function is to create a new generation of proletarian workers. They see the roots of the 1861 Act that criminalized terminations as an attempt to control both the population in Britain and the masses of the colonies. This derives from a central tenet of Marxist theory, that the state is a manifestation of class irreconcilability that acts in the common interests of capital, which in this specific case is to increase the birth rate. Holborow (2019) therefore sees the progress of decriminalization as being made possible by recent economic changes, such as the increase of women in the Irish workforce and the new priorities of Irish capital, where the birth rate is much less of a concern. The wording of the Irish Constitution itself is put forward as evidence for this. The text recognizes that the centrality of women's 'work in the home gives the state support' (Article 2.1, Bunreacht na hEireann 1937) and Holborow notes that 'women in a capitalist society perform the function of replenishing and reproducing the present and next generation of workers, intricately tied to profit accumulation' (Holborow, 2019: 27). The significance of this interpretation is that it locates state inaction in the collective interests of the capitalist class and that since control of women's bodies is justified in economic terms, the struggle for abortion rights is a key component of the class struggle.

This view is criticized for focusing too much on class distinctions when bodily autonomy affects women and pregnant people across social classes. If the purpose of criminalizing abortion is to control the bodies of working-class women specifically, why then does the law apply to middle-class women, too? Recent studies in this area have conclusively demonstrated that although the law applies formally to all, working class women suffer disproportionately from poor access to healthcare, abortion in particular. Research conducted by the Guttmarcher Institute in the US showed that women near the poverty line disproportionately required abortion access (Jones et al, 2010). In Ireland support for access to abortion has been most evident in areas of Dublin that are more likely to house working-class voters (Bohan, 2018). Access to a termination is always easier for those who have the means to travel and/or avail of private healthcare.

An alternative view arises from the radical feminist tradition, where the state and thus oppression is viewed as primarily patriarchal, rather than capitalist. In this view the state is characterized as male-dominated, male-orientated and predisposed to mistreat female bodies not just deliberately but also arbitrarily. West (1988: 61) stated that women are 'people who value intimacy, fear separation, dread invasion and crave individuation' and that state institutions, legal systems and jurisprudence have all failed to value such concerns, but rather the values of the powerful institutions, real or theoretical, which underpin state power. In Ireland, this meant the Catholic Church.

There is consensus that the retention of the 1861 Act and the 8th Amendment that entrenched it were driven by forces loyal to Church teaching. The Catechism of the Catholic Church defends the 'right to life and physical integrity from the moment of conception' (USCBC, 2020: 550: s 2273) and so in this sense the state is giving expression to the patriarchal ideology of the Church. There is certainly evidence that the manner in which abortion remained the concern of criminal, rather than medical, law was heavily determined by state and semi-state institutions that were subject to Church influence or control. Foucault (1991) argued that authorities used all manner of institutions, from hospitals and schools to asylums and prisons to render human bodies docile and useful to the state and the capitalist economy and thus developed this through the concept of 'Biopower' (Foucault, 1976). Feminists have taken issue with Foucault's genderless conception of these docile bodies, since he does not recognize the different way that women's bodies are set upon for regulation and control. It has become a major theme of poststructuralist feminism to apply Foucault's methods to an analysis of what they see as a highly gendered 'biopower', one that acts very differently and often, more violently, towards women.

However, it is possible to demonstrate that the institutions that policed women's bodies, sex lives and family lives were not only intensely gendered (Connolly, 2003) but also that they offered utility to a small, weak and poor Irish state. For example, Beaumont (1997) puts the abortion taboo in the context of a set of institutions that define Catholic womanhood more generally – docile, submissive, sexually pure, and so on. Her study notes that the influence of Catholic doctrine was so pervasive that women's organizations who resisted the second-class citizenship of Irish women often took issue only with the means by which the state restricted women's lives, rather than the principle of equality itself and that this can be traced back to Catholic hegemony in education, media and politics.

It was precisely through the biopolitical institutions explored by Foucault that the Catholic Church operated in Ireland, promoting traditional notions of womanhood and defining the concepts of 'deviance' and 'shame' (Fischer, 2016: 821). These included Magdalene Laundries, convents, reformatory and industrial schools and asylums as well as public schools and hospitals. It is true, however, that the report into abuse in such places has emphasized that they were not uniquely Catholic institutions, suggesting that there were secular, as well as religious, motivations for shaming unmarried mothers and others deemed to have deviated from the expected norms of Irish family life (Department for Justice and Equality, 2013).

Still, it is the case that strong religious organizations do play a role in the 'symbolic politics' (Welch et al, 1995: 1) where a person's views on the issue represents deeply held beliefs about ideology more broadly. Controlling bodily autonomy achieves more than simply preventing the termination of pregnancy simply because it results in aborted foetuses. It is also part of a whole range of technologies, laws and practices that determine how women see themselves and therefore their potential to resist authority. It also served to leave antiquated law fossilized on the statute books, reflecting 19th-century religious attitudes. This was also the case in Northern Ireland, where the Presbyterian and evangelical Churches, who once represented a majority of citizens, also opposed liberalization (Mitchell and Tilley, 2004).

Having ensured there was little space for public discussion of abortion, the political institutions found the issue very easy to ignore, outside of a few infrequent flashpoints. Laury Oaks (2002), analysing the effects of the case law of the 1990s, expertly deploys feminist criticism of state inaction and the traditional notions of the state as a pluralist machine. Far from the political institutions facilitating debate and responding to the needs of citizens, Oaks (2002) draws the conclusion that political parties and governments feared the difficulties of political decision-making and the threat of US-style lobbying and anti-abortionist violence, and so shrugged their responsibilities. This meant that even after public opinion, economic necessity and state ideology had shifted dramatically, the law remained unchanged.

The question of why anti-abortion laws survived well into the 21st century in both jurisdictions is not merely an academic question. Activists have had to understand accurately what forces are at work defending the criminalization of abortion in order to turn their attention to abolition of those laws and practices. If simply a question of adherence to Catholic doctrine they might pose questions about the need for a separation of Church and state, while economic arguments might mean more of a turn towards trade union work. But primarily the movements that emerged in the early 2010s discovered that the debate had too long been centred on notions of morality, Irishness and modernization. The debate would turn sharply towards questions of healthcare and provision and, put simply, 'the right to abortion was understood as a political question, about the sort of society people wanted' (Holborow, 2019: 20).

## Contemporary abortion rights activism in Ireland

The Good Friday Agreement signed in 1998 gave rise to a new hope across Northern Ireland, where a power-sharing framework between opposing sides was enshrined in a new Stormont government. This new Stormont first began to exercise devolved power in 1999 and was praised as the culmination of an optimistic 'peace process'. It very quickly transpired that any hopes that there could be space for women and minority rights were premature. As the Legislative Assembly required a majority from both the 'Unionist' and 'Nationalist' sides to pass legislation, it proved difficult to move beyond sectarian disagreements. Of course, women and minority group issues affected both nationalist and unionist women, but just as these had been sidelined during the Troubles as irrelevant to the constitutional struggles, they now became a threat to the large parties and their traditional voting blocs. There was a short-lived Women's Coalition that entered Stormont in its early days, but the necessity to pick a 'side' of the chamber to align with made talking about women's issues almost impossible (Cowell-Meyers, 2011: 411).

Murtagh (2008: 21) argued that it was the 'adverse political climate of polarisation' that denied the Women's Coalition the opportunity to advance politics in Stormont. This also seems to be the case in some of the elections where smaller parties faced a squeeze from the larger nationalist and unionist parties. The flagship policies of the larger parties were usually centred on constitutional, identity and legacy issues. Women's rights have tended to be divisive within these parties, particularly in the Social Democratic and Labour Party and Sinn Féin and thus rarely take central positions in their manifestos. This ensures that politicians can avoid debating or campaigning on matters of policy. On several social issues where the majority of the electorate might favour a change in the law, the base of their party might be split fairly equally and successive opinion polls highlight these gaps (White, 2019). Thus, the stonewalling of issues of bodily autonomy and other issues has been exacerbated by the sectarian divide and also by the devolved institutions set up to manage that divide.

None of the major political parties in Northern Ireland took a pro-choice position before June 2018. Research conducted by O'Brien and Watters prior to an election found that many Members of the Legislative Assembly were, by their own admission, ill-informed about abortion policy and the researchers noted anecdotally that the respondents to their survey often objected to even being asked their position on the decriminalization of abortion in the case of foetal fatal abnormality (O'Brien and Watters, 2018). Some questioned the validity of such research and took to social media to condemn the researchers. Smaller parties such as the Green Party and People Before Profit were vocal about abortion rights but could not put the issue onto the agenda without a breakthrough in the unionist and nationalist blocks. In the meantime, community and activist groups stepped in to provide informal and sometimes illegal support for women and pregnant people needing abortions. Although the number is impossible to quantify, one estimate is that between 1980 and 2016, over 170,000 travelled from Ireland to Britain for an abortion (McKay, 2018). This presents a paradox – the numbers suggest that abortion affected large sections of the community directly or indirectly. It makes sense that most people knew a close friend or relative who had travelled to access abortion. Yet the stigma and silence remained. Failure to legislate for abortion as recently as 2015, and in particular the special cases of rape, incest, threat to life of the mother and fatal foetal abnormality helped preserve the taboo in a kind of suspended animation (McDaid, 2016). It is useful, here, to recall the role played by healthcare professionals and law enforcement in forming the discourses of bodily autonomy. The culture of fear and silence in the spheres where abortion is normally discussed as healthcare meant that the political and social taboos reinforced each other.

The breakthrough came in 2012 when the mainstream media reported the death of Savita Halappanavar (Holland, 2012). Savita, a migrant dentist in her early 30s living in Galway, was 17 weeks pregnant when she died in a maternity ward of sepsis, after she was denied an abortion (Berer, 2013). Her death caused a wave of outrage across the island, with hundreds and then thousands marching on the streets. The case was significant because it demonstrated the shortcomings of what has been described as a 'safety valve' (Carnegie and Roth, 2019: 2) in Ireland's anti-abortion regime. The safety valve is the method by which the state can export the responsibilities of healthcare by explicitly legalizing travel to seek abortions abroad. The case helped emphasize that many more people now viewed abortion as a question of access to healthcare, not about morality or even rights, but about safety, security and life.

As the public mood shifted noticeably after Savita's death (McDonnell and Murphy, 2019) and the demand for justice for her family under the slogan of 'never again', this brought a new generation of activists into action. Unlike the activists who had fought the 8th Amendment to the Constitution in 1983, which effectively outlawed abortion, these activists had the internet and could mobilize quickly. The Citizens Assembly met in 2016 and recommended numerous changes to the Irish Constitution, including Equal Marriage and Abortion. Enda Kenny's Fine Gael-Labour government called a referendum on same-sex marriage in May 2016, and fell silent on abortion. The marriage amendment was then approved by an overwhelming majority in the public vote and by all but one of the counties in the Republic of Ireland. Many reproductive rights activists were involved in the campaign. It gave great confidence to those making the argument for three reasons. First, it demonstrated the weakened grip of the Church in matters of social policy. Second, it was clear that even more conservative rural areas of Ireland were more liberal than had previously been assumed. Third, there was now a clear blueprint for winning change in a way that had not been seen for many years. Assumptions about Ireland's supposed social conservatism proved unfounded and many more activists now saw success in a plebiscite as a real possibility. The success in the equal marriage referendum was followed immediately by an announcement by the Irish Labour Party to back the repeal of the 8th Amendment (McLoughlin, 2016).

The five years between Savita's death and 2017 saw the pro-choice movement test and replicate a number of new tactics that kept abortion rights on the agenda, and in doing so they successfully forced the Irish government to commit to reform. This was aided by Enda Kenny stepping down as Taoiseach. From November 2016 until April 2017 a Citizens Assembly met, with a mandate from the Oireachtas (parliament) to advise on constitutional change. The movement seized this opportunity. Artists and actors came out in support, for example Eva O'Connor's prize-winning performance poem 'It Shouldn't Have to Be This Hard' accumulated over five million views on BBC and Vimeo (O'Connor, 2017). University campuses across Ireland and the Irish diaspora across the world established societies and made use of social media for ordinary people to share their abortion stories helping to destigmatize and personalize the issue of choice. For example, the X-ile Project (X-ile Project, 2015) emerged to create 'an online gallery of people who have accessed abortion services outside of Ireland and Northern Ireland.

The website also encouraged participation from transgender, non-binary people, and anyone who can be pregnant (Ocasio, 2016). Other campaigns such as #welfarenotairfare developed, culminating in regular protests at the Irish embassy from the Irish diaspora in England. Students, lawyers, doctors, retired Irish people, organized together in the London Irish Abortion Rights Campaign, backing up media stunts with well-informed research and a multi-faceted action way of engaging in the movement. Existing organizations including I.M.E.L.D.A. (Ireland Making England the Legal Destination for Abortion), set up in 2014, joined a broad coalition of other pro-choice groups helping to keep abortion rights in the headlines. Indeed internationally, the Irish diaspora played their role both by keeping pressure on the Irish government and by setting up working groups and campaigns across the world. A women's strike was called for on International Women's Day in March 2017 and saw 10,000 march in Dublin and thousands march globally to demand reform in Ireland. Just two months after this campaign, the new Taoiseach Leo Varadkar responded to the swell of abortion rights protests, calling a referendum to be held in May 2018. This reflects the notion that carving out a public space, not simply to debate the merits of decriminalization, but to break a decades-long taboo, was essential in ending state inaction and forcing the hand of a reluctant political class.

In Ireland itself, groups and individuals from the Republic and from Northern Ireland volunteered in large numbers for the #togetherforyes campaign to repeal the 8th Amendment. Right-wing religious groups spent huge amounts of money, particularly on high-profile signage and advertising. There have been allegations that Joseph Scheidler, a prominent American anti-abortion campaigner, boasted that hundreds of thousands of dollars had poured into Ireland (Nagle, 2016). But older activists noted smaller numbers active in church groups opposing repeal and the Church was far more muted on the subject than had been the case in 1983 (McDonagh, 2017). It was the range of forces that gathered around repeal that made the difference and the public reacted by repealing the 8th Amendment on 25 May 2018.

Fletcher (2018: 258), reflecting on the Repeal movement, wrote that it 'made the impossible possible as moments of conversation, together with their silent pauses, at kitchen tables, information stalls, street platforms and media studios, assembled somehow and turned a deceptively simple "yes" out of a mess of collective joy, heart-breaking stories, legal exchange and reproductive connections'. The significance of the vote is difficult to overstate. The result was a majority of 66.4 per cent, which proved beyond what many seasoned campaigners, including ourselves, had expected. All but one county out of 26 returned a majority 'Yes' for Repeal. At the celebration rally at Dublin Castle later on the day of the count, a homemade sign caught the attention of cameras. It read 'The North is Next' and captured the imagination of broadcasters, who began interviewing celebrating activists about a possible change in the law north of the border and the #TheNorthIsNext campaign quickly emerged as the next focus. The fact that so many people from the North had canvassed and campaigned for Repeal made the shift possible. Meanwhile, in Northern Ireland, there was simultaneously a tightening of the implementation of the Offences Against the Person Act (1861) from the Police Service of Northern Ireland (PSNI) (Sheldon et al, 2020).

It was clear to activists that there was an increasing crackdown on abortion rights in Northern Ireland. This is evidenced by the increasing instances of houses being raided by the PSNI. They targeted feminists in possession of abortion pills and seized the medicine that is perfectly legal in the rest of the United Kingdom (Fenton, 2017). One escalation was the prosecution of a young woman who was found guilty of breaking the law after her flatmates phoned the police when they discovered she had procured an abortion through pills as she could not afford the travel to England (Sheldon et al, 2020). Another woman from Northern Ireland was prosecuted after assisting her teenage daughter in accessing abortion pills and faced up to five years in prison for doing so. She was only acquitted after the old law was repealed in October 2019 (Young, 2019).

As the confidence of the movement crystallized, individual stories became more widely acknowledged and celebrated. Sarah Ewart, who went public with her abortion story in 2016 and spearheaded a campaign to liberalize abortion laws, persuaded the High Court to rule that the denial of her right to terminate an unviable pregnancy was unlawful (Amnesty International, 2019). This drew much-needed attention to unusual but tragic stories of inevitable stillbirths that result from the denial of abortion rights. These stories appeared to have pushed public opinion in Northern Ireland towards a more sympathetic view on decriminalization, with Amnesty polls regularly showing that with each year the public would support decriminalization at increasingly high rates (Amnesty International, 2018). The gap between public opinion and politicians had been steadily growing, as more details emerged of institutional scandals that had devastated women's lives. Pressure arising from activism, especially around individual court cases, added to the growing body of evidence that the law in Northern Ireland fell foul of international human rights law (CEDAW, 2018).

The set of Catholic-dominated institutions that simultaneously oppressed women and hamstrung their potential to resist had long been in terminal decline. But some revelations discredited their legitimacy conclusively. The babies of unmarried women had often been taken from them and put into Catholic care homes. Notoriously, in 2016, a plot of 796 dead babies and children was found in an unmarked grave of a derelict care home in Tuam, County Galway (Garrett, 2017). Campaigners spoke of a system that for decades saw the Catholic Church protected for their crimes against women and children in these laundries discussed. Keating's (2004a) essential research on historic abuses of the Church and state argues that it was the desperation to appear as a successful state to the outside world that helped suppress these horrific abuses. He describes this as a process whereby:

> The state seems paralysed from action for fear of being left holding the baby and of sullying the reputation of the very organisation that acted as custodian of the state's founding myth, i.e. Ireland as the model Catholic nation. This culture of abuse, then, was aided and abetted by a covenant between church and state which resulted in the various religious orders doing as they pleased in relation to the running of these institutions. (Keating, 2004a: 164)

The combination of a Church reeling from successive scandals and the concomitant drop in church attendance meant Ireland North and South finally began to experience a secularization that it had long resisted. It was in this context in Ireland that the reproductive rights movement found its mass support. It struck many people as ironic that the Church and its campaigning 'pro-life' groups, which supposedly cherished life and dignity and would 'love them both', was responsible for the deaths of children and had enacted a suppression of those crimes. Catherine Corless, an amateur historian who meticulously uncovered the records of the deaths, spoke about the reaction of the authorities to finding their tiny, shrouded bodies dumped in a disused septic tank: 'If you come here, you'll find no mass grave, no evidence that children were ever so buried and a local police force casting their eyes to heaven and saying "Yeah, a few bones were found – but this was an area where Famine victims were buried. So?"' (Barry, 2017). The impact of the revelation struck another blow to the perceived authority of the Catholic Church in matters of family and morality.

With social conservatism on the back foot, and Stormont still not sitting to give a voice to the anger over inaction on decriminalization, activists in Northern Ireland took their campaign directly to Westminster. Amnesty International released a statement arguing that 'inaction is no longer an option. The UK Government cannot remain complicit in the harm caused by the existing abortion regime – the time for change is now' (Teggart, 2019).

## Northern Ireland

After a century and a half of ancient law criminalizing women for their reproductive choices, Articles 58 and 59 of the infamous 1861 Act were repealed on 22 October 2019. Since the Stormont-based executive was suspended, activists from Ireland focused their campaign on backbench MPs in Britain who successfully took advantage of a weakened Tory government by passing the repeal of the amendments. Traditionally the

British government would not intervene in what they considered devolved matters, and as recently as December 2018 had issued a statement reiterating this point after pressure from Amnesty International, stating:

> [T]he current situation in Northern Ireland should dislodge that principle, particularly in circumstances where the Government is working towards the restoration of devolved government in Northern Ireland ... [the] Government will keep this position under review in light of its international and domestic obligations, and in light of any relevant emerging legal judgments, as appropriate. (Parliament UK, 2019)

The new guidelines in Northern Ireland were also underpinned by the caveat that they would only go through so long as Stormont did not reconvene before then. While activists from across Ireland welcomed the long-awaited modernization of the law, the largest party in Stormont, the Democratic Unionist Party (DUP), whose right-wing ideology includes supporting the criminalization of abortion, were invited by the British Secretary of State for Northern Ireland to take their seats again if they wanted to have their say in the legislation. Smith, addressing the DUP on the Northern Ireland channel UTV, less than two weeks before the new policy would be rolled out, said:

> We need to get movement for decision-making across the board this week to help public services, help citizens in Northern Ireland get the decisions they need, but to shape that abortion law, reform that is best shaped in Northern Ireland, we need parties in talks this week and to be back in an Executive by next Monday. (Cross, 2019)

This controversial move showed that women's and pregnant people's bodies were still political objects for elites to exchange because inevitably, and publicly, the DUP's position on abortion has never wavered from anything other than a total ban on abortion. On one hand, the British establishment maintains that citizens of Northern Ireland are legally British, but on the other hand, shows no inclination to provide citizens in that state the same access to civil liberties and freedom as they do to the rest of the UK. So, neither the current British government, nor the Stormont government have taken action and it is here we see feminist resistance at its most decisive, placing the issue of reproductive justice onto the agenda despite concerted state resistance. Still, despite the best efforts of the anti-abortion movement, the campaign won and the law was passed. It remains to be seen how this will be implemented and funded but the campaign was successful in meeting its short-term aims.

Dictating solutions for Northern Ireland from Westminster can only be a temporary solution to the intractable democratic deficit. A particularly incisive criticism of the state of affairs in Northern Ireland published in October 2019 by the Institute for Government found that 'we repeatedly heard Northern Ireland described as an "immature" political system, with ministers focusing on short-term political point-scoring rather than making difficult long-term choices' (Sargeant and Rutter, 2019: 6). While it remains the case that politicians and the state continue to use our rights and bodies as election slogans, we will continue to demand a service that is locally provided to anyone who needs it. This should be regardless of their citizenship status, should be free and safe, and, ultimately, should be a service that is provided away from the shame and stigma that has dictated the actions and inactions of the states. At the time of writing (July 2021) there are already reports that agreements are being made between the DUP and Sinn Féin to exclude disability from the list of recognized grounds for a termination, indicating that there may be many political battles in the near future over what provision looks like.

## Conclusion

This chapter has outlined some of the historical reasons why Ireland's abortion laws remained stagnant and why the change has come rapidly in recent years. In particular we have noted the process by which Church authority became a cornerstone of the state and its institutions at a time when other states in Europe were becoming more secularized. The literature illustrates that this had a detrimental effect on the institutions that normally facilitate the development of discourse around reproductive health, so that attitudes as well as regulations failed to reflect the needs of the citizens and the political institutions mirror and reified the most conservative views. Where public debate did take place, elected representatives were often fearful of the consequences taking a public stance because of the power of US-backed anti-abortion groups as well as influential constituents in Ireland. It took the development of a new, internet-enabled younger generation of activists, freed from the demoralization of past defeats, to build spaces where informed and fact-based discussion could finally take place.

The contemporary movement to repeal the 8th Amendment and also to extend abortion rights to Northern Ireland exploited contradictions in state power. This was because the states relied on the longevity and rigidity of the historical law as a bulwark against reform, but the unyielding nature of both the 1861 Act and the 8th Amendment meant that only radical change was possible, as had been proven through successive High Court cases where evolution of the law proved impossible. It has been demonstrated that state institutions proved incapable of refining the law or even giving clarity to health professionals and it was campaigning by women's groups both in Ireland and the diaspora that made continuity of the status quo an impossibility.

However, obstructionism remains a key tactic in preventing the implementation of services for abortion in Northern Ireland. As recently as 19 July 2021, DUP leader Jeffrey Donaldson warned that commissioning the necessary services would threaten 'the credibility of our political institutions' in an attempt to make opposition to a liberalization of the abortion law a constitutional issue (Young, 2021). Health Minister Robin Swann came under considerable criticism too, during the COVID-19 pandemic, when, during the lockdown it became apparent that abortion services remained unavailable and pregnant people were still making the journey to England (Young, 2021). Such examples show a hostile ruling party to the huge gains made by activists across the island. Thus, decriminalization does not automatically mean comprehensive provision and it will be necessary to consider and address new methods by which the state might deny access to abortion in both jurisdictions. In that sense the victories of recent years are as yet incomplete and new confrontations with the state are inevitable.

Still, this chapter has also shown, through examination of recent sources, how the campaigns made use of new technologies and networks as well as all-island solidarity, to carve out a space for activism that had not previously been possible. This allowed for widespread discussion of individual accounts of crisis pregnancies and of terminations denied. This led to a subsequent 'normalizing' of abortion stories, where in the past only unusual circumstances might have merited media coverage. Such changes demonstrate the effective agency of campaigning groups rather than the inevitable outcome of economic and demographic changes. It has been clear in all of these events that the state has acted reluctantly, slowly and with little sense of purpose. But where it did act, for example in the post-repeal clampdown in Northern Ireland, the effect was to highlight abortion as a social crime, no longer carrying the same level of taboo that it had previously. The movement for bodily autonomy in Ireland has won a series of enormous victories and in the future we will continue to push for universal reproductive healthcare for everyone: free, safe, legal, local and on-demand.

## References

Amnesty International (2018) 'Northern Ireland abortion law poll', [online] available at: https://www.amnesty.org.uk/northern-ireland-abortion-law-poll [accessed 24 June 2019].

Amnesty International (2019) 'Northern Ireland abortion: Sarah Ewart in High Court to challenge the law', [online] available at: https://www.amnesty.org.uk/press-releases/northern-ireland-abortion-sarah-ewart-high-court-challenge-law [accessed 24 June 2019].

Barry, D. (2016) 'Airbrushed out of history? Elizabeth O'Farrell and Patrick Pearse's surrender, 1916', *The Irish History*, [online] 10 March, available at: https://www.theirishstory.com/2016/03/10/airbrushed-out-of-hist ory-elizabeth-ofarrell-and-patrick-pearses-surrender-1916/ [accessed 21 March 2020].

Barry, D. (2017) 'Ireland wanted to forget. But the dead don't always stay buried', *The New York Times*, [online] 28 October, available at: https:// www.nytimes.com/interactive/2017/10/28/world/europe/tuam-ireland-babies-children.html [accessed 21 March 2020].

Beaumont, C (1997) 'Women, citizenship and Catholicism in the Irish free state, 1922–1948', *Women's History Review*, 6(4): 563–85.

Berer, M. (2013) 'Termination of pregnancy as emergency obstetric care: The interpretation of Catholic health policy and the consequences for pregnant women', *Reproductive Health Matters*, 21(41): 9–17.

Bohan, C. (2018) 'It's Yes: Ireland has voted to repeal the Eighth Amendment', *Thejournal.ie*, [online] 25 May, available at: https://jrnl.ie/ 4034416 [accessed 20 July 2020].

Carnegie, A, and Roth, R. (2019) 'From the grassroots to the Oireachtas: Abortion law reform in the Republic of Ireland', *Health and Human Rights*, 21(2): 109–20.

CEDAW (2018) 'Observations of the Government of the United Kingdom of Great Britain and Northern Ireland on the report of the inquiry concerning the Committee on the Elimination of Discrimination against Women under article 8 of the Optional Protocol to the Convention on the Elimination of All Forms of Discrimination against Women', [online] available at: https:// tbinternet.ohchr.org/Treaties/CEDAW/Shared%20Documents/GBR/ INT_CEDAW_ITB_GBR_8637_E.pdf [accessed 26 March 2020].

Connolly, E. (2003) 'Durability and change in state gender systems: Ireland in the 1950s', *European Journal of Women's Studies*, 10(1): 65–86.

Cowell-Meyers, K. (2011) 'A collarette on a donkey: The Northern Ireland Women's Coalition and the limitations of contagion theory', *Political Studies*, 59(2): 411–31.

Cross, G. (2019) 'Secretary of State warns Stormont must return by Monday if parties want say on abortion reform', *The Belfast Telegraph*, [online] 14 October, available at: https://www.belfasttelegraph.co.uk/news/north ern-ireland/secretary-of-state-warns-stormont-must-return-by-mon day-if-parties-want-say-on-abortion-reform-38593795.html [accessed 26 March 2020].

Department for Justice and Equality (2013) *Report of the Inter-Departmental Committee to Establish the Facts of State Involvement with the Magdalen Laundries*, [online] available at: http://www.justice.ie/en/JELR/Pages/Magdalen Rpt2013 [accessed 22 March 2020].

Engels, F. (2019/1884) *Origin of the Family, Private Property and the State*, London: Forgotten Books.

Farrell, M. (1990) *The Orange State*, London: Pluto Press.

Fenton, S. (2017) 'Northern Irish police raid women's homes in crackdown on abortion pills', *The Independent*, [online] 23 March, available at: https://www.independent.co.uk/news/uk/crime/northern-ireland-abortion-pill-raids-police-women-homes-workplaces-a7627211.html [accessed 12 October 2019].

Finnegan, F. (2001) *Do Penance or Perish: A Study of Magdalen Asylums in Ireland*, Kilkenny: Congrave Press.

Fischer, C. (2016) 'Gender, nation, and the politics of shame: Magdalen laundries and the institutionalization of feminine transgression in modern Ireland', *Journal of Women in Culture and Society*, 41(4): 821–43.

Fletcher, R. (2018) '#RepealedThe8th: Translating travesty, global conversation, and the Irish abortion referendum', *Feminist Legal Studies*, 26(3): 233–59.

Foucault, M. (1976) *The Will to Knowledge: The History of Sexuality* (volume 1), London: Penguin Books.

Foucault, M. (1991) *Discipline and Punish*, Harmondsworth: Penguin Books.

Garrett, P.M. (2017) 'Excavating the past: Mother and baby homes in the Republic of Ireland', *The British Journal of Social Work*, 47(2): 358–74.

Girvin, B. (1996) 'Church, state and the Irish constitution: The secularisation of Irish politics?', *Parliamentary Affairs*, 49(4): 599–615.

Hearne, D. (1992) 'The Irish citizen 1914–1916: Nationalism, feminism, and militarism', The *Canadian Journal of Irish Studies*, 18(1): 1–14.

Holborow, M. (2019) 'Ireland's abortion victory: Women's lives, the liberal agenda and the radical left', *International Socialism*, 160: 19–38.

Holland, K. (2012) 'Savita Halappanavar's death may stir Ireland to change over abortion', *The Guardian*, [online] 18 November, available at: https://www.theguardian.com/commentisfree/2012/nov/18/savita-halappanavar-death-abortion-ireland-change [accessed 22 March 2020].

Houses of the Oireachtas (2018) 'Democratic programme', Dáil Eireann 100, available at: https://www.dail100.ie/en/long-reads/democratic-programme/ [accessed 26 March 2020].

Jones, R., Finer, L., and Singh, S. (2010) 'Characteristics of U.S. abortion patients', *The Guttmacher Institute*. Available at: https://www.guttmacher.org/sites/default/files/report_pdf/us-abortion-patients.pdf [accessed 20 July 2021].

Kasstan, B. (2018) 'Irish voters repealed the eighth: Now it's time to ensure access to abortion care in law and in practice', *Reproductive Health Matters*, 26(52): 51–3.

Keating, A. (2004a) 'Church, state, and sexual crime against children in Ireland after 1922', *Radharc*, 5/7: 155–80. Available at: www.jstor.org/sta ble/25122348, [accessed 28 July 2020].

Keating, A. (2004b) 'Censorship: The cornerstone of Catholic Ireland', *Journal of Church and State*, 57(2): 289–309.

Luddy, M. (1995) *Women in Ireland 1800–1918*, Cork: Cork University Press.

MacKinnon, C.A. (1989) *Towards a Feminist Theory of the State*, Cambridge, MA: Harvard University Press.

McAuliffe, M., Gillis, L., Ní Chléirigh, É. and Almqvist, M. (2016) *'We were there' – 77 women of the Easter Rising*, Dublin: Four Courts Press.

McDaid, M. (2016) 'With reproductive rights from Victorian times, how could I move back to Ireland?', *The Irish Times*, [online] 15 February, available at: https://www.irishtimes.com/life-and-style/abroad/generat ion-emigration/with-reproductive-rights-from-victorian-times-how-could-i-move-back-to-ireland-1.2535419 [accessed 26 March 2020].

McDiarmid, L. (2015) *At Home in the Revolution: What Women Said and Did in 1916*, Dublin: Royal Irish Academy.

McDonagh, M. (2017) 'Ireland's abortion debate is happening without Catholic church', *The Post*, [online] 2 October, available at: https://unh erd.com/2017/10/irelands-abortion-debate-happening-without-catho lic-church/ [accessed 26 March 2020].

McDonnell, O. and Murphy, P. (2019) 'Mediating abortion politics in Ireland: Media framing of the death of Savita Halappanavar', *Critical Discourse Studies*, 16(1): 1–20.

McKay, S. (2018) 'Ireland's nasty no campaign', *Foreign Policy: Dispatch*, [online] 24 May, available at: https://foreignpolicy.com/2018/05/24/irela nds-nasty-no-campaign/ [accessed 1 October 2019].

McKee, E. (1986) 'Church-State relations and the development of Irish health policy: The mother-and-child scheme, 1944–53', *Irish Historical Studies*, 25(98): 159–94.

McLoughlin, E. (2016) 'Joan Burton vows to hold abortion vote if re-elected', *Irish Examiner*, [online] 16 February, available at: https://www. irishexaminer.com/ireland/joan-burton-vows-to-hold-abortion-vote-if-re-elected-382111.html [accessed 2 May 2020].

Mitchell, C. and Tilley, J. (2004) 'The moral minority: Evangelical protestants in Northern Ireland and their political behaviour', *Political Studies*, 52(3): 585–602.

Murtagh, C. (2008) 'A transient transition: The cultural and institutional obstacles impeding the Northern Ireland women's coalition in its progression from informal to formal politics', *Irish Political Studies*, 23(1): 21–40.

Nagle, A. (2016) 'Why American pro-life dollars are pouring into Ireland', *The Atlantic*, [online] 30 January, available at: https://www.theatlantic.com/sexes/archive/2013/01/why-american-pro-life-dollars-are-pouring-into-ireland/266981/ [accessed 26 March 2020].

Northern Ireland Office (2020) 'Changes to the law in Northern Ireland: Updated information', [online] 25 March, available at: https://www.gov.uk/government/news/changes-to-the-law-in-northern-ireland-updated-information [accessed 20 May 2020].

Ó Buachalla, S. (1985) 'Church and state in Irish education in this century', *European Journal of Education*, 20(4): 351–9.

O'Brien, M. and Watters, R. (2018) 'Reproductive justice activism by spreadsheet: Documenting assembly election candidates' attitudes towards abortion reform in Northern Ireland', presented at *Abortion and Reproductive Justice: The Unfinished Revolution III* conference at Rhodes University, Grahamstown, South Africa, July 2018.

O'Connor, E. (2017) 'It shouldn't have to be this hard', [online] available at: https://vimeo.com/113618478 [accessed 26 March 2020].

Oaks, L. (2002) 'Abortion is part of the Irish experience, it is part of what we are: The transformation of public discourses on Irish abortion policy', *Women's Studies International Forum*, 25(3): 315–33.

Ocasio, A. (2016) 'The X-Ile project helps Ireland to "face the 8th"', *Queens Free Press*, [online] 30 June, available at: https://www.queensfreepress.com/2016/06/30/the-x-ile-project-helps-ireland-to-face-the-8th/ [accessed 29 March 2020].

Offences Against the Person Act (1861) Articles 58 and 59, available at: https://www.legislation.gov.uk/ukpga/Vict/24-25/100/crossheading/attempts-to-procure-abortion [accessed 12 October 2019].

Parliament UK (2019) 'Abortion law in Northern Ireland', (Section 5) Responsibility Under International Human Rights Obligations, [online] 20 April, available at: https://publications.parliament.uk/pa/cm201719/cmselect/cmwomeq/1584/158408.htm [accessed 26 March 2020].

Purséil, N. (2008) *Catholic Stakhanovites? Religion and the Irish Labour Party, Essays in Irish Labour History: A Festschrift for Elizabeth and John W. Boyle*, Dublin: Irish Academic Press.

Sargeant, J. and Rutter, J. (2019) *Governing Without Ministers: Northern Ireland Since the Fall of the Power-Sharing Executive*, Institute for Government. Available at: https://www.instituteforgovernment.org.uk/sites/default/files/publications/governing-without-ministers-northern-ireland.pdf [accessed 26 March 2020].

Sheldon, S., O'Neill, J., Parker, C. and Davis, G. (2020) '"Too much, too indigestible, too fast"? The decades of struggle for abortion law reform in Northern Ireland', *Modern Law Review*, 83(4): 761–96.

Teggart, G. (2019) 'Northern Ireland abortion: Westminster inquiry mounts pressure on UK government to reform law', Press Release (Amnesty International), available at: https://www.amnesty.org.uk/press-releases/ northern-ireland-abortion-westminster-inquiry-mounts-pressure-uk-gov ernment-reform [accessed 21 March 2020].

USCBC (2020) Catechism of the Catholic Church. *Libreria Editrice Vaticana*, [online] available at: http://ccc.usccb.org/flipbooks/catechism/index.html [accessed 21 March 2020].

Welch, M., Leege, D. and Cavendish, J. (1995) 'Attitudes toward abortion among U.S. Catholics: Another case of symbolic politics?', *Social Science Quarterly*, 76(1): 142–57.

West, R. (1988) 'Jurisprudence and gender', *University of Chicago Law Review*, 55(1): 1–72.

White, B. (2019) 25th October 2019: LT NI Opinion Panel Poll-Project – *NI Quarterly 'Tracker' Poll* October 2019: Final Results Report (Version 1) Date (Base Version 1): 25th October 2019 for *Lucid Talk*. Available at: https://www.lucidtalk.co.uk/single-post/2019/10/29/lt-ni-opinion-panel-quarterly-tracker-poll-october-2019 [accessed 20 June 2022].

X-ile Project (2015) Available at: http://www.x-ileproject.com/about [accessed 1 October 2019].

Young, D. (2019) 'Mother cleared over online abortion pills after law change', *Irish News Online*, [online] 23 October, available at: https://www.irishnews. com/news/healthcarenews/2019/10/23/news/mother-cleared-over-onl ine-abortion-pills-after-law-change-1746666/ [accessed 23 October 2019].

Young, D. (2021) 'Jeffrey Donaldson warns against British government intervention on North's abortion law', *Irish News Online*, [online] available at: https://www.irishnews.com/news/northernirelandnews/2021/07/19/ news/jeffrey-donaldson-warns-against-british-government-intervention-on-north-s-abortion-law-2391901/ [accessed 19 July 2021].

# 4

# At the Limits of 'Acceptable' Speech: A Feminist Analysis of Official Discourse on Child Sexual Abuse

*Katie Tucker*

## Introduction

This chapter draws upon doctoral research into institutional responses to child sexual abuse (CSA) in England between the years of 2010 and 2015. This period was referred to as a 'watershed' (BBC, 2015a) for both public awareness and reporting of CSA, both in terms of recent and historical cases (see IICSA, 2021). This heightened awareness was prompted by a number of high-profile cases coming to public attention within a relatively short space of time. These cases include, but are not limited to, large-scale abuse in a number of English towns and regions, including: Blackburn with Darwen, Bristol, Derby, Kent, Newcastle, Oldham, Oxford, Peterborough, Preston and Telford (see *Express*, 2017). In addition to these cases, abuse perpetrated by high-profile individuals such as Cyril Smith, Gary Glitter and Sir Jimmy Savile, among others, were brought to light, in part, due to the unprecedented Metropolitan Police investigation, codenamed Operation Yewtree.[1]

This chapter focuses on the ways in which CSA was put into official discourse in the period 2010 to 2015. Focusing on the high-profile cases of abuse in the English towns of Rochdale and Rotherham,[2] the chapter considers how the discursive framing of the problem developed in this period. The chapter considers the official responses to the cases in Rotherham and Rochdale through an examination of official discourse. Recognizing the long history of problems set out by feminists, with identifying and dealing with CSA (see, for instance, Rush, 1980; Gordon, 1988; La Fontaine, 1990; Smart, 1999, 2000, 2016), the chapter considers the recent discursive history through these two case studies. Starting from a recognition of the importance of definitions, and aiming to engage with what Ballinger (2016: 9) highlights as the 'politics of naming' (see also Chapter 2 in this volume), the analysis considers the discursive construction of the problem – including the perpetrators and victims – and the proposed solutions as contained in official discourse. The aim here is to examine the extent to which the 'watershed' period of 2010 to 2015 changed the dominant discourse and whether, after these high-profile cases, feminist interventions were acknowledged or shut down.

## Background

In 2011 and 2012 respectively, the northern towns of Rochdale and Rotherham became the focal point of public attention concerning CSA. In both towns, revelations highlighted widespread abuse involving groups of male perpetrators and thousands of victims (Jay, 2014) and exposed historic institutional failures to protect children. In both towns, the perpetrators were predominantly British-Pakistani men and media emphasis on the dynamic between 'Asian men' and White victims, gave rise to the 'Asian grooming gang' panic that dominated news reporting of CSA in England (see Cockbain and Brayley, 2012; BBC, 2015b). The nature and extent of abuse in these cases meant that the 'Asian grooming gang' framing was the focal point for public debate around CSA, and arguably, became the lens through which CSA was then viewed (Cockbain and Brayley, 2012). Andrew Norfolk's (2011) *Times* exposé into 'grooming gangs' in the Midlands and Northern England (Rotherham, Telford, Derbyshire) further framed the issue of child sexual exploitation around 'race' and ethnicity and claimed to uncover a 'conspiracy of silence on UK sex gangs' (Norfolk, 2011). The media focus, reflected in much political discussion in this pivotal moment, was not upon the wider causes and effects of abuse and exploitation as discussed in this chapter, but instead emphasized the 'dangerous masculinities of Muslim men' (Tufail, 2015: 30).

The effects of structural inequalities in terms of 'race', ethnicity and gender are demonstrated throughout the cases in question. Structural inequality in these terms refers to inequalities that are both maintained and created through the way in which society itself is organized. In the case of Rotherham and Casey's (2015) report, 'Asian' ethnicity is presented as a relevant characteristic to the perpetration of abuse. Further, the victims' characteristics as White, working-class girls was also seen as synonymous with abuse; however, there is no critical discussion of inequality in the official discourse, nor the intersections that bring these inequalities into existence. Crenshaw (1989) argues that the experiences of Black women have been theoretically erased. It is here in this space, which demands the critical analysis of the multiple systems of power that create specific experiences, that there is, as Gilroy (2000: 45) argues, an 'urgent need for future work'. In intersectional terms, structural inequalities such as gender and 'race' must therefore be discussed in terms of their ability to collude through discriminatory power. It is this power that sees these issues 'render invisible experiences of the more marginal members of specific social categories and [these inequalities then] construct a homogenized "right way" to be its member' (Yuval-Davis, 2006: 195). Social divisions are examples of macro power, however it must be highlighted that these divisions involve real people (Yuval-Davis, 2006). These people experience the world, and their daily lives, in differing ways, especially in terms of discrimination and exclusion, and these experiences then create individual identities.

Social divisions such as 'race', class and ethnicity also have certain characteristics in common. Intrinsically, these divisions are seen as 'normal' or 'natural', existing due to biological elements related to genetics. These divisions with their claims to scientificity then 'create, in specific historical situations [such as experienced by both the victims and perpetrators of CSA in Rochdale and Rotherham] hierarchies of differential access to a variety of resources – economic, political and cultural' (Yuval-Davis, 2006: 199). For example, 'race' as a division remains an important mechanism for 'limiting and restricting access to privilege, power and wealth' (Smedley and Smedley, 2005: 22) and focus on this division, and its dislocation from other forms of structural inequality, is especially prevalent in the analysis to follow.

Although it could be argued that any institutional acknowledgement and recognition of sexual harm against children, as has been the case in England since the Rochdale and Rotherham cases, is welcomed from a feminist perspective, there are dangers associated with changing definitions of the problem and the state's role therein. The issues with (re)definition have long been acknowledged by feminists (Rush, 1980; Gordon, 1988; Smart, 1999, 2000, 2016) and ideas of what constitutes harm and abuse have evolved and changed. Historically, CSA has been defined as 'moral corruption', 'immorality', 'molestation', 'tampering', 'ruining' and 'juvenile/child prostitution' (Jackson, 2000). The importance of the use of language when examining CSA is intrinsic to its wider understandings. Thanks to feminist interventions (see, for instance, Rush, 1980; Renvoize, 1993; Bartley, 2000; Smart, 2000), 'child prostitution' has now been removed from legal, political and official discussions of CSA due to the implied agency and consent inherent within the term prostitution (House of Commons Home Affairs Committee, 2013). However, there remain issues with definition highlighted within these cases that will be further explored in what follows.

## Some critical feminist insights into child sexual abuse

The study of CSA has long occupied feminists, beginning in the 1870s, the movement against child abuse (Gordon, 1988) was a product of feminist thought and began by problematizing the sanctity of the Victorian family and opposing corporal punishment. This movement grew to include a focus on the routine sexual abuse of children, then described as 'juvenile prostitution' (Jackson, 2000). The movement then saw a pushback after the Second World War (Smart, 1999), and ground that had been gained in highlighting abuses within the family was quickly rescinded, with discourse shifting to prioritize the ideals of the private sphere, against the backdrop of a moral panic concerning 'foreign disease' brought home by servicemen (Gordon, 1988; Smart, 1999, 2000). This then saw the discourse shift to concentrate on the failure of mothers to domesticate and control their daughters and state responses were framed around 'moral neglect' and the promiscuity of the victim (Gordon, 1988).

After gaining ground and the pushback after the Second World War, women again began to break the silence on CSA and continued the struggle throughout the 20th century. The initial (re)cognition in the early 20th century was achieved due, in part, through women gaining common ground with the struggles of the right to vote, housing, healthcare, social care, access to contraception and the opposition to nuclear arms (Driver and Droisen, 1989). This (re)discovery of the presence of CSA in all arenas was a pivotal moment in the history of feminist interventions. However, several feminists (see Stanley et al, 1999; Browne, 2014; Millett, 2016; Smart, 2016) have since warned that this (re)discovery should not be seen as disconnected from the struggles of the present. It is important to note here that although feminists persisted in the struggle to have CSA recognized, it was not even constituted as abuse in law until the 1970s – before this abuse was defined as 'unlawful carnal knowledge, incest, a slip and so on' (Smart, 1999: 393). The historical discursive struggles exist then, as an intrinsic part of the process of 'framing the idea of CSA as a recognisable, problematic and harmful behaviour' (Smart, 1999: 393). These problems were then, and remain today, further heightened, due to the ongoing crises of definition, making it difficult to adopt coherent policy towards CSA (Smart, 1999). As this brief history demonstrates, the issue of CSA has long been a priority for feminists, particularly the importance of the discursive framing of the issue.

Having CSA recognized as a gendered problem is at the heart of the feminist struggle. 'Patriarchy is the most important contributor to child sexual abuse' (Bolen, 2001: 34). Patriarchy as used within the Women's Movement refers to male domination and to the power relationships by which men dominate women (Millett, 2016). The challenge must be to patriarchy as a 'fact of nature', to the passive and domestic woman versus the rational and physical man (Belsey and Moore, 1997: 3). Feminism for the 21st century, then, must both acknowledge and continue to challenge this *Patriarchal Equilibrium* (Bennett, 2006: 54). Further, for Smart (1989: 50), 'the root problem of CSA for feminism is that of masculine sexuality'. What Smart (1989) is arguing here is not that masculine sexuality is always violent, but that heterosexual masculine sexuality has the ability, in a patriarchal power structure, to dominate discourses and to disqualify and silence women and children's experiences of violence, and that it is a critique of this dominance and avoidance of accountability that feminism must centralize. Centralizing a critique to these power relations is key for feminist analyses of CSA. As Bell (1992) argues in her work on incest, it is the existence of unequal power relations that is fundamental to feminist struggles against the sexual abuse of children. Rather than understanding the exercise of power as a rigid structure, unmovable without patriarchy, critical feminist analyses acknowledge that the fluid concepts of power, gender and sex exist in an array of practices, experiences and strategies (Campbell, 2014). Foucault's arguments put forward within the *History of Sexuality* (1990) further argue that power is exercised through bodies and that sexuality is the primary locus of power exercised through these bodies. Since power and identity are formed within discourses, utilizing a Foucauldian model of power and discourse within this chapter provides a context for understanding how CSA is discursively framed, and furthermore, how this framing can be challenged through feminist intervention.

Browne (2014) calls for a revival of 1970s feminism, arguing that the focus should shift back to a reappraisal of patriarchy; that of structural male power rather than the current focus upon a generalization of power abuse, especially in relation to sexual violence. Walklate (2008) argues for both CSA and violence against women more generally to be situated within societal male/female relations so that it can be talked about, debated and its depoliticization challenged, rather than somehow remaining outside of discourse. Following Millett (2016), sexual politics as a system of oppression must be eliminated, however, policy responses may be hindered if male dominance remains the key to politics. The feminist goal, then, should be to challenge this dominance and provide critical analysis of all issues affecting the public acknowledgement of CSA.

Rather than drawing upon these years of feminist (and other) theoretical and practice-based insights into CSA, institutions and subsequently the official discourse now appear to be claiming to 'learn lessons' (Klonowski, 2013: 9; Casey, 2015: 38) from what they have determined to be a new and growing 'phenomenon' of exploitation. A focus on the apparent novelty of new cases has seen the issue of CSA further (re)defined. Moreover, a critical discussion of masculinity, and a gender order that sees CSA persist to such a large scale, remains absent from the official discourse. It is through the engagement with the feminist struggle to have the prevalence of CSA recognized in all its forms that this chapter aims to make a critical contribution. This is done via a focus on these two case studies, and the official discourse therein, to demonstrate the contemporary framing and consequences of this discourse for children, families and communities.

## The power of discourse

Crucial to the understanding of CSA is the discursive framing of the problem. The way in which CSA is put into discourse – what is included and what is excluded – shapes the responses and the very acknowledgement of the problem. As Foucault (1981) has argued, analysis should not only be geared towards what is present in discourse, but also what limits it. Feminists have long recognized both the importance of discourse in this context and its role in shaping dominant understandings of CSA (see Rush, 1980; Gordon, 1988; Bell, 1992; Smart, 1999, 2000, 2016; Whittier, 2009, 2016).

Feminist scholars have also documented the importance of the relationship between power and discourse (see, for instance, Gavey, 1989; Butler, 1990; Weedon, 1997). Drawing upon Foucault, Weedon (1997: 105) defines discourse as 'ways of constituting knowledge, together with the social practices, forms of subjectivity and power relations which inhere in such knowledges and relations between them'. Discourse, then, produces both knowledge and meaning and is a site of power, power to define what is, and what is not, 'important' when analysing knowledge formations. Foucault has been a key reference point in this work as he recognized that 'in every society the production of discourse is at once controlled, selected, organised and redistributed by a … number of procedures' (Foucault, 1981: 52). From this position, discourses are not simply the language that we use, but discourse should be understood as 'a system which structures the way that we perceive reality' (Mills, 2003: 55). Those feminist scholars who have been drawn to, and developed, Foucault's theory of discourse have emphasized the fact that discourse is always a site of conflict and contestation (Sawicki, 1991).

Utilizing a Foucauldian feminist understanding of discourse for a critical examination of CSA directs us not only to the dominant discourse(s), but also requires us to consider the processes of constraint and restriction. An analysis of discourse involves the careful reading of texts (in this case the two official reports discussed further in this chapter) with a view to 'discerning discursive patterns of meaning, contradictions and inconsistencies' (Gavey, 1989: 467). Discourse analysis identifies the role a discourse plays within society and crucially reveals the 'polymorphous techniques of power' (Foucault, 1990: 11) which enable the dominance of certain discourses while others remain subjugated.

Official discourse is central to understandings of CSA and remains the state's key tool for information output. Official discourse has been defined as 'the realisation of power in the creation of a distinct object that is fashioned from the discourses of law, epistemology, social science and common-sense' (Burton and Carlen, 1979: 34). This form of discourse includes statutory inquiries, legislation, policing strategies and reports undertaken or commissioned by any government agency. As official discourse is the state's way of 'proclaiming legal and administrative rationality' (Burton and Carlen, 1979: 48) it is central to the administration of state power. As Phoenix and Oerton (2005: 4) point out, official discourse on law and order is 'necessarily engaged in a symbolic erasure of the very material realities that generate the "problem" to which official discourse addressed itself'. Moreover, as Cohen (2001: 114) warns, 'official discourse is inevitably a mixture of blatant lies, half-truths, evasions, legalistic sophistries, ideological appeals and credible factual balances' and, therefore, as this chapter aims to do, requires critical intervention.

In order to provide a critique of the discursive framing of CSA, this chapter focuses in on data analysed in the shape of two of the many official reports commissioned following the 'scandals' in Rochdale and Rotherham. These reports, examples of official discourse, are two independent reviews into the respective councils' response to the issue of CSA in the towns. The first report is the self-commissioned review into Rochdale Metropolitan Borough Council conducted by Anna Klonowski (2013) and the second is the government-commissioned review into Rochdale Metropolitan Borough Council, by Louise Casey (Casey, 2015).

The report authored by independent consultant Anna Klonowski (2013) into child sexual exploitation issues at Rochdale Metropolitan Borough Council was commissioned by the council in 2012 and tasked to 'undertake an independent review of the arrangements within the Council and the Council's multi-agency working arrangements relating to child sexual exploitation' (Klonowski, 2013: 3). This review's remit was to undertake fieldwork in the shape of interviews, in and around the council with both current, and past, employees to uncover the council's stance on CSA, and to assess whether this stance was a contributing factor to the abuse perpetrated in the town.

The 2015 report into Rotherham Metropolitan Borough Council's handling of CSA was undertaken by Louise Casey (2015). Casey, former Victims Commissioner and now Dame, at the time of undertaking her report held the role of Director General of the Casey Review Team (2015–17) (Gov. uk, 2021). Her inspection was ordered after Professor Jay's (2014) damning report into the failings of social care responses in the borough. Jay's (2014) report found that a minimum of '1400 children were sexually assaulted over the full inquiry period 1997–2003' in Rotherham (Jay, 2014: 1). The inspection report (Casey, 2015) was commissioned by the then Home Secretary Theresa May, with the ultimate aim of uncovering whether the council, and all subsequent agencies therein, were fit for purpose. This data provides an insight into the official discursive framing of CSA in the period in question, and demonstrates how official understandings shaped institutional responses.

The official discourse critically analysed in the context of this chapter, then, is in the shape of the two aforementioned official reports into local authority responses to CSA. The justification for the inclusion of these two reports over others produced in this 'watershed' (BBC, 2015a) period, are that they represent key reference points in the official and public discourse on CSA. These reports form only part of a myriad of official contributions in this time period.[3] However, the constraints of this chapter prevent a critical analysis of all, and the focus of the reports, the point of their publication and the fact they are commissioned by the councils to examine institutional failings, all mean that these reports warrant critical analysis. Furthermore, through analysis of the themes arising from this data sample, they allow the chapter to highlight what Burton and Carlen (1979: 51) refer to as the 'hegemonic and legitimating strategies of the state'.

Following Weedon (1997: 122), this analysis aims to 'understand the intricate network of discourses, the sites where they are articulated and the institutionally legitimized forms of knowledge to which they look for their justification'. The analyses aim to consider the discursive strategies implemented in official discourse and examine the extent to which patriarchal interests have shaped the discursive framing of CSA in relation to the cases of Rochdale and Rotherham (Weedon, 1997). It is through an engagement with the feminist struggle to have the prevalence of CSA recognized in all its forms that this chapter aims to make a critical contribution.

Due to the issues with (re)definition, when this chapter refers to CSA, it is referring to the overarching act of the sexual abuse of children, in all its complexities. However, child sexual exploitation (which is abbreviated to CSE within both official reports) will be included when discussing institutional responses, due to their prioritization of this, and my responsibility to present the data as I find it.

## The language of exploitation

The cases of CSA perpetrated in both Rotherham and Rochdale were predominantly referred to as child sexual exploitation within the media, political and official dominant discourses of the time (see Norfolk, 2011; Klonowski, 2013; Casey, 2015; South Yorkshire Police and Crime Commissioner, 2015). The repercussions of referring to CSA as 'exploitation' over abuse are reminiscent of the persistent crisis of definition, highlighting that CSA remains a contested discursive field. Furthermore, referring to CSA as 'exploitation' disavows the crucial point highlighted by feminist interventions, that gendered power relations are always involved in this abuse. This contemporary contestation is predominantly due to the meaning attached to the language of exploitation. This framing constructs exploitation as 'an emerging form of abuse: a new social problem' (Hallett, 2017: 1). Exploitation is also referred to as a 'phenomenon' (Klonowski, 2013: 93, Casey, 2015: 34), as something new to be tackled and afraid of, instead of something depressingly normal and ingrained in our society (as evidenced in Rush, 1980; Renvoize, 1993; Smart, 1999, 2000, 2016; Whittier, 2009; Pearce, 2019).

The definition of exploitation relied upon within the data analysed, refers to exploitation as an '"exchange" for the victim performing sexual activities, or it can happen through grooming' (Klonowski, 2013: 95; Casey, 2015: 15). Referring to exploitation as an 'exchange' has dual consequences. First, the language of 'exchange' can help to identify agency when those involved take part out of necessity, seeking to meet unmet needs (Hallett, 2017), such as financial gain, companionship and security. Second, however, the language deployed within these reports sees all cases of exploitation as synonymous with 'grooming' and, therefore, frames exploitation very narrowly, failing to recognize the existence of the many cases that exist outside of a grooming model.

The reports do acknowledge some issues with language, for example Klonowski (2013) highlights in her report into Rochdale Metropolitan Borough Council, before 2009 the language of 'child prostitution' would have been used to describe the victims and survivors involved in the Rochdale cases. She highlights that the use of the language of 'child prostitution' by government agencies and social care practitioners reflects a 'lack of understanding as to the inequity of power in such relationships and the "choices" that the young people have allegedly made when entering into such relationships' (Klonowski, 2013: 6).

The government intervened in 2013 to provide new guidelines stating that 'all references in guidance and regulation to "prostitution" when speaking of children should be amended to "child sexual exploitation"' (House of Commons Home Affairs Committee, 2013: 9). However, there are also issues with the dismissal of agency here. Phoenix (2019) argues that we must keep the language of prostitution, as the needs of economic necessity and poverty also may shape choices made by young people. Furthermore, she places importance on 'talking about young people in prostitution because we need a frame of reference in which to address the question of what *justice* in the context of the harms of commercial sexual exchange means and how it can be achieved' (Phoenix, 2019: 57, emphasis in original). Acknowledging the feminist arguments for and against the use of the language of prostitution in official accounts, then, further demonstrates the contested nature of the field.

'Child sexual exploitation' is problematized through Klonowski (2013) and Casey's reports. Casey (2015: 5) describes the issue as 'complex and hard to tackle', as 'undoubtedly, a very difficult problem for public services to deal with as there are many complexities involved'. Casey (2015: 91) also recognizes some of the issues presented by the changing definitions, stating that: 'The absence of a clear definition and strong shared understanding of CSE in its different forms, including on-line and street grooming, has led to poor use of resources and confusion amongst CSE team workers as to the boundaries of their role.' Although it is positive to see this recognition of the issues caused by inadequate, inconsistent and ambiguous language, the official discourse presented here still neglects to locate the crucial issue of the outright abuse of power and authority involved when adults sexually abuse children. Furthermore, the concept of exploitation, with all its complexities, still ignores the gendered power relations at play in these cases.

## Abnormalization in action

Both reports seek to identify the specific contextual factors that led to widespread CSA in Rochdale and Rotherham. In this sense the reports arguably construct the sexual abuse of children as abnormal in that they frame the issue of child sexual exploitation as a result of specific geographic, cultural, ethnic and occupational factors. For Foucault (2016), the process of abnormalization is continually presented against what is regarded as the 'norm'. The 'norm' then, as Foucault (2016: 50) points out, 'lays claim to power. The norm is not simply and not even a principle of intelligibility: it is an element on the basis of which a certain exercise of power is founded and legitimised'. This framing, then, requires critical analysis to understand how the causes of CSA are understood. Furthermore, there is a need to understand the power relations at play and, intrinsically, what is excluded from discourse, and this is done through analysis of the positioning of CSA and exploitation as a result of a set of abnormal contextual factors.

Firstly, and crucially, the ethnicity of the perpetrators of abuse was a focus within official discourse and the responses to that abuse from both councils. It is pertinent here to discuss the fact that 'race', ethnicity and gender are fundamental to the analysis of these cases. There exist tensions between attempting to protect racially minoritized men from racism perpetrated by state agencies and protecting children from men's violence (Meetoo and Mirza, 2007). These tensions exist due to the existence of a patriarchal system that, as Meetoo and Mirza (2007: 9) argue, 'uses violence extensively to subjugate women [and children] – it is not an issue of racial or ethnic differences. It is a question of the economic, political and social development of a society and the levels of democracy and devolution of power within communities'. The communities affected in both Rochdale and Rotherham are described as the 'Pakistani Heritage Community' (Casey, 2015: 5) and there are explicit sections of both reports analysed that deal specifically with 'the race issue' (Casey, 2015: 32) and the use of 'disruption techniques' (Klonowski, 2013: 23) to hinder the activities of 'migrant workers' (Klonowski, 2013: 29). The 'disruption techniques' (more on this to follow) referred to by Klonowski in the case of Rochdale, are interwoven with the focus on ethnicity and serve as racialized surveillance as they are geared directly towards a specific ethnicity and occupation. This 'liberal multiculturalism' (Meetoo and Mirza, 2007) functions throughout the data analysed to add to the abnormalization of a culture and privilege a focus on 'race' and ethnicity over one on gender, and further disregards feminist interventions in this area (see Gill, 2004; Anitha, 2008; Chapter 9, this volume).

The data demonstrates this 'gender blind multicultural discourse' (Meetoo and Mirza, 2007: 12) as workshops with a sample of council employees were conducted in the process of Klonowski's (2013) review into the Rochdale abuses, and questions were posed regarding their experiences with what they refer to as 'CSE', and whether these experiences had impacted their practice. A key theme to come out of these workshops was that 'questions/concerns were raised that there may have been a reluctance to act quickly because of "political correctness", a fear of being accused of racism or prejudice, fear of reprisals within communities' (Klonowski, 2013: 103). Here, the official discourse is focusing on how employees are alleging fears of being labelled as 'racist', fears of breakdowns in community cohesion, and ultimately trust if they report CSA to those in positions of power within the council. Questions then arise, on the back of this discursive framing, as to why these fears exist, and whether they should ever be prioritized within institutions tasked with the safety and protection of children.

The focus on ethnicity in the official data analysed is further evident through an emphasis on the professions of those involved in the sexual abuse of children in the towns. First, taxi drivers and those working in fast food restaurants in Rochdale are the focus of concern for Klonowski (2013), due to the trial and subsequent imprisonment (and in some cases deportation), of nine 'Asian' men employed in what is defined as 'the night-time economy' (Home Office, 2020: 25), for their involvement in the sexual abuse of children in Rochdale. Klonowski (2013: 33) dedicates an entire theme of her report to the: 'use of "disruption techniques"', to "disrupt the activities of taxi drivers and those running fast food establishments"'. It is pertinent here to mention, then, that these 'disruption techniques' demonstrate a problematic conflation of ethnicity and migrant status within the official discourse. The presumption appears that those who work in the aforementioned industries are members of a certain or the same ethnic group. This is further emphasized through the prioritization of official discourse on the policing of minoritized communities, through a focus on 'migrant' workers: 'Migrant workers can use taxi driving as a legitimate employment if they are joining a family or friend's company/workforce' (Klonowski, 2013: 29). Klonowski (2013: 79) goes on to provide two key recommendations calling for clarity at a national level regarding 'the grounds and circumstances upon which authorities can suspend and/or revoke licences for taxi drivers and fast-food establishments, thereby enabling more robust disruption tactics for CSE'.

As with the case of Rochdale, Casey (2015: 16) argues that Rotherham Metropolitan Borough Council failed in its duty to safeguard children and to 'govern the landscape in which child sexual abuse was played out in the town'. The landscape focused on within the data here includes a concentration on private hire vehicles (taxis), as the main arena where abuse took place. For one of the main tasks of the report, Casey (2015: 7), was directed to consider whether only 'fit and proper persons' were permitted to hold a taxi licence. This 'fit and proper persons' test was implemented in legislation (Local Government Act, 1976) due to taxis being used by many vulnerable people such as the elderly, intoxicated, those with special needs, and non-English-speaking tourists. This focus on taxi drivers sees an entire profession abnormalized and responsibility is placed on the drivers themselves to disrupt and prevent CSA.

Intertwined with this concentration on taxi drivers in Rotherham is the council's apparent inability to discuss the issue of 'race', so much so that 'staff perceived that there was only a small step between mentioning ethnicity of perpetrators and being labelled a racist' (Casey, 2015: 34). A former social worker told Casey's (2015: 35) team that 'if we mentioned Asian taxi drivers, we were told we were racist and the young people were seen as prostitutes'. By focusing on ethnicity and the taxi driving occupation as determining factors for CSA, the official discourse prioritizes these factors over a critical interpretation of gender. Therefore, the emphasis here is on the apparent risks associated with the taxi industry, and the process of racialization for some men who work within it, however the fact the perpetrators were all men is ignored, and this adds further to the 'invisibility of gender and violence in multicultural discourse' (Meetoo and Mirza, 2007: 13).

The focus on ethnicity was reproduced within official discourse and subsequent institutional responses in Rotherham, and this is clearly reflected in Casey's (2015) report. Casey (2015: 32) addresses what she refers to as 'the race issue' in an early subsection of the report, arguing that 'Rotherham Metropolitan Borough Council struggled historically and into the present day with the issue of race. It seems that with an intention of not being racist, their ways of dealing with race does more harm than good'. Furthermore, interviews undertaken by Casey and included in the report present the issue of 'race' as contentious as 'staff and council members lacked the confidence to tackle difficult issues for fear of being seen as racist or affecting community cohesion' (Casey, 2015: 10). As with the case in Rochdale, there were also claims of 'institutionalised political correctness' (Casey, 2015: 6) that the report claims affected the council's ability to protect children, and to deal with, and ultimately prevent, CSA.

Although it is important to recognize the myriad ways that CSA plays out, to place the sole onus on one community, one ethnicity or one occupation, is to disavow the wider causes and prevalence of CSA in many spaces. CSA occurs in many institutions, within the protected space of the family home, and within all communities (Pearce, 2019).

A further 'phenomenon' (Klonowski, 2013: 93), related to ethnicity is the issue of 'localised grooming' (House of Commons Home Affairs Committee, 2013) first identified in response to the cases of CSA in Rochdale and Rotherham. There have been many terms utilized when attempting to define instances of organized and large-scale CSA. For example, 'grooming gangs' (Cockbain, 2013; Tufail, 2015), 'group-based child sexual exploitation' (Home Office, 2020), 'gang associated sexual violence' (Beckett et al, 2013), 'child sexual exploitation in gangs and groups' (Children's Commissioner, 2013) and 'on-street grooming' (Norfolk, 2011). The range of terminology used within official discourse to capture the large-scale sexual abuse of children further adds to the crises of definition (Smart, 1999). In reference to the case in Rochdale, it was the term 'localised grooming', preferred by the House of Commons Home Affairs Committee (2013), that Klonowski (2013) utilized in her report.

Localized grooming then, is defined as 'a model of child sexual exploitation in which a group of abusers target vulnerable children, including, but not confined to, those who are looked after by a local authority' (House of Commons Home Affairs Committee, 2013: 5). Issues with the discursive framing of CSA as confined to the 'vulnerable' highlights the innocence and fragility of children. As Tufail (2015: 36) argues, while vulnerability is an important concept, it is necessary to move beyond this, as the term adopts a 'politically neutral position'. The focus on vulnerability does not, for instance, incorporate the overwhelmingly working-class position of the victims in these cases, and therefore serves to limit the discourse. Instead, the focus should be on the failures of institutions to recognize abuses and protect working-class girls from systemic CSA by men in positions of power. This also requires a focus on a critical reappraisal of an official discourse that abnormalizes both perpetrators and victims, and ignores the patriarchal relations that fuel these abuses (Browne, 2014).

Through the focus on 'disruption techniques', Klonowski's (2013) report into Rochdale Council seems to be interweaving this 'phenomenon' of 'localized grooming' with the portrayal of taxi drivers, and in turn a specific ethnicity and 'migrant' status, as dangerous to young, vulnerable, White girls. It is this dangerous portrayal of 'Asian' men that has seen a huge rise in racism (Tufail, 2015), and this is encapsulated in the response to the cases of abuse in Rochdale and Rotherham by those on the far right. These cases happened at a time when the right-wing was ramping up support in the towns, and there was a real 'background threat of the British National Party or the English Defence League exploiting the problems in Rotherham for their own divisive ends' (Casey, 2015: 35). These threats were realized, as the far right did indeed exploit these cases, and as the prosecutor in the Rochdale trial argued, used the cases of CSA in cities like Rotherham and Rochdale to stir up hate and recruit their activists (Afzal, cited in Chakelian, 2018). Again, this racialized discourse serves to construct CSA as a problem belonging to a specific subset of society, and abnormalizes 'Asian' men against the backdrop of dominant White culture in Britain. 'Asian' masculinity is readily represented as dangerous, however recognition of a hegemonic and toxic masculinity that transcends communities and perpetuates the sexual abuse of children is totally absent in official discourse. This focus, then, dislocates CSA from other forms of men's violence and hinders the protection of children.

The focus on 'race' in the official discourse around Rochdale and Rotherham disavows the wider prevalence of abuse in the home (Gordon, 1988) and, instead, sees both policy and practice focus on already marginalized communities, and not on those abuses perpetrated by, and in the homes of, those racially and class-privileged (Whittier, 2016). This dangerous myth that CSA exists largely in specific communities serves to locate the problem as outside of the mainstream, and abnormalizes the communities in focus and the very issue of CSA itself.

It is important here to note that these reports focus explicitly on 'abuse outside of the family' (Klonowski, 2013: 67). However, there exist references to families within the official discourse. Casey's (2015: 101) report discusses family life and the likelihood of CSA being brought about due to the victim's place within a: ' "chaotic and vulnerable" family'. This idea of problematic family life as a fundamental factor for abuse arguably relates to the wider government focus on 'troubled families' (Cameron, 2011). This discourse deflects responsibility from institutions such as the council, tasked with the safety of children, and instead sees families blamed for creating an environment where abuse can occur.

Casey (2015: 15) also refers to those who have a 'difficult family background' as being prime targets for the grooming process. Included within the idea of 'difficult backgrounds' are children in care. Casey (2015: 15) states that children in care are especially vulnerable to grooming, but that, on occasions, 'predators are also sometimes able to exploit those from stable backgrounds'. She describes the grooming process as one where the children are treated like adults, given gifts, attention, alcohol and drugs for sex, and that they feel as though they are in a reciprocal, loving relationship. Casey

(2015: 15) states that 'this is a powerful thing, especially for young children or young people who may have difficult family backgrounds and crave love and attention'. This claim shifts some of the blame onto the decisions made by the child and serves to blur some of the legal issues around consent and agency (see Phoenix, 2019). Furthermore, the gendered elements of the crime are disavowed, and instead, the 'difficult family', pitted against the 'stable' family, is discursively framed as the cause of abuse. References to family backgrounds as a marker for abuse sees the blame placed on families for their children's victimization, and again, we see further disavowal of the wider structural causes, the gendered elements and the power relations involved in CSA.

## Conclusion

The limits to discourse presented here mirror the wider institutional responses found during the course of doctoral studies. First, the official discourse omits any real discussion of the gendered elements of the crime of CSA. This is crucial for a feminist analysis and, furthermore, is the only tangible link between both cases under examination and arguably the vast majority of cases of CSA. To suggest that CSA is a product of a specific community, ethnic group or social class is to negate a discussion of the intersections involved, and the wider power relations at play, that allow for the issue to remain prevalent in the 21st century. An effect of the omission of a critical interpretation of gender hides the role of men as the predominant perpetrators of CSA and reinforces guilt in women and children.

As the official reports by Klonowski (2013) and Casey (2015) demonstrate, CSA in the English towns of Rochdale and Rotherham was discursively framed as a problem of troubled families and confined to specific places and spaces. Both past (Rush, 1980; Gordon, 1988; Radford and Stanko, 1991) and more recent feminist interventions (see Smart, 2016) into CSA demonstrate this narrow focus as a dangerous myth. This myth perpetuates the problem and serves to ignore the prevalence of abuse in the home. This discourse sees official responses geared towards specific individuals and geographical areas, over a focus on a hegemonic masculinity (Connell and Messerschmidt, 2005), in a patriarchal society, that allows for CSA and violence against women to continue. As Phoenix and Oerton (2005: 17) argue: 'The great silence at the heart of official discourse of sex is that there "really" is a persistent and intransigent "problem", maybe not with sex per se, nor with sexual relations between adults, or even adults and children, but with men, and what men do.'

Official discourse, then, closes down opportunities for state interventions that are reflective of feminist demands. Through the obvious omission of a critical discussion of masculinity, the official discourse here is shaped by the state's inability to respond effectively to feminist concerns. As Bumiller (2008: 13) argues, 'by far the broadest reach of state power is its ability to transform sexual violence into a social, legal and medical problem'. This transformation is highlighted in the discursive framing of CSA in Rochdale and Rotherham, as a problem unrelated to men and masculinity. Further to this is the effect of official discourse in limiting what is sayable. Foucault describes this ability as 'logophilia':

> It is as though these taboos, these barriers, thresholds and limits were deliberately disposed in order, at least partly, to master and control the great proliferation of discourse, in such a way as to relieve its richness of its most dangerous elements; to organise its disorder so as to skate round its most uncontrollable aspects. (Foucault, 1981: 21)

These limits are demonstrated throughout the official discourse. Fundamentally, if men consist of 92 per cent (ONS, 2020) of the perpetrators of CSA, and 100 per cent in the cases of Rochdale and Rotherham, the question remains as to why the focus of attention is not levied towards this overwhelming gendered disparity. These statistics further emphasize the dangers of the narrow focus on specific ethnicities, communities and individuals, over a critical (re)appraisal of patriarchal relations that allow for this abuse to continue, throughout generations and across society, in the face of feminist interventions (Browne, 2014).

Second, reference to the abnormality of perpetrators, victims, families, ethnicities and communities sees the discourse of CSA confined to specific arenas and results in legitimized state interventions to correct this 'abnormality'. As Foucault (2016) argues, the notion of abnormality requires the problematization of the very notion of 'normality'. The common-sense notion of 'normality' disavows wider harms and closes down space for critique. State interventions such as the institutional focus on 'troubled families' and the policing of racially minoritized communities sees the prevalence of CSA disavowed, sees victims and their families blamed, and does not allow for the state to 'learn lessons', provide justice and ultimately protect children from future abuses. Issues with definition also see the issue abnormalized and hinder any real progress.

Responsibilization is also apparent through the victim-blaming discourse that portrays children as sexual beings, and through the policing of specific communities, families and professions. Through this discourse children are blamed for their own victimization, and the responsibility for abuse is put in their hands, or in the hands of their 'troubled families'. Professions are also responsibilized, and in particular, taxi drivers were given specific training and tasked with preventing cases of CSA, over state agents such as police officers. Although these discourses seem to overlap, the responsibilization strategy within the official response serves to deflect responsibility from failed state agencies (social services, police, local authorities and wider government), and instead gives responsibility to individuals and maintains that victim-survivors and their families play a part in their own abuses.

Disavowal is also evidenced throughout the official discourse. It is clear that the local authorities were aware of the presence of CSA in their jurisdictions, though they were reluctant to report said abuses on grounds of 'political correctness' (Casey, 2015: 9; Klonowski, 2013: 103). However, even with all of the evidence in front of them, professionals remained resolute that the issue was not widespread. Furthermore, both councils disavow the gendered elements of the crime and even with the evidence of men making up 92 per cent of the population of convicted CSA perpetrators (ONS, 2020), the focus remains on ethnicity, communities, victim-blaming, troubled families and individual professions, yet nowhere is there a critical appraisal of gender.

The pertinent question for a feminist analysis, then, is if we do indeed have a case of conscious disavowal in official discourse on CSA, how can we prioritize a critique of the power of patriarchal institutions to override moral judgement? CSA is an issue that is depressingly normal, as feminists have argued for decades (see Rush, 1980; Radford and Stanko, 1991; Smart, 1999, 2000, 2016; Browne, 2014). The constant redefining of CSA causes innumerable harms, as the focus shifts from uncovering prevalence and causes, to instead understanding newly (re)defined 'phenomena'. Moving forward, there is an obvious need to acknowledge the prevalence of CSA and to recognize the gendered elements that make it possible. Only then can we aim to prevent it in the first place.

Following Foucault (1981), and adopting his stance for a feminist analysis, going forward the focus should not be on only what is *present* in discourses around CSA, but also the *limits*. As well as highlighting the problems in what *is* said, feminist critique should focus on what is *not* said – what is restricted and controlled within official discourse. Although the rise in public awareness of CSA subsequent to these cases is a positive step, as evidenced in this chapter, there are enduring problems in this ever-moving field. Feminist study in the 21st century, then, should continue to engage in critical analysis of the official discursive framing of the problem, because, as these cases starkly demonstrate, and as Rush (1980: 15) argued back in 1980, 'adult child sex is not a phenomenon that emerges from nowhere but is a legacy from the past which continues in our everyday life'. CSA is an enduring injustice, causing immeasurable harms, that feminist interventions in the 21st century must continue to highlight and challenge.

## Notes

[1] Operation Yewtree was a large-scale police investigation into CSA. This Operation began with the allegations against Sir Jimmy Savile, and grew to include other high-profile

individuals such as Rolf Harris, Stuart Hall, Fred Talbot, Ray Teret, Max Clifford and Dave-Lee Travis. Yewtree was seen to have been a turning point in historic reporting of CSA and exploitation (see Gray and Watt, 2014; Lampard and Marsden, 2015; Spindler, 2018, for further information).

2   For further information on the cases of Rotherham and Rochdale see, for instance, Gladman and Heal (2018) and BBC (2017).

3   The official reports/discourses analysed within the course of doctoral studies relate directly to Rotherham, Rochdale and abuses perpetrated by Jimmy Savile. They are within the specific time frame of 2010–15 and include examples from Ofsted, NSPCC, Local Government Association, House of Lords and House of Commons Joint Committees, HMIC, Department for Education, Children's Commissioner, Association of Chief Police Officers, Barnardo's and All Party Parliamentary Groups.

## References

Anitha, S. (2008) 'Neither safety nor justice: The UK government response to domestic violence against immigrant women', *Journal of Welfare & Family Law*, 32(3): 189–202.

Ballinger, A. (2016) *Gender, Truth and State Power: Capitalising on Punishment*, London: Routledge.

Bartley, P. (2000) *Prostitution: Prevention and Reform in England, 1860–1914*, London: Routledge.

BBC (2015a) 'Norfolk Chief Constable: Child sex abuse "challenge of the century"', *BBC News*, [online] 28 July, available at: https://www.bbc.co.uk/news/uk-england-norfolk-33688374 [accessed 8 April 2021].

BBC (2015b) 'Rotherham child abuse: The background of the scandal', *BBC News*, [online] 5 February, available at: https://www.bbc.com/news/uk-england-south-yorkshire-28934963 [accessed 22 April 2021].

BBC (2017) 'Three girls', *BBC iPlayer*, [online] available at: https://www.bbc.co.uk/programmes/b08rgd5n [accessed 8 April 2021].

Beckett, H., Brodie, I., Factor, F., Melrose, M., Pearce, J., Pitts, J., Shuker, L. and Warrington, C. (2013) '"Its wrong but you get used to it": A qualitative study of gang-associated sexual violence towards, and exploitation of, young people in England', University of Bedfordshire and The Children's Commissioner, [online] available at: https://uobrep.openrepository.com/bitstream/handle/10547/305795/Gangs-Report-final.pdf?sequence=1&isAllowed=y [accessed 14 April 2021].

Bell, V. (1992) *Foucault and Feminism: The Case of Incest*, doctoral thesis, University of Edinburgh, [online] available at: https://era.ed.ac.uk/handle/1842/20015 [accessed 11 August 2021].

Belsey, C. and Moore, J. (1997) *The Feminist Reader* (second edition), London: Macmillan.

Bennett, J. (2006) *History Matters: Patriarchy and the Challenge of Feminism*, Pennsylvania: University of Pennsylvania Press.

Bolen, R.M. (2001) *Child Sexual Abuse: It's Scope Our Failure*, New York: Plenum Publishers.

Browne, V. (2014) 'The persistence of patriarchy: Operation Yewtree and the return to 1970's feminism', *Radical Philosophy*, 188: 9–19.

Bumiller, K. (2008) *In an Abusive State: How Neoliberalism Appropriated the Feminist Movement Against Sexual Violence*, London: Duke University Press.

Burton, F. and Carlen, P. (1979) *Official Discourse: On Discourse Analysis, Government Publications, Ideology and the State*, London: Routledge.

Butler, J. (1990) *Gender Trouble: Feminism and the Subversion of Identity*, London: Routledge.

Cameron, D. (2011) *Troubled Families Speech*, [online] available at: https://www.gov.uk/government/speeches/troubled-families-speech [accessed 15 April 2021].

Campbell, B. (2014) 'Neoliberal neopatriarchy: The case for gender revolution', Open Democracy, [online] available at: https://www.opende mocracy.net/5050/beatrix-campbell/neoliberal-neopatriarchy-case-for-gender-revolution [accessed 11 July 2021].

Casey, L. (2015) *Report of Inspection of Rotherham Metropolitan Borough Council*, [online] available at: https://assets.publishing.service.gov.uk/government/uploads/system/uploads/attachment_data/file/401125/46966_Report_of_Inspection_of_Rotherham_WEB.pdf [accessed 8 April 2021].

Chakelian, A. (2018) 'Grooming rings are the biggest recruiter for the far right: Rochdale and Telford prosecutor', *New Statesman*, [online] available at: https://www.newstatesman.com/politics/uk/2018/03/child-sexual-abuse-grooming-rings-are-biggest-recruiter-far-right-rochdale-and-telf ord-prosecutor [accessed 29 April 2021].

Children's Commissioner (2013) *'If only someone had listened': Office of the Children's Commissioner's Inquiry into Child Sexual Exploitation in Gangs and Groups*, [online] available at: https://childrenscommissioner.gov.uk/wp-content/uploads/2017/07/If_only_someone_had_listened.pdf [accessed 14 April 2021].

Cockbain, E. (2013) 'Grooming and the "Asian sex gang predator": The construction of a racial crime threat', *Race and Class*, 54(4): 22–32.

Cockbain, E. and Brayley, H. (2012) 'The truth about "Asian sex gangs"', *The Guardian*, [online] available at: https://www.theguardian.com/commen tisfree/2012/may/08/asian-sex-gangs-on-street-grooming [accessed 24 May 2021].

Cohen, S. (2001) *States of Denial: Knowing about Atrocities and Suffering*, Cambridge: Polity Press.

Connell, R.W. and Messerschmidt, J.W. (2005) 'Hegemonic masculinity: Rethinking the concept', *Gender & Society*, 19(6): 829–59.

Crenshaw, K. (1989) 'Demarginalizing the intersection of race and sex: A black feminist critique of antidiscrimination doctrine, feminist theory and antiracist politics', *University of Chicago Legal Forum*, 1: 139–68.

Driver, E. and Droisen, A. (1989) *Child Sexual Abuse: A Feminist Reader*, New York: New York University Press.

*Express* (2017) 'The list of Britain's towns and cities shamed by Asian grooming gangs', *Express*, [online] available at: https://www.express.co.uk/news/uk/839509/Britain-towns-cities-asian-grooming-gangs-Newcastle-Rochdale-Rotherham [accessed 23 June 2021].

Foucault, M. (1981) 'The order of discourse' in R. Young (ed) *Untying the Text: A Post-Structuralist Reader*, London: Routledge, pp 53–72.

Foucault, M. (1990) *The History of Sexuality* (volume 1), London: Penguin.

Foucault, M. (2016) *Abnormal: Lectures at the Collège de France 1974–1975*, London: Verso.

Gavey, N. (1989) 'Feminist poststructuralism and discourse analysis', *Psychology of Women Quarterly*, 13(4): 459–75.

Gill, A.K. (2004) 'Voicing the silent fear: South Asian women's experiences of domestic violence', *The Howard Journal of Criminal Justice*, 43(5): 465–83.

Gilroy, P. (2000) *Against Race: Imagining Political Culture Beyond the Color Line*, Cambridge, MA: Harvard University Press.

Gladman, A. and Heal, A. (2018) *Child Sexual Exploitation after Rotherham: Understanding the Consequences and Recommendations for Practice*, London: Jessica Kingsley Publishers.

Gordon, L. (1988) 'The politics of child sexual abuse: Notes from American history', *Feminist Review*, 28(1): 56–64.

Gov.uk (2021) *Dame Louise Casey CB*, [online] available at: https://www.gov.uk/government/people/louise-casey [accessed 28 June 2021].

Gray, D. and Watt, P. (2014) *Giving Victims a Voice: A Joint Report into Sexual Allegations made against Jimmy Savile*, [online] available at: https://www.nspcc.org.uk/globalassets/documents/research-reports/yewtree-report-giving-victims-voice-jimmy-savile.pdf [accessed 8 April 2021].

Hallett, S. (2017) *Making Sense of Child Sexual Exploitation: Exchange, Abuse and Young People*, Bristol: Policy Press.

Home Office (2020) 'Group-based child sexual exploitation: Characteristics of offending', [online] available at: https://assets.publishing.service.gov.uk/government/uploads/system/uploads/attachment_data/file/944206/Group-based_CSE_Paper.pdf [accessed 13 September 2021].

House of Commons Home Affairs Committee (2013) 'Child sexual exploitation and the response to localised grooming', [online] available at: https://publications.parliament.uk/pa/cm201314/cmselect/cmhaff/68/68i.pdf [accessed 26 April 2021].

IICSA (Independent Inquiry into Child Sexual Abuse) (2021) Available at: https://www.iicsa.org.uk/ [accessed 19 May 2021].

Jackson, L.A. (2000) *Child Sexual Abuse in Victorian England*, London: Routledge.

Jay, A. (2014) *Independent Inquiry into Child Sexual Exploitation in Rotherham 1997–2013*, [online] available at: https://www.rotherham.gov.uk/downlo ads/file/279/independent-inquiry-into-child-sexual-exploitation-in-rotherham [accessed 8 April 2021].

Klonowski, A. (2013) *Report of the Independent Reviewing Officer in Relation to Child Sexual Exploitation Issues in Rochdale Metropolitan Borough Council During the Period 2006–2013*, [online] available at: http://www.rochdale. gov.uk/pdf/2013-05-23-independent-reviewing-officer-report_into-csc-issues-v1.pdf [accessed 8 April 2021].

La Fontaine, J. (1990) *Child Sexual Abuse*, Cambridge: Polity Press.

Lampard, K. and Marsden, E. (2015) *Themes and Lessons Learnt from NHS Investigations into Matters Relating to Jimmy Savile*, [online] available at: https://assets.publishing.service.gov.uk/government/uploads/system/uploads/attachment_data/file/407209/KL_lessons_learned_report_FI NAL.pdf [accessed 1 May 2021].

Local Government Act (1976) Available at: https://www.local.gov.uk/sites/default/files/documents/events%20presentations%20-%20Taxi%20li censing%20regional%20event%20NW%2021%20February%202017%20-%20Principles%20in%20determining%20fitness%20-%20Alan%20Tolley. pdf [accessed 22 July 2021].

Meetoo, V. and Mirza, H.S. (2007) '"There is nothing honourable about honour killings": Gender, violence and the limits of multiculturalism', *Women's Studies International Forum*, 30(3): 187–200.

Millett, K. (2016) *Sexual Politics*, New York: Columbia University Press.

Mills, S. (2003) *Michel Foucault*, Oxon: Routledge.

Norfolk, A. (2011) 'Revealed: Conspiracy of silence on UK sex gangs', *The Times*, [online] available at: https://www.thetimes.co.uk/article/revealed-conspiracy-of-silence-on-uk-sex-gangs-gpg5vqsqz9h [accessed 21 February 2021].

ONS (Office for National Statistics) (2020) 'Child sexual abuse in England and Wales: Year ending December 2019', [online] available at: https://www.ons.gov.uk/peoplepopulationandcommunity/crimeandjustice/artic les/childsexualabuseinenglandandwales/yearendingmarch2019#what-do-we-know-about-perpetrators-of-sexual-abuse-before-the-age-of-16-years [accessed 27 May 2021].

Pearce, J. (ed) (2019) *Child Sexual Exploitation: Why Theory Matters*, Bristol: Policy Press.

Phoenix, J. (2019) 'Child sexual exploitation, discourse analysis and why we still need to talk about prostitution' in J. Pearce (ed) *Child Sexual Exploitation: Why Theory Matters*, Bristol: Policy Press, pp 43–62.

Phoenix, J. and Oerton, S. (2005) *Illicit and Illegal: Sex, Regulation and Social Control*, Cullompton: Willan.

Radford, J. and Stanko, E.A. (1991) 'Violence against women and children: The contradictions of crime control under patriarchy' in K. Stenson and D. Cowell (eds) *The Politics of Crime Control*, London: SAGE, pp 188–202.

Renvoize, J. (1993) *Innocence Destroyed: A Study of Child Sexual Abuse*, London: Routledge.

Rush, F. (1980) *The Best Kept Secret: Sexual Abuse of Children*, New York: McGraw-Hill.

Sawicki, J. (1991) *Disciplining Foucault: Feminism, Power and the Body*, London: Routledge.

Smart, C. (1989) *Feminism and the Power of Law*, London: Routledge.

Smart, C. (1999) 'A history of ambivalence and conflict in the discursive construction of the child victim of sexual abuse', *Journal of Legal Studies*, 8(3): 391–409.

Smart, C. (2000) 'Reconsidering the recent history of child sexual abuse 1910–1960', *Journal of Social Policy*, 29(1): 55–71.

Smart, C. (2016) *Observations through a Rear-view Mirror: Revisiting Women, Crime and Criminology*. Presentation delivered at Liverpool John Moores University, 16 March, [online] available at: https://www.youtube.com/watch?v=seThS8qNZOk&feature=youtu.be [accessed 24 July 2020].

Smedley, A. and Smedley, B.D. (2005) 'Race as biology is fiction, racism as a social problem is real', *American Psychologist*, 60(1): 16–26.

South Yorkshire Police and Crime Commissioner (2015) 'Child sexual exploitation', [online] available at: https://southyorkshire-pcc.gov.uk/openness/legacy-information/child-sexual-exploitation/ [accessed 28 March 2021].

Spindler, P. (2018) 'Operation Yewtree' in M. Erroga (ed) *Protecting Children and Adults from Abuse after Savile*, London: Jessica Kingsley Publishers, pp 212–34.

Stanley, L., Manthorpe, J. and Penhale, B. (eds) (1999) *Institutional Abuse: Perspectives across the Life Course*, London: Routledge.

Tufail, W. (2015) 'Rotherham, Rochdale, and the racialised threat of the "Muslim grooming gang"', *International Journal for Crime, Justice and Social Democracy*, 4(3): 30–43.

Walklate, S. (2008) 'What is to be done about violence against women?', *British Journal of Criminology*, 48(1): 39–54.

Weedon, C. (1997) *Feminist Practice and Poststructuralist Theory* (second edition), Oxford: Blackwell.

Whittier, N. (2009) *The Politics of Child Sexual Abuse*, New York: Oxford University Press.

Whittier, N. (2016) 'Where are the children? Theorizing the missing piece in gendered sexual violence', *Gender and Society*, 30(1): 95 108.

Yuval-Davis, N. (2006) 'Intersectionality and feminist politics', *European Journal of Women's Studies*, 13(3): 193–209.

# 5

# Universities, Sexual Violence and the Institutional Operation of Power

*Kym Atkinson*

## Introduction

The extent of sexual violence experienced by women university students has, in recent years, garnered increased media, political, academic and institutional attention, in the UK and internationally. In England and Wales, the National Union of Students' (NUS) (2010) report, *Hidden Marks*, found that one in seven women students had experienced a serious or physical sexual assault and 68 per cent had experienced some form of verbal or non-verbal harassment, in and around their institution. The study highlighted the extent of sexual violence experienced by women university students, as well as a range of issues in relation to students' limited awareness of institutional support and low levels of reporting and accessing support. While research and activism around the issue pre-dates the publication of *Hidden Marks*, it can be viewed as a turning point and a catalyst due to the range of media, political, institutional, academic and activist responses which followed (for an overview of these developments see Phipps and Smith, 2012; Lewis and Marine, 2018, 2019; Towl and Walker, 2019; Marine and Lewis, 2020).

Despite this increased focus on the issue, much has remained the same and further issues have been documented. The Office for National Statistics (ONS) (2017) found that students (6.4 per cent) were more likely to have been victims of sexual assault in the previous year than adults in other occupations. Testimonies online (Strategic Misogyny, 2017), and social media accounts such as *Do Better Academia*, have confirmed the nature and extent of sexual violence on campus as well as the problematic nature of institutional responses. Moreover, media reports have highlighted a range of issues, including prevalence (Batty et al, 2017; Reynolds, 2018; Batty, 2019), the failure of universities to respond adequately to incidents, victims and survivors (Jokic, 2020; Lawthom, 2020; Page et al, 2020; Pittam, 2020; Hall, 2021), and staff sexual misconduct against students (Batty, 2018). Universities were also found to be using non-disclosure agreements (NDAs) in cases of sexual violence (Weale and Batty, 2016), while *The Guardian* found that £90 million was spent over two years on upholding NDAs, some of which related to allegations of bullying, discrimination and sexual misconduct (Murphy, 2019).

These issues have emerged in a context where, as Field (2018: 1) has argued, 'higher education has been hijacked by an increasingly aggressive neo-liberal ideology'. The marketization of higher education, via the removal of the majority of public funding, and the increase in student fees, has resulted in competition between universities, a business model approach in which success depends on how well universities market themselves, an increase in student numbers, and ultimately, what Collini (2018: 1) argues is 'a change in the character and above all the ethos of universities'. Within this neoliberal, marketized context where profit maximization is the priority, evidence that universities are not providing adequate levels of health, wellbeing and support services has been documented (Shackle, 2019). In terms of sexual violence, this context is important as neoliberal rationalities are argued to be shaping, not only university practices, but also student behaviour and the performances of masculinities (Phipps, 2017).

This chapter presents findings from PhD research which explored the nature and extent of women students' experiences of sexual violence at one university in England and the institutional responses to this violence.[1] The purpose of this chapter is to consider these students' experiences in the particular context in which they took place and to explore the dominant discourses which shape university responses to sexual violence. In order to do this, a feminist poststructuralist framework (Weedon, 1987) is utilized which builds on the concepts of power, discourse and truth. This perspective allows for an exploration of the ways in which the exercise of power, via discourses, constructs a 'truth' about sexual violence which shapes women's behaviour and university responses to sexual violence. Alongside this feminist poststructuralist framework, this chapter asserts that feminist epistemologies, and feminist praxis, are essential, not just to understanding women students' experiences of sexual violence, but in creating an alternative 'truth' about sexual violence. Therefore, this chapter develops radical, theoretically informed victim- and survivor-led responses which directly challenge current policies and practices in the neoliberal university which are failing women students physically, psychologically and emotionally.

## The legal and policy context in UK universities

Prior to October 2016, if sexual violence was alleged by a student, universities often followed guidelines set out in the Zellick Report (1994), which provided guidance for universities on how to handle circumstances where a student's alleged misconduct might also constitute a criminal offence. The guidelines advised against universities investigating cases of manifestly serious violence, described as 'incidents where conviction is likely to lead to a custodial sentence or are triable only on indictment' (Swanton, 2015: 1). This included various forms of sexual violence. The report was criticized by the End Violence Against Women Coalition (EVAW) (2015) for its failure to meet legal obligations under the Public Sector Equality Duty and its incompatibility with the Human Rights Act (1998).

The problematic nature of the Zellick guidelines were a key part of a campaign by the NUS to improve institutional responses to sexual violence (NUS, 2016). Following NUS campaigning, and alongside the academic, activist and media responses in the area, a taskforce to address the issue of sexual violence on campus was created by Universities UK (UUK) which was responsible for developing and coordinating guidance in relation to the prevention, support and response needs of students and staff and for developing the responsibilities of institutions to consider these needs. The aim was to provide a national template which universities could use 'to support the development of an institution-wide response' (UUK, 2016: 1). This resulted in the *Changing the Culture* report (UUK, 2016), which highlighted a number of themes and identified key components relating to the response to, and prevention of, sexual violence, harassment and hate crime. It looked at various forms of harassment and hate crime with a separate focus on sexual violence, noting that 'such cases are particularly complex and sensitive' (UUK, 2016: 45). A range of recommendations were made which broadly highlighted that universities have 'a clear responsibility to respond appropriately to any student or staff member who experiences sexual violence' (UUK, 2016: 49). This was a clear shift away from previous approaches, such as the guidance offered by Zellick, and a move towards understanding the impact incidents of sexual violence may have had on student and staff wellbeing, academic attainment and student retention, issues which were clearly highlighted within the NUS's (2010) *Hidden Marks* study.

In 2017, following the *Changing the Culture* report, the Higher Education Funding Council for England made money available to universities to address the issue of sexual violence on campus and implement measures in relation to student safeguarding (Office for Students [OfS], 2018). This work, now taken over by the OfS, the independent regulator for higher education in England, awarded £4.7million to 119 projects across the higher education sector (OfS, 2020). Moreover, one year after the production of *Changing the Culture*, UUK (2018) assessed the progress that had been made, as well as barriers to progress in implementing the recommendations made by the UUK (2016) taskforce. This qualitative research found that there had been 'significant but highly variable progress' (UUK, 2018: 6). In 2019, UUK quantitatively assessed the progress that had been made (UUK, 2019), stating that there were improvements in a range of areas, but that progress was still variable and specific challenges remained in terms of resources and funding.

Chantler et al (2019) also carried out a survey and interviews with staff at 54 universities in England, Wales and Scotland to establish what had been achieved since the *Changing the Culture* report. They found that institutions were at very different stages of developing an institutional agenda in terms of creating working groups, producing plans and reviewing policies, and found that, at times, it was key individuals who were pushing the agenda forward, rather than institutions necessarily being committed to change. When asked about barriers that they faced when trying to address the issues, two key challenges were identified by participants. First, out of 68 respondents, 37 noted a disparity between the verbal support of the institution and the level of commitment and support in the form of resources, money and dedicated staff time. Second, institutional resistance was cited by survey respondents. For 33 participants, resistance took the form of institutional concern for reputational risk, 24 stated that their institutions denied or minimized the issue, 16 noted difficulties in achieving senior level buy-in, and seven noted barriers from ethics committees.

In terms of legal developments, the UUK taskforce commissioned Pinsent Masons LLP to produce guidance for the sector on how to handle student disciplinary issues where alleged misconduct may have constituted a criminal offence (Pinsent Masons, 2016). These guidelines broadly related to all such incidents but, as with *Changing the Culture*, the guidelines provided specific guidance in relation to sexual misconduct. Pinsent Masons argued that, when handling incidents of student misconduct, 'the imposition of disciplinary sanctions must be seen in the context of the contractual relationship between the university and the student' (Pinsent Masons, 2016: 2). In order to ensure disciplinary actions taken by a university were in line with this contractual relationship, Pinsent Masons recommended producing a code of conduct, which provided possible sanctions that might be imposed on students, as well as the publication of a disciplinary framework. The guidelines, again, represented a further move away from the Zellick guidelines with the acknowledgement that universities should be handling issues internally. In instances where the allegation might constitute a criminal offence, the report recommended first that the criminal process should take priority. If a criminal process did take place, the internal disciplinary process should be suspended until the end of the criminal process. If the alleged incident was not being dealt with through a criminal process, universities should consider whether to investigate the matter under internal disciplinary regulations (Pinsent Masons, 2016).

The OfS has also published a statement of expectations (OfS, 2021a) to guide universities in producing policies and practices to address harassment and sexual misconduct. The recommendations cover a range of expectations in terms of clearly communicating institutional approaches to the issues, engagement with students in the development of processes, prevention and training, the development of policies and reporting mechanisms and support for reporting students. These recommendations, however, while intended to provide a consistent approach, will not be connected to institutional conditions of registration. That is, the OfS will not use its powers of enforcement in relation to the statement of expectations, although this will be reviewed at a later date (OfS, 2021b).

The next section outlines the feminist poststructuralist theoretical framework utilized which asserts that dominant discourses about sexual violence have the effect of shaping women students' behaviours and university responses to the issue. The section, therefore, focuses on the body as a site of surveillance, noting the ways in which disciplinary practices are gendered, specifically through limiting women's space, movement and behaviours, purportedly to avoid sexual violence while at university.

## The gendered operation of disciplinary power

The relevance of the body, for feminist poststructuralists, is that 'it is the place where power relations are manifest in their most concrete form' (McNay, 1992: 16). Foucault (1980: 57–8) argued that 'nothing is more material, physical, corporeal than the exercise of power'. In response to this, Cahill (2000: 47) stated, 'far from being in any sense natural or primary then, the body is the location of inscription'. The body, and its functions, is the site of the inscription of power dynamics (Diamond and Quinby, 1988; Sawicki, 1990) and the body is produced through the exercise of power, via discourses (McNay, 1992). Feminist poststructuralists have critiqued and developed Foucault's work, highlighting the ways in which disciplinary practices are gendered (Bartky, 1990; Bordo, 1993; Cooper, 1994) and ensure women's compliance with socially constructed norms of femininity, such as bodily comportment and appropriate ornamentation of the body. Ultimately, they uncover the manufacture of the gendered, self-disciplining subject by highlighting the gendered operation of disciplinary power through adherence to, and internalization of, culturally and historically specific norms (Foucault, 1995). For Bartky (1988: 62), this effectively 'fragments and partitions the body's time, space, and its movements' (Bartky, 1988: 62). The self-disciplining subject, who alters her physical appearance in terms of ornamentation, also alters her physical movements, in relation to how much or how little space she takes up, as well as geographically, in the spaces she goes to or avoids. For Cahill (2000: 54), 'women's limitation of the space within which her body can move seems to gesture not towards self-inflicted harm, but rather toward harm inflicted by other bodies ... to go beyond that space is to enter an arena where her body is in danger of being violated'.

The limitation of women's spatial movements is an effect of disciplinary practices and discourses around women's safety, deployed by institutions such as universities, which construct a 'truth' about sexual violence and impose responsibility on students to avoid sexual violence. Implicit within such discourses is that danger is located within women students' bodies. Highlighting the embodied nature of violence, Vera-Gray (2018: 11) explored the habitual 'safety work' women undertake in order to avoid men's violence. These norms, of appropriate feminine bodies, behaviours and movements, ensure that spatial and geographic limitations are placed on women, based on the need to avoid sexual violence. University deployment of discourses on women's safety, therefore, place the responsibility to avoid assault on women students, encouraging this bodily self-discipline, and expressing the 'power dynamic which blames women for sexual assault' (Cahill, 2000: 56).

Before applying this theoretical argument to sexual violence in universities, the chapter considers the central role of feminist epistemology, and feminist praxis, in relation to unmasking the nature and extent of sexual violence in universities.

## Feminist epistemology and feminist praxis

In addition to the utilization of feminist poststructuralism, to centralize the role of discourse in the construction of a 'truth' about sexual violence, this chapter is concerned with utilizing feminist methodologies to uncover this construction based on utilizing experiential accounts from women who had direct experience of sexual violence during their time at university.

Critiques of 'traditional' methodologies and developments in feminist methodologies centre around epistemology and which knowledge is deemed reliable, valid and is valorized as the 'truth' about men's violence and women's lives more generally (for an overview of these developments, see Chapter 2, this volume). Key to these accounts is the 'insurrection of subjugated knowledges' (Foucault, 2003: 7). That is, unearthing specific knowledge which has, at particular points in history, been blocked, ignored or discarded, in addition to uncovering discourses which have been given validity. Knowledge is, therefore, not objective but inherently linked to the exercise of power. Truth is, moreover, understood as a social construction, one which develops from a person's position and experience in the social world. There is a need, therefore, for the 'insurrection of subjugated knowledges' that have been 'masked', to be 'reveale[d] ... by using ... the tools of scholarship' (Foucault, 2003: 7).

As outlined in the introduction to this collection, resistance to injustice requires responses built on feminist praxis and, therefore, a focus on the question – what is this knowledge for? (Stanley, 1990). Building responses on feminist praxis requires a prioritization of the potential value of research and how the social world can be changed to improve the situation at hand. In terms of sexual violence at university, the focus should be on how research can produce knowledge which helps us to understand the nature of sexual violence and, therefore, improve the experience of those who are victims and survivors in terms of, for example, reporting and working towards changing the structures which enable the continuation of sexual violence with the ultimate aim of prevention. Stanley's (1990) outline of the symbiotically related and mutually beneficial nature of theory and research is also required to produce purposeful knowledge to address the issue of sexual violence at university. In addition to the interrelated nature of theory and research, policy is also a part of this symbiotic relationship. Specifically, while theory and methodology are knitted together through feminist praxis, they are done so in order to work towards practical and useful policy change which is based upon the experiences of students.

The subjugation of women's testimonies of sexual violence at university not only disqualifies these testimonies but, also, supports the further subjugation and disqualification of future testimonies. Following Smart (1995: 45), the aim here is not to establish a feminist 'truth', but to 'analys[e] the power effects that claims to truth entail'. Therefore, in order to understand women's experiences of sexual violence at university, the dominant discourses – the 'truth' – about these experiences needs to be deconstructed, from a range of sources. This chapter, therefore, goes on to analyse the withering effects of these 'truths' – state-defined official discourses – upon the women who have experienced sexual violence.

## The institutional operation of power

Following feminist poststructuralist insights, so far, this chapter has indicated that, in terms of experiencing, testifying to and understanding experiences of sexual violence at university, it is not just what is said that is of importance, but also the discourses and frameworks through which experiences and testimonies are interpreted. These discourses and frameworks differ across institutions, although with some persistent, common themes, resulting in different, social constructions of sexual violence, victims and perpetrators, and different responses to what might or might not be perceived as an issue that needs to be institutionally addressed. There are two dimensions to this: the role, place and ideological construction of the neoliberal university; and connecting criminal justice and institutional justice.

*The role, place and ideological construction of the neoliberal university*

Universities, as institutions, are instruments of discourses and power relations. For Foucault, institutions are 'instruments for the finer, more elemental workings of power' (Caputo and Yount, 1993: 4). Foucault (1986) also argued that institutions should be analysed from the standpoint of power relations, rather than power relations being analysed from the standpoint of institutions. Overall, 'the fundamental point of anchorage [of power relations], even if they are embodied and crystallized in an institution, is to be found outside the institution' (Foucault, 1986: 222).

Universities operate in a neoliberal, marketized and corporatized societal context (Ozga, 2008; Brady, 2012; Brooks et al, 2016). Brady (2012: 344) states that power has been relocated away from the academy to the marketplace, which has resulted in 'a utilitarian preoccupation with extrinsic outcomes'. The findings in the research, presented in this chapter and drawn from interviews with students and stakeholders, demonstrated that neoliberal, marketized and corporatized discourses affected the way in which universities were responding to sexual violence and how prevention initiatives were framed and developed.

Joanna, a stakeholder interviewee, who played a leadership role in the university's Feminist Society, highlighted this as an issue, arguing that the university prioritized profit and a marketized approach to education, resulting in the university operating as a business first. She also noted that, in this context, the university was not providing an adequate level of support services for students:

'[W]hy would I not expect the people who run this organization, who are in charge, to provide adequate services? ... [I]f you want to think of the university as a business, rather than an academic institution, then the very least you could do is provide the services for your students.'

Neoliberal governmentality, moreover, operates via discourses of responsibility and risk management. In relation to sexual violence, gendered discourses of responsibility and risk management were evident in university prevention initiatives. It is important to note that several stakeholders acknowledged issues with framing the question of sexual violence around discourses of safety and the need for students to protect themselves. For example, Elizabeth, who had a leadership role in student services, stated: "I think it is very difficult to give prevention tips to students. How do you do that? Because it is dependent on somebody else's behaviour."

There were, however, interviewees who noted prevention initiatives which were centred on the perceived risk of sexual violence for women students and were based on safety tips, advising students on how to stay safe. Kristin, a university counsellor, noted work that she had undertaken in her role, developed around the idea of student safety. This, however, was specifically in relation to students protecting themselves from being victims of sexual violence. The counselling team provided a variety of workshops throughout the academic year, she noted:

> 'I've added a new group ... the group is called "It won't happen to me" ... and that is around safety, being aware of your surroundings, what you can do to, you know, take care of yourself. ... We will have a group as well about how to keep yourself safe as best you can.'

The construction of safety in the programme developed by the counselling team, then, stands in contrast to that described by Elizabeth, through its messaging on individual responsibility for safety. Therefore, despite explicit contestation of such discourses by some, they were still evident. Such prevention initiatives construct the issue as being in the body of women students, and the 'risk' as a result of their existence in public spaces, particularly in the night-time economy.

Stringer (2014: 2) suggested that 'the ideal neoliberal citizen' is someone who takes responsibility for protecting themselves against the risk of victimization and, therefore, the effect of such discourses is the responsibilization of women students. As already discussed, feminist poststructuralist insights have shown how gendered discourses on women's bodies as dangerous and violable induce individual discipline and self-surveillance. In line with this, the student participants discussed the multiple forms of 'safety work' (Kelly, 2013; Vera-Gray, 2018), which they undertook to try to avoid sexual violence, such as always keeping their phone in their hand, always being with someone that they knew when in public spaces, taking taxis rather than walking short distances, not going to certain places which were perceived as risky and buying a car to avoid public transport. All student participants who had experienced sexual violence described undertaking such behaviours and Nicola described the range of strategies she undertook in order to avoid harassment:

> 'When I'm walking on the university campus there's always young men, there's always groups of men and I don't feel comfortable or safe around them ever. Like, to be honest no, it doesn't feel safe and then I alter my behaviour. ... I just like walk faster or I'll be like hyper aware. Like if I hear a noise, I'll be like uhh, or if I see someone behind me, I'm like, why are they behind me? It's weird like I read years ago that if like you jingle your keys around you are less likely to get attacked.'

The effects of these gendered discourses are compounded when, as Stringer (2014) argues, neoliberalism replaces the concept of structural oppression with personal responsibility. Rather than sexual violence being understood as a result of the operation of power and gender inequality in the university, it is explained through a lack of personal responsibility. This was exemplified through Meredith's choice not to tell anyone about her experience of sexual violence, she said: "I had a boyfriend at the time so it was like, I didn't speak to him about it because … he would have been like why have you gone back to a hotel with all the lads?" Moreover, Caitlin, who worked for the local Rape Crisis service, noted the persistence of responsibilizing, victim-blaming attitudes within and outside of the university: "I've been to many meetings where there is that kind of victim blame, we need to change, the student needs to do this, the student needs to do that. And they need to get in the right taxi."

Gendered discourses on risk, therefore, ensure women students are responsibilized to take care of themselves, avoid certain areas, watch their drinks and to be alert to danger. Not only does this place limitations upon their bodies, movements and choices, but failure to adequately self-discipline and take responsibility for their own safety plays a role in determining the extent of the woman's perceived 'culpability' in the violence she experiences (Ballinger, 1997: 123). Further to the effect that neoliberal discourses responsibilize women students and construct them as within or outside of acceptable norms, these discourses operate to shift the focus, and therefore the responsibility, away from the institution. The responsibilization of women students to 'protect' themselves from the risk of victimization deflects attention away from the role of the institution in supporting the discourses which provide the 'cultural scaffolding' of sexual violence (Gavey, 2005: 2).

In responding to the issues of sexual violence on campus, universities have focused on the creation of policies, legalistic responses and reporting mechanisms which, for Lewis and Marine (2019: 1284), 'appear to have fallen victim to neoliberal commodification'. The stakeholders in this research were involved in a range of work, but there was a clear focus for some on the importance of policy development and mechanisms for reporting. Ahmed (2012) explored the role and effects of the language of equality and diversity and the experiences of those doing diversity work in universities. She argued that equality often becomes a performance indicator, and that institutional commitment to equality becomes a 'paper trail' and 'tick box exercises' which 'do nothing to bring about the effect they name' (Ahmed, 2012: 17). This limited focus allows institutions 'to "show" that they are following procedures but are not really "behind" them' (Ahmed, 2012: 114). She argues that by showing or stating that they are committed to diversity, institutions are then able to not commit to diversity. What are presented as commitments to diversity can be understood as 'non performatives' (Ahmed, 2012: 116), that is, actions or performances which do not bring about what they name. Therefore, in the context of this research, through producing a policy on sexual violence outlining the university's position and process of responding to the issues, the existence of this policy creates the opportunity for the institution to demonstrate that they are committed to change. However, the ability to demonstrate this commitment through the existence of the policy can have paradoxical effects, as the policy can then be used to deny that there is a problem.

The stakeholders in this research seemed genuinely committed to addressing the issue of sexual violence on campus, more than performatively. They acknowledged a problem and were working to create change, with several stakeholders challenging the dominant discourses which limit university responses. However, it is the broader institutional, neoliberal context which impeded some of this work. As Ahmed (2012) notes, a document and statement of commitment needs to be supplemented with other and further work to address the issues, and develop other forms of institutional pressure such as reminders from committed staff, resources and funding, As noted by one stakeholder, Elizabeth, all of these were limited within the institution of the research: "I'd like to see some resources identified to be able to support this work because I'm currently doing this with existing resources." Elizabeth did, however, think that the creation of policies was important. While she agreed with the point that policies, on their own, would not create transformational change, she felt she was able to use a policy to then lobby for the further work and action that needed to be taken in order to create real change. While this demonstrates a commitment on her part, it also highlights the limited institutional commitment as there was still a requirement from committed individuals to take the work further beyond policy creation.

## Connecting criminal justice and institutional justice

The failures of the criminal justice system in responding to women's reports of sexual violence have been well documented (Madigan and Gamble, 1989; Temkin and Krahé, 2008; Meloy and Miller, 2010; Walby et al, 2015; Centre for Women's Justice, 2019). As discussed in the introduction to this collection, this has led to feminist engagement with the state to different extents, resulting in some successes, but also highlighting the contradictions in engaging with the institutions which have consistently failed to address the root causes of sexual violence (Ballinger, 2009); have co-opted and institutionalized calls for radical, transformative change (Richie, 2012); and which, through policies and practices, reflect and complement the violence which feminists seek to redress (Richie, 2012; Connell and Pearse, 2015; Davis, 2016). Therefore, despite a range of seemingly positive reforms, as Ballinger (2009) argues, reforms have had little impact on the actual extent of sexual violence, nor have they addressed the social context which enables sexual violence. This can also be said for university policies, when neoliberal solutions come in the form of monitoring mechanisms, statements of commitment and legalistic responses, the root causes of the problem, that is the context of gendered and structural inequality, remains veiled and effectively unchallenged.

Smart (1989) considered the power of law specifically and warned that feminists should not rely on the law for justice or accept its significance in regulating the social order. Given the operation of legal discourses which limit the ability for women to testify to the harms of sexual violence (Smart, 1989; Lees, 1997; Howe, 2008), discredit those testifying (Tuerkheimer, 2017) and limit opportunities to achieve criminal 'justice', the law creates its own, and further, harms. Smart's (1989) argument, that the law has the potential to produce further harms, and her concern with the extension of the power of the law into new modes of regulation, can be applied to the context of the university and the power of the discourses which are (re)produced through the institution. For example, the inclusion of 'vexatious complaints' within student conduct policies, which was the case in this research, positions this as a significant issue, which is contrary to the available evidence from wider research which points out that the percentage of vexatious complaints about sexual violence are similar to vexatious complaints in other crimes (Kelly et al, 2005). Nonetheless, this inclusion brings into effect a 'truth' about sexual violence and, therefore, the context and discursive production of gendered inequality is reproduced.

Bumiller (2008: 36), in analysing institutional, governmental and state level responses to sexual violence, outlined the operation of what she termed 'expressive justice'. Due to cultural anxieties raised by sexual violence, the state is required to respond to demands for justice and to create order. Following Garland (2001, cited in Bumiller, 2008), the sovereign response is produced, whereby 'the state reassures an anxious public by demonstrating its ability to protect citizens with immediate and authoritative police power' (Bumiller, 2008: 36). For Bumiller (2008), politicians act in 'expressive mode', concerned more with the outrage that crimes of sexual violence provoke, rather than with actually controlling crime. Bumiller's (2008) argument is that the deployment of expressive justice in relation to sexual violence increases the power and legitimacy of the police and the state to control sex crimes without affecting the capacity to effectively 'respond to the prevalent and ordinary conditions of sexual violence' (Bumiller, 2008: 37).

Bumiller's analysis is applicable to the university and was exemplified through a statement from Sajid Javid, the former Secretary for Business, Innovation and Skills, during an interview, undertaken at the time when the issue of sexual violence on campus was beginning to gain media attention. He stated, 'I will end this evil of campus harassment' (cited in Lanigan, 2015: 1). After expressing his outrage at the 'evil' of campus harassment, Javid proposed a taskforce to help reduce violence against women and girls on university campuses. He subsequently stated that he believed 'police should be involved in cases such as alleged rape at university, even if students have gone to staff about the issues in confidence' (Lanigan, 2015: 1), further reinforcing the legitimacy of the criminal justice system. As Bumiller (2008: 37) states, 'by declaring war against sexual terrorism, police power is legitimated and the state maintains its monopolistic power to control sex crimes'. Moreover, the more routine and everyday experiences of sexual violence are not responded to with such expressive outrage, as they do not fit within dominant discourses of 'real rape', 'real victims' and 'real perpetrators'. This further contributes to the construction of a 'truth' about sexual violence in universities whereby notions of behaviour which is condemnable are reinforced and the normality of sexual violence is mystified.

As noted in the introduction to this collection, reliance on the criminal justice system to respond to sexual violence does little to reduce the frequency of sexual violence, or feelings of justice. In part, this is due to the individualization of the problem, which deflects responsibility away from institutions of the state, to individuals deemed 'bad'. For Phipps (2019: 5), however, when the problem is individualized, the person who will be believed is the person with the most 'compelling and commodifiable story'. In the specific context of universities, naming and shaming strengthens 'institutional airbrushing' (Phipps, 2019: 5). This means that universities, and management, more concerned with their image and reputation, as a result of the marketized, corporatized and neoliberal agenda, 'merely remove the individual "blemish", while the systemic malaise remains' (Phipps, 2019: 5). As a result, this airbrushing passes the problem onto other institutions. In the context of universities, the individualization of prevention strategies, and dominance of discourses of risk and responsibility, as discussed in this chapter, are unable to transform the conditions in which sexual violence persists. A feminist conceptualization of justice is therefore required.

The operation of neoliberal, institutional and criminal justice discourses within universities results in the construction of a 'truth' about sexual violence, built around, as outlined in this chapter, individualism, responsibility and risk management. This 'truth' limits the parameters in which the broad and varied range of experiences of sexual violence, across the student population, can be rendered intelligible. In turn, this deflects the responsibility of the institution to respond to incidents, through limiting the intelligible instances which they are required to respond to. Although contested by some stakeholders, and all student participants, these discourses were found to shape the university's responses to sexual violence and framed some prevention initiatives, which meant that responsibility was deflected away from structural issues and the role of the institution, to the individual. In sum, the individualization of prevention and protection, the 'truth' that is constructed about sexual violence through discourses of responsibility and risk, and the deflection away from structural problems within the university are incompatible with, and unable to transform, the social conditions in which sexual violence against women students occurs.

## Envisioning a feminist utopia: a question of women's safety in the 21st century

As neoliberal discourses on safety, responsibility and risk management were found to affect not only how the institution was responding to sexual violence, but also how women students were moving about the institution in order to avoid sexual violence, addressing the issue of sexual violence at university necessitates an approach which acknowledges the need to resist the individual, structural *and institutional* exercise of power. The discussion which follows sets out a framework for addressing the issues and working towards a feminist conceptualization of safety for student victims/survivors of sexual violence, built on feminist praxis.

Russell Jacoby has made the point that: 'The choice we have is not between reasonable proposals and an unreasonable utopianism. Utopian thinking does not undermine or discount real reforms. Indeed, it is almost the opposite; *practical reforms depend on utopian dreaming – or at least utopian thinking drives incremental improvements*' (Jacoby, 2005, cited in Sim, 2009: 162, emphasis in original). Therefore, following Jacoby, in order to envision a feminist utopia, it is important to move beyond 'incremental improvements' and address the roots of sexual violence. While discourses of safety and protection are necessary in moving forward and imagining a world free from sexual violence, the co-optation of victims into law and order rhetoric serves to enhance punitive, individualized responses to crime (Bumiller, 2008; Duggan, 2018) and results in the dichotomizing of 'good' and 'bad' victims (Duggan, 2018) in the criminal justice system and wider state institutions.

There is, therefore, a need for clarity concerning what safety means for women. Brown (2020: 78) argues for 'reconceptualis[ing] safety in ways that address harm while resisting the vigilantism of "call out culture" and permanent exile as solutions'. This means addressing the issue of harm, rather than just criminality. It also means recognizing that the safety of all women is key. While there is a need for institutional accountability, there is also a need to recognize the limitations of punitive, retributive responses whereby, at times, the perpetrator is removed from one institution to another (The 1752 Group, 2018; Phipps, 2019). As a long-term solution, moving the individual perpetrator to another institution, where perhaps, women do not have the same access to this limited notion of safety and protection, does nothing for the safety of all women.

Brown and Schept have also argued for a reconsideration of safety and call for an 'insurrectionary safety' whereby: 'Safety … is not simply about those who have harmed or been harmed, but a movement beyond disciplinary neoliberal frames of responsibilisation and internalisation to community and state accountability' (Brown and Schept, 2016, cited in Sim, 2021: 16). Therefore, the questions we should ask are: 'How can we organise our communities to be safe? What should we do when various kinds of harm, with different kinds of needs, occur? What are the collective ways and forums in which we can pursue this work?' (Brown and Schept, 2016, cited in Sim, 2021: 16). In doing this, they suggest that dominant discourses of harms as private and individualized, particularly relevant in the case of sexual violence, should be rendered visible as structural violence. Neoliberal, individualizing discourses which responsibilize women students and rely on criminalization do 'not reduce harm or future harm and is at cross-purposes with stopping abuse and violence' (Brown and Schept, 2016: 449). Therefore, it is this visibility, they argue, which can lead to community accountability. Moreover, their point that institutions should consider how safety can be organized collectively, within and across communities, is reinforced by Phipps (2019) who argues that safety should not 'reinforce the stigmatisation and alienation of marginalised people'. The safety of women in any institution or community can be connected to the safety of women more generally.

Challenging dominant discourses of safety and protection, Sim (2021) argues, requires connecting the lack of safety experienced by a range of marginalized groups. Building on this argument, without denying the specificity of violence experienced by particular groups, sexual violence against women university students, and their lack of safety inside and outside of the institution, could be connected intersectionally to the lack of safety generated by gender-based violence more generally, racist and homophobic violence, homelessness, poverty, austerity and state confinement. By connecting issues of safety between different groups, violence, harms and deaths are not individualized but 'represent a *normal* outcome of the state's failure to offer even a modicum of protection to those at the bottom of the ladder of inequality' (Sim, 2021: 18, emphasis in original).

## Conclusion

By undertaking research with women students, victims and survivors of sexual violence and stakeholders, this chapter has critically analysed how the institution in which the research took place – a university in England – was responding to sexual violence. Overall, the chapter highlights the failure of institutional policy and practices to adequately respond to students in a way which reflects the realities of sexual violence. It has, therefore, outlined a framework built on feminist praxis to respond to this failure, which acknowledges the need for radical transformation in how universities conceptualize the issue of sexual violence against women students, including 'the production of new discourses and so new forms of power and new forms of the self' (Ramazanoglu, 1993: 24). In practice, this means contesting and resisting dominant discourses which construct a 'truth' about sexual violence and the broader reality of victims' and survivors' experiences in order to develop theoretically informed, victim- and survivor-led responses.

## Note

[1] The research was undertaken at one post-1992 university in England. The primary data were collected between February 2017 and December 2017. Mixed methods were employed in the form of an online survey of 144 women students enrolled at the university, five interviews with students who had experienced sexual violence and five stakeholders who were responsible, in different ways, for managing and/or responding to incidents at the university. Participants were recruited through internal university emails, social media accounts, Student Union societies and interviewees were also recruited through snowball sampling. The institution where the research took place, and all participants, are anonymous, with pseudonyms used. For an in-depth discussion of methods, see Atkinson (2020). This chapter focuses on the findings from the student and stakeholder interviews.

## References

The 1752 Group (2018) *Silencing Students: Institutional Responses to Staff Sexual Misconduct in the UK*, [online] available at: https://1752group.com/wp-content/uploads/2018/09/silencing-students_the-1752-group.pdf [accessed 10 September 2020].

Ahmed, S. (2012) *On Being Included: Racism and Diversity in Institutional Life*, London: Duke University Press.

Atkinson, K. (2020) *'An Amplified Space': A Feminist Poststructuralist Analysis of Sexual Violence at University*, unpublished PhD thesis, Liverpool John Moores University.

Ballinger, A. (1997) *Dead Woman Walking: Executed Women in England and Wales, 1900–1955*, PhD thesis, University of Sheffield.

Ballinger, A. (2009) 'Gender, power and the state: Same as it ever was?' in R. Coleman, J. Sim, S. Tombs and D. Whyte (eds) *State, Power, Crime*, London: SAGE, pp 20–34.

Bartky, S. (1988) 'Foucault, femininity and the modernization of patriarchal power' in I. Diamond and L. Quinby (eds) *Feminism and Foucault: Reflections on Resistance*, Boston: Northeastern University Press, pp 61–86.

Bartky, S. (1990) *Femininity and Domination: Studies in the Phenomenology of Oppression*, New York: Routledge.

Batty, D. (2018) 'Sexual misconduct by UK university staff is rife, research finds', *The Guardian*, [online] 3 April, available at: https://www.theguardian.com/world/2018/apr/03/sexual-misconduct-by-uk-university-staff-is-rife-research-finds [accessed 20 January 2021].

Batty, D. (2019) 'More than half of UK students say they have faced unwanted sexual behaviour', *The Guardian*, [online] 26 February, available at: https://www.theguardian.com/education/2019/feb/26/more-than-half-of-uk-students-say-they-have-faced-unwanted-sexual-behaviour [accessed 20 January 2021].

Batty, D., Weale, S. and Bannock, C. (2017) 'Sexual harassment "at epidemic levels" in UK universities', *The Guardian*, [online] 5 March, available at: https://www.theguardian.com/education/2017/mar/05/students-staff-uk-universities-sexual-harassment-epidemic [accessed 20 January 2021].

Bordo, S. (1993) 'Feminism, Foucault and the politics of the body' in C. Ramazanoglu (ed) *Up Against Foucault*, London: Routledge, pp 179–202.

Brady, N. (2012) 'From "moral loss" to "moral reconstruction"? A critique of ethical perspectives on challenging the neoliberal hegemony in UK universities in the 21st century', *Oxford Review of Education*, 38(3): 343–55.

Brooks, R., Byford, K. and Sela, K. (2016) 'Students' unions, consumerism and the neoliberal university', *British Journal of Sociology of Education*, 37(8): 1211–28.

Brown, M. (2020) 'Transformative justice and new abolition in the United States' in P. Carlen and L.A. Franca (eds) *Justice Alternatives*, London: Routledge, pp 73–87.

Brown, M. and Schept, J. (2016) 'New abolition, criminology and a critical carceral studies', *Punishment & Society*, 19(4): 440–62.

Bumiller, K. (2008) *In an Abusive State: How Neoliberalism Appropriated the Feminist Movement Against Sexual Violence*, Durham, NC: Duke University Press.

Cahill, A. (2000) 'Foucault, rape and the construction of the feminine body', *Hypatia*, 15(1): 43–63.

Caputo, J. and Yount, M. (1993) 'Introduction: Institutions, normalization and power' in J. Caputo and M. Yount (eds) *Foucault and the Critique of Institutions*, Pennsylvania: The Pennsylvania State University Press, pp 3–26.

Centre for Women's Justice (2019) 'Police failure to use protective measures in cases involving violence against women and girls', [online] available at: https://static1.squarespace.com/static/5aa98420f2e6b1ba0c874e42/t/5c91f55 c9b747a252efe260c/1553069406371/Super-complaint+report. FINAL.pdf [accessed 20 August 2021].

Chantler, K., Donovan, C., Fenton, R. and Bracewell, K. (2019) 'Findings from a national study to investigate how British universities are challenging sexual violence and harassment on campus', Briefing paper, University of Central Lancashire, available at: http://clok.uclan.ac.uk/30179/1/13.10.19%20Briefing%20Paper.pdf [accessed 13 July 2020].

Collini, S. (2018) 'The marketisation of higher education', *Fabian Society*, [online] 22 February, available at: https://fabians.org.uk/the-marketisation-of-highereducation/ [accessed 10 December 2020].

Connell, R.W. and Pearse, R. (2015) *Gender: In World Perspective*, Cambridge: Polity Press.

Cooper, D. (1994) 'Productive, relational and everywhere? Conceptualising power and resistance within Foucauldian feminism', *Sociology*, 28(2): 435–54.

Davis, A. (2016) 'Feminism and abolition: Theories and practices for the twenty-first century' in A. Davis (ed) *Freedom is a Constant Struggle*, Chicago: Haymarket Books, pp 91–110.

Diamond, I. and Quinby, L. (1988) 'Introduction' in I. Diamond and L. Quinby (eds) *Feminism and Foucault: Reflections on Resistance*, Boston: Northeastern University Press, pp ix–xx.

Duggan, M. (2018) 'Victim hierarchies in the Domestic Violence Disclosure Scheme', *International Review of Victimology*, 24(2): 199–217.

EVAW (2015) 'Spotted: Obligations to protect women students' safety & equality', legal briefing, EVAW.

Field, D. (2018) 'The marketisation of British universities: Neoliberalism and the privatisation of knowledge', *The A-Line*, [online] available at: https://alinejournal.com/the-reading-room/the-marketisation-of-britishunive rsities-neoliberalism-and-the-privatisation-of-knowledge/ [accessed 10 September 2020].

Foucault, M. (1980) 'Two lectures' in C. Gordon (ed) *Power/Knowledge Selected Interviews and Other Writings 1972–1977*, New York: Pantheon, pp 78–108.

Foucault, M. (1986) 'The subject and power' in H. Dreyfus and P. Rainbow, *Michel Foucault: Beyond Structuralism and Hermeneutics*, Brighton: The Harvester Press, pp 208–29.

Foucault, M. (1995) *Discipline and Punish: The Birth of the Prison*, New York: Random House.

Foucault, M. (2003) *Society Must be Defended*, London: Penguin Books.

Garland, D. (2001) *The Culture of Control: Crime and Social Order in Contemporary Society*, Oxford: Oxford University Press.

Gavey, N. (2005) *Just Sex: The Cultural Scaffolding of Rape*, East Sussex: Routledge.

Hall, R. (2021) 'Complaining to universities about harassment "often a waste of time"', *The Guardian*, [online] 25 April, available at: https://www.theg uardian.com/world/2021/apr/25/complaining-to-universities-about-har assment-often-a-waste-of-time [accessed 6 May 2021].

Howe, A. (2008) *Sex, Violence and Crime: Foucault and the 'Man' Question*, Oxon: Routledge Cavendish.

Jokic, N. (2020) 'I told my university I was harassed online: They asked me what a hashtag was', *The Guardian*, [online] 20 April, available at: https://www.theguardian.com/education/2020/apr/20/i-told-my-university-i-was-harassed-online-they-asked-me-what-a-hashtag-was [accessed 20 January 2021].

Kelly, L. (2013) 'Thinking in 10s: What we have learnt, what we need to know and do', inaugural lecture at the launch of the Durham Centre for Research into Violence and Abuse, Durham University, 16 May.

Kelly, L., Lovett, J. and Regan, L. (2005) *A Gap or a Chasm? Attrition in Reported Rape Cases*, Home Office Research Study 293, [online] available at: https://www.researchgate.net/profile/Jo_Lovett/publication/2387132 83_Home _Office_Research_Study_293_A_gap_or_a_chasm_Attrition_ in_reported_rap e_cases/links/00b7d52a09b4935e0e000000/Home-Office-Research-Study293-A-gap-or-a-chasm-Attrition-in-reported-rape-cases.pdf [accessed 15 November 2020].

Lanigan, R. (2015) 'Government orders tough new inquiry into sexist "lad culture" at university', *The Tab*, [online] 6 September, available at: https://thetab.com/2015/09/06/government-orders-tough-new-inquiry-into-sexist-lad-culture-at-university-52547 [accessed 21 October 2020].

Lawthom, J. (2020) 'Cardiff students "felt silenced" after sex assault claims', *BBC News*, [online] available at: https://www.bbc.co.uk/news/uk-wales-54012443 [accessed 20 January 2021].

Lees, S. (1997) *Ruling Passions: Sexual Violence, Reputation and the Law*, Buckingham: Open University Press.

Lewis, R. and Marine, S. (2018) *Gender Based Violence in University Communities*, Bristol: Policy Press.

Lewis, R. and Marine, S. (2019) 'Guest editors' introduction', *Violence Against Women*, 25(11): 1283–9.

Madigan, L. and Gamble, N. (1989) *The Second Rape: Society's Continued Betrayal of the Victim*, New York: Lexington Books.

Marine, S. and Lewis, R. (2020) *Collaborating for Change: Transforming Cultures to End Gender-based Violence in Higher Education*, Oxford: Oxford University Press.

McNay, L. (1992) *Foucault and Feminism*, Boston: Northeastern University Press.

Meloy, M.L. and Miller, S.L. (2010) *The Victimisation of Women: Law, Policies and Politics*, Oxford: Oxford University Press.

Murphy, S. (2019) 'UK universities pay out £90m on staff "gagging orders" in past two years', *The Guardian*, [online] 17 April, available at: https://www.theguardian.com/education/2019/apr/17/uk-universities-pay-out-90m-on-staff-gagging-orders-in-past-two-years [accessed 20 January 2021].

National Union of Students (2010) *Hidden Marks: A Study of Women Students' Experiences of Harassment, Stalking, Violence and Sexual Assault*, London: National Union of Students.

National Union of Students (2016) 'Stand by me: Campaign briefing', [online] [accessed 6 May 2021, URL no longer active].

Office for National Statistics (2017) 'Statistical bulletin: Crime in England and Wales: Year ending December 2016', [online] 27 April, available at: https://www.ons.gov.uk/peoplepopulationandcommunity/crimeand justice/bulletins/crimeinenglandandwales/yearendingdec2016#latest-viol ent-crime-figures-continue-to-present-a-complex-%E2%80%98picture [accessed 20 January 2021].

Office for Students (2018) 'Evaluation of safeguarding students catalyst fund projects', *Thematic Analysis Report 1*, [online] available at: https:// www.officeforstudents.org.uk/media/bd771e1c-b650-49d1-bd60-a6188d084506/ofs2018_safeeval.pdf [accessed 27 November 2020].

Office for Students (2020) 'Student safety and wellbeing: What are we doing?', [online] available at: https://www.officeforstudents.org.uk/adv ice-and-guidance/student-wellbeing-and-protection/student-safety-and-wellbeing/what-are-we-doing/ [accessed 20 January 2021].

Office for Students (2021a) 'Statement of expectations', [online] available at: https://www.officeforstudents.org.uk/advice-and-guidance/student-wellbeing-and-protection/prevent-and-address-harassment-and-sexual-mis conduct/statement-of-expectations/ [accessed 15 May 2021].

Office for Students (2021b) 'Frequently asked questions', [online] available at: https://www.officeforstudents.org.uk/advice-and-guidance/student-wellbeing-and-protection/prevent-and-address-harassment-and-sexual-mis conduct/frequently-asked-questions/ [accessed 15 May 2021].

Ozga, J. (2008) 'Governing knowledge: Research steering and research quality', *European Educational Research Journal*, 7(3): 261–2.

Page, T., Fenton, R. and Keliher, J. (2020) 'Universities fail sexual violence survivors: Will new rules change the culture?' *The Guardian*, [online] 9 January, available at: https://www.theguardian.com/education/2020/jan/ 09/universities-fail-sexual-violence-survivors-will-new-rules-change-the-culture [accessed 20 January 2021].

Phipps, A. (2017) '(Re)theorising laddish masculinities in higher education', *Gender and Education*, 29(7): 815–30.

Phipps, A. (2019) 'The fight against sexual violence', *Soundings*, 71: 62–74.

Phipps, A. and Smith, G. (2012) 'Violence against women students in the UK: Time to take action', *Gender and Education*, 24(4): 357–73.

Pinsent Masons (2016) *Guidance for Higher Education Institutions: How to Handle Alleged Student Misconduct which may also Constitute a Criminal Offence*, London: Universities UK.

Pittam, D. (2020) 'Students "felt silenced by De Montford University" after alleged groping', *BBC News*, [online] 9 September, available at: https:// www.bbc.co.uk/news/uk-england-leicestershire-53910544 [accessed 20 January 2021].

Ramazanoglu, C. (1993) *Up Against Foucault*, Oxon: Routledge.

Reynolds, E. (2018) 'Universities are home to a rape epidemic: Here's what they can do', *The Guardian*, [online] 2 March, available at: https://www.theguardian.com/commentisfree/2018/mar/02/universities-rape-epidemic-sexual-assault-students [accessed 20 January 2021].

Richie, B. (2012) *Arrested Justice: Black Women, Violence and America's Prison Nation*, New York: New York University Press.

Sawicki, J. (1990) *Disciplining Foucault: Feminism, Power and the Body*, London: Routledge.

Shackle, S. (2019) '"The way universities are run is making us ill": Inside the student mental health crisis', *The Guardian*, [online] 27 September, available at: https://www.theguardian.com/society/2019/sep/27/anxiety-mentalbreakdowns-depression-uk-students [accessed 10 September 2020].

Sim, J. (2009) *Punishment and Prisons: Power and the Carceral State*, London: SAGE.

Sim, J. (2021) '"Help me please": Death and self-harm in male prisons in England and Wales' in M. Coyle and D. Scott (eds) *The Routledge International Handbook of Penal Abolition*, Abingdon: Routledge, pp 119–30.

Smart, C. (1989) *Feminism and the Power of Law*, London: Routledge.

Smart, C. (1995) 'Feminist approaches to criminology, or postmodern woman meets atavistic man' in C. Smart (ed) *Law, Crime and Sexuality*, London: SAGE, pp 32–48.

Stanley, L. (1990) 'Feminist praxis and the academic mode of production: An editorial introduction' in L. Stanley (ed) *Feminist Praxis: Research Theory and Epistemology in Feminist Sociology*, London: Routledge, pp 20–60.

Strategic Misogyny (2017) 'Strategic Misogyny: Connecting stories of sexism at universities', [online] available at: https://strategicmisogyny.wordpress.com/ [accessed 20 January 2021].

Stringer, R. (2014) *Knowing Victims: Feminism, Agency and Victim Politics in Neoliberal Times*, London: Routledge.

Swanton, G. (2015) 'Education bulletin – Zellick revisited – dealing with allegations of rape', *ShakespeareMartineau*, [online] 8 September, available at: http://www.shma.co.uk/pressrelitem/924/Education-bulletin---Zellick-revisited-- -dealing-with-allegations-of-rape/ [accessed 6 May 2021].

Temkin, J. and Krahé, B. (2008) *Sexual Assault and the Justice Gap: A Question of Attitude*, Oxford: Hart Publishing.

Towl, G. and Walker, T. (2019) *Tackling Sexual Violence at Universities: An International Perspective*, Oxon: Routledge.

Tuerkheimer, D. (2017) 'Incredible women: Sexual violence and the credibility discount', *University of Pennsylvania Law Review*, 166(1): 1–58.

Universities UK (2016) *Changing the Culture: Report of the Universities UK Taskforce Examining Violence against Women, Harassment and Hate Crime Affecting University Students*, London: UUK.

Universities UK (2018) 'Changing the culture: One year on', [online] March, available from: https://www.universitiesuk.ac.uk/policy-and-analysis/repo rts/Documents/2018/changing-the-culture-one-year-on.pdf#search= changing%20the%20culture [accessed 13 December 2020].

Universities UK (2019) 'Changing the culture: Tackling gender-based violence, harassment and hate crime: Two years on', [online] October, available at: https://www.universitiesuk.ac.uk/policy-and-analysis/reports/ Documents/2019/uuk-changing-the-culture-two-years-on.pdf [accessed 13 July 2020].

Vera-Gray, F. (2018) *The Right Amount of Panic: How Women Trade Freedom for Safety*, Bristol: Policy Press.

Walby, S., Olive, P., Towers, J., Francis, B., Strid, S., Krizsán, A., Lombardo, E., MayChahal, C., Franzway, S., Sugarman, D., Agarwal, B. and Armstrong, J. (2015) *Stopping Rape: Towards a Comprehensive Policy*, Bristol: Policy Press.

Weale, S. and Batty, D. (2016) 'Sexual harassment of students by university staff hidden by non-disclosure agreements', *The Guardian*, [online] 26 August, available at: https://www.theguardian.com/education/2016/aug/ 26/sexual-harassment-of-students-by-university-staff-hidden-by-non-dis closure-agreements [accessed 20 January 2021].

Weedon, C. (1987) *Feminist Practice and Poststructuralist Theory*, Oxford: Blackwell.

Zellick, G. (1994) *Final Report of the Taskforce on Student Disciplinary Procedures, London: Committee of Vice-Chancellors and Principles of the Universities of the United Kingdom*.

# 6

# Gender, Policing and Social Order: Restating the Case for a Feminist Analysis of Policing

*Will Jackson and Helen Monk*

## Introduction

In March 2021, the Sarah Everard case brought the policing of women in Britain into the public spotlight in a manner not witnessed for decades. The murder of Sarah reignited debates about women's experiences of men's violence and highlighted the police's role as both perpetrators of that violence (the man who raped and murdered Sarah was a serving Metropolitan Police officer[1]) and as ineffective protectors. The police response to the vigil held in Sarah's memory in the days after her death was widely criticized for being aggressive and disproportionate (Graham-Harrison, 2021) and brought women's experience of policing into sharp relief, for many people for the first time. Despite the exoneration of police in a subsequent report by the police inspectorate (HMICFRS, 2021), the policing of the vigil raised significant questions about women's rights to protest the institutional and societal failure to tackle men's violence. Furthermore, in an echo of women's struggles in the past, the vigil exposed the ways in which the police respond to defiant women. While the work of pioneering service providers and campaigning organizations such as Women's Aid, Rape Crisis, Southall Black Sisters and Sisters Uncut have long highlighted the failures of police responses to men's violence, the Everard case arguably shone a light on the police as an organization marked by institutional misogyny and centrally involved in the maintenance of a gendered order.

This chapter seeks to reassert the case that policing is, and always has been, a feminist issue. By examining current police responses to women in a range of contexts, the chapter argues that policing requires a renewed feminist analysis that should be central to a feminist criminology in the 21st century. Starting from the public debate and activist responses to the Everard case, the chapter begins by examining a range of contemporary issues that highlight problems in the police response to women and girls and, as a result, points to the enduring relevance of gender to analyses of policing. We suggest that considering the police response to women as both victims and offenders remains a key task for feminist criminology, but the case studies highlighted in the first part of the chapter suggest that this binary framing of women's interaction with police limits the terrain of our analysis. We seek to argue that the police institution in Britain is characterized by a view of gender roles that affects *all* police interactions with women. We argue that women's experience of police power has always been, and continues to be, affected by the role of gender in the vision of order pursued by police. There is therefore a need to understand the gendered forms that policing takes and the role that policing plays in (re)producing gender norms.

To consider the place of this work in contemporary feminist criminology, the chapter proceeds by considering a body of feminist work that sought to highlight and understand the policing of women in the 1980s. Following feminist activist and scholarly work in the 1970s that highlighted the extent and nature of men's violence against women (for example, Amir, 1971; Russell, 1973; Pizzey, 1974; Brownmiller, 1975; Dobash and Dobash, 1979), feminist social scientists produced a concerted body of work that sought to understand the reasons why the problem endured. Here, the law (in statute and in practice), the criminal justice system, and the police in particular, were identified as key objects of analysis (Hanmer and Maynard, 1987; Edwards, 1989a; Hanmer et al, 1989a; Smart, 1989). As the first point of contact with many victims of men's violence against women, the police were subject to pioneering empirical and theoretical work that aimed to examine and explain problems with policing and the response to women. A wider body of critical feminist work also sought to examine the experiences of women as the objects of policing (Chadwick and Little, 1987; Morris, 1987; Cain, 1989; Dunhill, 1989; Worrall, 1989). The experiences of women from working-class and Black and racially minoritized backgrounds, lesbians, sex workers, and women involved in political activism were explored by feminist researchers in order to document and understand the experiences of those women marked by police as disorderly.

This chapter therefore considers how the question of policing was framed in these foundational feminist analyses and considers the extent to which the central ideas remain relevant and useful to us today. From this point, the chapter will conclude by restating the case for a feminist analysis of policing. We seek to demonstrate that feminist theory and a critical theory of police power can be brought together in a mutually beneficial way to enhance our collective understanding of the general role of police in reproducing the current social order.

## Failing to protect women from men's violence

The Everard case and the police response to the vigil were undoubtedly significant for highlighting the nature and extent of men's violence against women and for exposing the way that police respond to women involved in public displays of defiance. The identification of the suspect in the case as a serving Metropolitan Police officer was shocking to many observers, and the heavy-handed response to the vigil on Clapham Common[2] reinforced a view of police as a threat to women's safety, rather than a source of protection. However, the case should not be viewed as an isolated example of institutional sexism and misogyny in the police. Following the police response to the vigil, female officers and campaigners spoke out about the 'institutionalised misogyny' in the police describing a force characterized by 'toxic masculinity' within which women are objectified and fetishized (Wolfe-Robinson and Dodd, 2021). In Britain, examples abound of the police's differential treatment of women and their apparent complicity in the proliferation of a culture of normalized misogyny. The examples that follow must be considered against the backdrop of a punitive state that, despite its commitment to 'law and order', continues to demonstrate an unwillingness to mobilize all available resources in efforts to deal effectively with men's violence against women. It is to these contemporary case studies of police responses to women and girls that the chapter now turns.

While it is fair to recognize significant change to police policy and practice in recent decades in regard to the response to men's violence against women, the overall effectiveness of the police response continues to lead to allegations of systematic failure. In 2019, the Centre for Women's Justice (CWJ) submitted a super-complaint to the police inspectorate accusing police of a 'systemic failure' to protect women as a 'highly vulnerable section' of the population from multiple forms of men's violence (Oppenheim, 2019). The CWJ highlighted enduring failings in police training and guidance, arguing that police in Britain continue to fail to mobilize the available resources at their disposal to tackle domestic violence, rape, harassment and stalking (Oppenheim, 2019). CWJ and other leading women's organizations[3] have demonstrated that while there have been welcome changes to police policy, failings in police practice are caused by the endurance of 'ancient patriarchal attitudes which pervade the criminal justice system' (CWJ et al, 2020: 13) and limit the capacity of police to deal effectively with men's violence.

The failure of police to protect women and girls from violence and sexual exploitation has also been highlighted in Britain in the last decade by a series of high-profile sexual abuse cases. Well-publicized cases of sexual abuse of girls in Rotherham and Rochdale (discussed further in Chapter 4, this volume), as well as cases in other towns and cities in Britain, have exposed the failures of multiple institutions tasked with safeguarding vulnerable girls and young women. Police attitudes towards victims' culpability has been cited as a cause of inaction that led to thousands of girls being victims of rape and sexual exploitation (Syal, 2013; Ramesh, 2014; Laville, 2015). In a reflection of the problems with police responses in this context, calls have been made for the prosecution of senior police officers in Greater Manchester for their mishandling of investigations – in part due to a prioritization of burglaries and car crime over the sexual abuse of children (Walker, 2020). Despite reforms to police policy and practice in recent decades in Britain, police views of gender roles and gendered behaviour continue to affect the level of protection victim-survivors of men's violence are afforded.

## Police as perpetrators of men's violence against women

Problems in the police's institutional responses to men's violence are also reflected in the manner in which police officers accused of raping, beating or coercing women and children are dealt with. A *Channel 4 News* investigation in 2021 (Stephenson, 2021) found that one woman per week in Britain is coming forward to report their partner in the police for abusing them and/or their children, leading one former police commander to refer to officer perpetrated domestic abuse as an 'epidemic' within the force (cited in Stephenson, 2021). The role of police officers as perpetrators of violence against women is also laid bare by the problem of 'abuse of position for sexual purpose', which demonstrates that 'police are abusing their power to target victims of crime they are supposed to be helping, as well as fellow officers and female staff' (Laville, 2012). While the police inspectorate has sought to frame this issue as involving only a 'tiny proportion of police officers and staff' (Billingham in HMICFRS, 2019: 1), they have conceded that the abuse of victims and suspects is 'the most serious corruption issue facing the police service' (Grierson, 2016). Observers have suggested that this is yet another reflection of the 'macho culture' in policing that encourages 'profound sexism' and has enabled male officers to be 'openly predatory' (Laville, 2016). While there have been 'cultural changes in the police service' (Laville, 2016), an increase in senior female officers, and the apparent end of openly expressed sexism, this problem persists.

These institutional failings are linked by an underpinning culture of misogyny, but in the dominant framing, culpability is attributed to individual officers who are easily dismissed as 'bad apples' as problems in policing invariably are. The revelations about undercover policing of political activists in recent years, however, have been much harder to distance from the institution itself. The targeting of women activists by undercover officers has been central to the controversy that followed from initial revelations about the officer Mark Kennedy in 2011 (Evans and Lewis, 2013).[4] At least 20 undercover officers deceived women into intimate relationships while they infiltrated political groups from the 1970s to 2010 (Evans, 2021a). At least three of them fathered children with women they met while undercover (Evans, 2021a), disappearing from the women's lives at the end of their deployment. The lack of informed consent in these cases means that women have publicly reported that they regard their relationship as rape (Evans, 2021b) with one woman reporting feeling 'raped by the state' (cited in Lewis et al, 2013).

The targeting of women as political activists is further demonstrated in recent studies of women's experience at protests in Britain. Ethnographic research has suggested that women's experiences of violent policing in protest spaces is reflective of the gendered nature of public order policing (Monk et al, 2019). This work documented experiences of sexual violence by police officers in the response to women's involvement in environmental protests. Women have been marked as out of place in protest spaces and police attitudes about gender roles appear, again, to determine the responses to women. The position of police as both perpetrators of violence against women and ineffective protectors needs to be understood in relation to the culture of sexism and misogyny that appear to continue to pervade the institution and the enduring attitudes about gender roles that shape police perceptions of crime and disorder.

## Feminist criminological analyses of policing

The issues highlighted in the previous section make clear that policing should be a key concern of feminist scholarship and activism in the 21st century. The two key dynamics of police engagement with women – as victim-survivors and as suspects – should position the institution at the centre of a feminist criminology that seeks to understand and challenge the state as it both perpetrates and sanctions violence against women. While there is important work in this area, feminist criminological work on policing has not kept pace with other areas of research and scholarship in recent years. The field of 'gender and policing' has been dominated by important work on women's experiences in the police (Heidensohn, 1995; Westmarland, 2001; Kringen, 2014), but work considering women as the object of police has not been developed to the same extent as criminological work on women's experiences of prison or the law.

However, in the early years of feminist criminology, significant work was published in Britain that focused on policing, incorporating it into wider analyses of women's experience of the criminal justice system. It is our contention that this work still has much to offer contemporary feminist criminology. We want to argue that by bringing this foundational work into dialogue with a critical theory of police power, there is an important contribution to make to feminist work for the 21st century. This section of our chapter will provide a review of feminist criminological analyses of the police developed in the 1980s to outline how women's experiences of policing were studied and theorized. We argue that much of the required theoretical toolkit for contemporary analyses was provided in this early feminist work in criminology, and there is much to be gained by revisiting a number of classic, and some lesser known, texts.

Pioneering work in feminist criminology highlighted the relative neglect of women in the study of crime (Heidensohn, 1968; Bertrand, 1969; Klein, 1973), and from the 1970s, empirical and theoretical interventions sought to challenge the 'silence of criminologists' (Smart, 1976: 180) and address the invisibility of women in criminological discourse. At the same time, feminist activists and those agencies tasked with helping women were highlighting endemic problems in the criminal justice system's response to women (Hanmer, 1989). In response, in the 1980s, feminist scholars produced significant work on women's experiences of punishment and the criminal justice system (Carlen, 1983; Heidensohn, 1985; Dobash et al, 1986; Morris, 1987; Worrall, 1989) as well as on the impact of the law on women's lives (Brophy and Smart, 1985; Smart, 1989, 1995).

For Maureen Cain, writing in 1989, feminist criminology had three central concerns: men and women's (un)equal treatment in the criminal justice system; female crime; and women's victimization (Cain, 1989). It is possible to trace these three lines of enquiry to important feminist analyses of the police. An expansion in the use of victimization studies in the 1980s also helped to highlight problems in policing and in doing so, exposed an institution long insulated by the state to a feminist critique (Hanmer, 1989). In essence, the feminist critique of police developed in this period sought to examine how the 'all-pervasiveness of patriarchal attitudes in society, in law and in policing has had certain fundamental consequences for what is policed and who are protected' (Edwards, 1989a: 31).

Broadly, foundational feminist analyses of police and policing in Britain had two central focal points: police responses to women as victims of men's violence and the policing of 'deviant' women. Alongside the drive to expose criminology's failure to take women's victimization seriously, early feminist work in criminology sought to highlight the enduring failure of the law and criminal justice system to deal effectively with men's violence against women. This was not a new line of critique. Problems in the police and judicial response to men's violence identified in the 1970s and 1980s paralleled those identified by campaigners for women's suffrage in the early 20th century (Radford, 1989). In fact, feminists had been campaigning for men's violence to be treated as a crime, and policed accordingly, since the 19th century (Hanmer et al, 1989a). This demand had led to calls for police reform and specifically demands for the introduction of women officers to encourage women to report victimization and to remove the possibility of abuse of women by police men (Radford, 1989).

The unwillingness of institutions of criminal justice to tackle men's violence was understood to be a product of social attitudes towards gender roles, the family and violence that infused the police and legal system. As Frances Heidensohn argued, 'in cases of rape and of domestic violence, police views about women, about their behaviour, morals and roles are made explicit' (1985: 52). The enduring attitude of police towards men's violence against their partners – reflected in the phrase 'just a domestic' – was based on a central distinction drawn between 'police problems' and 'family problems' (Edwards, 1989a: 93). Responding to so-called 'domestic' violence was not 'real' police work; in comparison to violence against a stranger in a public place, violence against a woman by her partner in the privacy of their home was viewed 'as a quite different crime ... if a real crime at all' (Morris, 1987: 183). The protection of victims in cases of domestic violence (or lack thereof) was understood to be the product of private attitudes regarding 'sex roles, appropriate conduct and family ideologies' (Edwards, 1989a: 91) and the effectiveness of police interventions rested on the police perceptions of the character of both the offender and victim. Crucially, this work highlighted the role that police play in (re)producing the idea of the deserving victim.

The status of a real or a legitimate victim was understood as being determined by police attitudes towards gender roles (Morris, 1987; Edwards, 1989a; Hanmer et al, 1989a, 1989b) but was also affected by class and 'race' stereotypes of both the victim and the offender. Racist and discriminatory attitudes held by police were emphasized as key factors in determining the response victims received. As Edwards argued, 'such commonly held views are conflated with perceptions of the normality of domestic violence' in particular communities (1989a: 92). Black women's experiences were compounded by having to deal with police racism as well as victimization (Hague et al, 1989) and police stereotypes reaffirmed the idea that violence is a cultural phenomenon linked to racially minoritized communities rather than being rooted in gender relations. This meant that 'Black and Asian women lose out on protection because of racist and cultural perceptions but they lose out even more because their protection is seen as of lesser importance' (Edwards, 1989a: 97). Gendered behaviour was key to determining who is seen to warrant police protection but 'race', class, immigration status and sexuality was also key in determining a woman's status as a deserving victim (Hanmer et al, 1989).

Scholars recognized that feminist campaigns have had a tremendous impact and influence on the evolution of police policy and training (Edwards,

1989a) and this has continued since the 1980s (Hanmer and Itzin, 2001). The enduring attitudes towards women, men and the place of violence in heterosexual relationships continued to determine the effectiveness of the responses to victims, even as it appeared that police were responding to pressure from feminists. The historical unwillingness on the part of police to intervene in dealing with men's violence within marriage (McCann, 1985) exposed the power of *discretion* that has always been central to the exercise of police power. The capacity of individual officers and police forces to exercise discretion meant that even where reform to policy appeared progressive, the reality of police practice continued to be affected by police perceptions. Ultimately, 'wife assault' has long been construed as less serious than other forms of assault and this determines the nature of the police response.

The resistance of the police institution to respond effectively to victim-survivors was ultimately explained in relation to the place of men's violence in the current social order. As Hanmer et al explained: 'There is no way the police or other agents of the state, the courts, or judiciary, can truly treat men's violence as a serious crime without undermining the social order it serves so well' (1989a: 11). The key contributions to work on police responses to men's violence published in the 1980s highlighted problems of police policy and practice, but also made clear that there was a need to examine the *structural* role of police. The failure to adequately protect women from men's violence is not therefore a problem reducible to the attitudes of individual officers, but is instead reflective of the wider social function of the police institution. For Radford (1989), the state's response to men's violence serves only to discriminate between acceptable and excessive violence and this needs to be understood as a process connected to the conservative function of police.

As outlined in the introduction to this collection, the police's prominent role in 'keeping order' needs to be understood in relation to their drive to reproduce the current *social order*, in reality this involves 'maintaining existing gender, sexuality, race and social class power relationships' (Hanmer et al, 1989a: 5), and sanctioning the violence required to maintain a system of hetero-patriarchy is part of this. Indeed, 'the ideology of hetero-patriarchy in part depends on a closely woven system of ideas about the security and safety of the family home for women' (Hanmer et al, 1989b: 188), and the distinction between the public and private, (re)produced by police, is pivotal to reaffirming the idea that the place of women and their safety is in the home. As Hanmer et al argued, 'the way that police intervene in gendered interpersonal crime is essential to the continuing credibility of this ideology' (1989b: 188). The role of the police is to protect the status quo and 'the failure to provide an adequate response to men's violence is perfectly consistent with this role' (Radford, 1987: 41).

## Women as the object of policing

In this same period, a significant body of criminological work documented the politicization of policing in Britain (Scraton 1985, 1987; Farrell, 1992; Reiner, 1992). In these analyses, the police response to widespread urban disorder, industrial unrest and protest movements in this decade was reflective of the heightened political nature of policing, as Britain drifted into what Stuart Hall (1980) referred to as the 'law and order society'. In this context, research and scholarship focused on the distinct experiences of working-class and Black and racially minoritized communities, highlighting the ways in which class and 'race' served as markers of disorder in this decade (Scraton, 1985; Gilroy, 1987; Cashmore and McLaughlin, 1991). While the salience of gender was arguably underplayed in most of the critical criminological analyses of policing in the 1980s, important feminist work on women's experiences did seek to highlight how gender served to mark out certain groups of women as the object of police.

Research comprehensively examined how formal and informal modes of social control police women in relation to their subordinate position in society and coerce women to self-police their own actions, behaviours and appearance (Smart and Smart, 1978; Hutter and Williams, 1981; Mason, 2002). In contrast, the history of the police features far fewer confrontations between women and police and women have rarely been considered dangerous by the state (Radford, 1987). However, feminist analyses of women's history have highlighted how the lives of women and girls have been controlled through the law and how women marked as disorderly have long been subject to the exercise of police power. This work illustrates that women's experience of policing is less frequent and less formal, but it is distinct and we need to understand how gender norms are (re)produced in the police response to women as suspects as well as victims. Scholarship has sought to demonstrate that the police response to deviant women, like the response to women as victims, is determined by the police perception of a woman's conformity to gender norms. The police concern with disorder is always informed by the vision of a *gendered order* and the police response to women needs to be considered in terms of gendered social control.

Bland's (1985) history of the policing of women in the First World War, for example, demonstrated how, even with the incorporation of women in policing, including feminists and suffragettes, the policing of women has always involved elements of surveillance and coercion. The moral policing of women in the early 20th century was based on (feminist) ideas of appropriate femininity and legitimate sexual behaviour and was not transformed by the involvement of feminists. As already noted, the role of women in the police from the 1970s has been key to developing policy and practice in the response to men's violence, but the longer history would suggest that women's involvement is not sufficient to effectively disturb the central function of the institution.

It is perhaps in the policing of sex work that the state's attempt to regulate 'disorderly' women is most obvious and most well established. The focus on the policing of street prostitutes in early feminist criminological work (Smart, 1976; Heidensohn, 1985; Chadwick and Little, 1987; Morris, 1987; Radford, 1987; Edwards, 1989b) is a reflection of the fact that they are the group of women that most frequently come into contact with the police. But this is not only a feature of the late 20th century. The Contagious Diseases Acts of 1864 and 1866 were introduced to strengthen the policing of prostitution in the 19th century and in Susan Edwards' analysis, these Acts stand as 'testaments in British History to the extraordinary powers of the police in the control and surveillance of working-class and largely poor and powerless women' (1989a: 33). The policing of prostitution is an enduring feature of modern policing (Howell, 2011; Sanders and Laing, 2018). The fact that this concern has persisted across the last two centuries is understandable if we recognize that it is 'only when women have broken away from being responsible to, and controlled by, individual men that they have been deemed worthy of state policing' (Radford, 1987: 42).

Feminist scholars argued that the historic focus on the woman rather than her male client – the defining feature of the policing of sex work – is reflective of a 'double standard of morality' (Chadwick and Little, 1987: 265). The primary concern with the woman is not simply a result of her having refused male control, but is also a reflection of the emphasis on the 'abnormal sexuality of women' (Chadwick and Little, 1987: 265) that is contrasted with the normal male sex-drive and ultimately renders prostitution intelligible. Feminist scholarship has argued that the prostitute is thus distinguished from the 'respectable' woman based on this construction of abnormal sexuality (Smart, 1976) and through the power of discretion, police are able to determine which women warrant policing (Morris, 1987). Feminist work sought to highlight that in the dominant view, the deviant woman involved in selling sex lacks the moral fibre that would ordinarily restrain a 'normal' female sexuality and, importantly, reinforces the virtue of legitimate work.

The recognition that women become a concern to the police when they reject informal modes of social control and act autonomously as women, connects many feminist analyses of policing. As already noted, a woman's ability or willingness to conform to expected standards of gendered behaviour determines their treatment by police. Jill Radford (1987) argued that 'by stepping outside of the normal parameters of male control' certain groups of women such as lesbians and prostitutes are 'frequently denied the kind of protection that may be afforded to "decent" women' (Radford, 1987: 43). An array of work in the 1980s highlighted how many groups of women were marked as deviant or disorderly. As with police responses to women as victims, police perceptions of the undeserving, unrespectable or disorderly woman is affected by other factors. Critically, the intersection of 'race', class and sexuality with gender serves to mark out certain groups of women as 'police property' (Lee, 1981).

The idea of police property captures the characterization of certain groups who are 'disproportionately at the receiving end of the use or abuse of police powers' (Reiner, 2009: 231) but also signifies that police discriminate against certain groups with relative impunity. Research conducted in the 1980s highlighted the experiences of certain groups of women who experienced distinct forms of targeted and disproportionate policing, and whose accounts and complaints were routinely discredited or ignored. These groups included Black women (Heaven and Mars, 1989; Chigwada, 1991), immigrant women (Shutter, 1989), Irish women in Britain (O'Shea, 1989), Nationalist women in Northern Ireland (McAuley, 1989), women as welfare claimants (Chadwick and Little, 1987), lesbians (Natzler, 1989) and women involved in protest (Chadwick and Little, 1987; Johnson, 1989). Foundational work in the 1980s highlighted the effects that cultural assumptions about minority communities had on perceptions of female deviance held by police. Assumptions about Black and Asian women, for example, were the focus of work on police responses to women as victims, suspects, witnesses, parents and members of the public (Chigwada, 1991). Importantly, research highlighted how gender intersects with 'race', class, sexuality and age to frame the respectable woman that is reproduced by police. This work also sought to demonstrate that the impact of 'race' is not uniformly experienced by all non-White women. While space here limits the extent to which we are able to examine the specific experiences of diversely situated women, what they arguably had in common was the challenge they posed to the 'natural' role of women that is central to police perceptions of good order.

## Feminist analyses of police for the 21st century

Here, we have argued that feminist work developed in the 1980s provided a range of key insights that could help us make sense of current problems in policing in Britain and beyond. While recognizing the importance of developments in feminist theory and praxis in the late 20th century, there is also a much longer history that we need to consider in our attempts to understand policing today. The experiences of women under the conditions of slavery and colonialism reflect the gendered form that policing has always taken in the drive to (re)produce order (see Cunneen, 2001; Correia and Wall, 2018). This arguably remains a defining feature of contemporary policing and we must consider this long history to understand the historical continuities in the policing of women. However, in this specific contribution, it is our contention that the insights drawn from foundational feminist work in the 1980s, in particular, should inform the work we do today as we seek to advance a gendered analysis of police and policing. We want to suggest that this foundational feminist work can, and should, inform recent scholarship that has sought to develop a critical theory of police power. We believe that bringing these two sets of ideas together will help us better understand the policing of women historically and in the contemporary period.

While there has been important empirical and theoretical work on policing in (critical) criminology, we want to argue that the most useful insights to inform a feminist theory of police power come from outside the discipline. Scholarship in political and social theory has arguably been more successful in unpicking the liberal myths that underpin the orthodox history of policing and in outlining the historical continuities in the function of police. In doing so, this work presents a challenge to the vast majority of current work on policing, including much of what passes as 'critical' in police studies and criminology. Contributing primarily to Marxist analyses of the police and state, such work has argued that the central concern of police is, and has always been, *order* rather than crime (Neocleous, 2000, 2021; Rigakos, 2016; Correia and Wall, 2018). In dismantling the argument that police are primarily concerned with, and involved in, the response to crime, this work demonstrates that the focus of the institutions of policing has, in fact, been consistently on 'those who challenge the order of capital and the state' (Neocleous, 2000: 115). Police power here is understood to be *productive*; police work is not simply based on a vision of what is unacceptable in the current social order – what constitutes *disorder* – but is driven by a clear vision of what is desirable, necessary and orderly. This critical account offers us a way to make sense of policing in the 21st century by helping to expose the continuities that link contemporary police policy and practice with the historical function of the institution.

Recognizing the central role police play in the production and reproduction of bourgeois order, this work has primarily focused on the links between police, order and social class. However, more recent work has sought to develop the central insights drawn from this critical theory of police power and use it to better understand the place of 'race' in the vision of order pursued by police (Correia and Wall, 2018; Seigel, 2018; Brucato, 2021). In these contributions, racial disparities in the experiences of policing exist because Blackness is always a sign of disorder in a social order based on White supremacy; the 'good order' fabricated by police has always been racialized. The historical roots of the association of Blackness and disorder are affected by particular colonial histories and histories of slavery, but the centrality of 'race' in contemporary capitalism is a result of the fact that 'race has been fundamental to capitalism from the first' (Seigel, 2018: 24). In recognition of this, the critical account of police history is being revised and developed to centralize the place of 'race' in this history and to better understand the relationship between policing and 'race' today.

We want to suggest that a parallel development in this critical theory of police is required to accurately grasp the place of gender in the (re) production of social order enabled through the exercise of police power. Starting from a recognition that the ideal citizen-subject produced through police power is always gendered, we argue that women's experiences of police power are a reflection of the idealized version of femininity that underpins the police vision of good order. There is, therefore, a mutually beneficial exchange of ideas to come from an integration of feminist work on policing and the critical theory of police power advanced in recent years. We have previously argued that key insights from this critical work can be integrated with feminist theory to centralize the place of gender in a theory of police power (Monk et al, 2019). Here, we want to suggest that feminist work on policing can advance theories of policing and, in turn, provide a theoretical framework through which we can adequately grasp the central features of contemporary policing.

One of the central issues on which these two bodies of work converge is the importance of the power of *discretion*. By considering the capacity for discretion that remains central to modern policing, we can understand why women's experiences of policing are distinct and explain the concentration of the use and abuse of police power among certain groups of women. In addition, it is the power of discretion that explains why problems with policing persist through the long and short histories we have considered. In the face of 50 years of modern feminist campaigns (and a longer history of feminist activism from the 19th century), and despite rounds of reform to police policy, the impact of police attitudes on the use of discretion explains why 'ancient patriarchal attitudes' continue to affect policing. A critical theory of police power requires us to understand the place of discretion in the general operation of police and the relation to the law. As Mark Neocleous has argued: 'To say that "the police enforce the law" fails to recognize the enormous range of police discretion which, far more than legal codes, shapes the way the police behave' (Neocleous, 2000: 100). From this perspective, the misuse of police powers and the problem of police corruption is better understood as part of the normal operation of police power.

## Conclusion

Contemporary evidence continues to suggest that police play a role in monitoring, regulating and reformulating acceptable forms of femininity. In addition, contemporary work suggests that experiences of police violence are still concentrated among women from historically oppressed populations (Ritchie, 2017). The over- and under-policing of women in different settings, as well as women's continued experiences of police violence, including of rape and sexual violence, reflect the fact that police power remains a patriarchal power central to the (re)production of a gendered social order. The ideal citizen-subject produced through police power is always gendered and women's experiences of police power are a reflection of the idealized version of femininity that underpins the vision of good order (Monk et al, 2019). The prevalence of sexual violence perpetrated by police is a reflection of the social function of sexual violence against women which is deployed to keep women in their place. Rape and sexual violence perpetrated by police are thus 'a form of terror that emerges out of the routine operation of police power' (Correia and Wall, 2018: 47) in the (re)production of order.

The nature and extent of the problems associated with police responses to women in the 21st century demand a renewed programme of feminist work. The endurance of informal means of social control that serve to regulate and constrain the behaviour of women and girls requires continued critical analysis, but we must also develop our understandings of the role of the state and formal agencies of control. We learn from the counter-history and critical theory of police today, that our analytical approach must reject the false separation of police from other institutions of control that affect women's lives. Understanding the links between formal and informal means of social control is not new to feminist theory, but our call here, in this chapter, is to retain and renew the focus on the police institution in feminist criminology. The central function of police in the reproduction of social order means that any feminist critique of gender relations and the violence therein must take seriously the place of police in (re)producing a culture of normalized misogyny and maintaining a system of hetero-patriarchy.

## Notes

[1] At the time of writing (July 2021), PC Wayne Couzens has pleaded guilty to the rape, kidnap and murder of Sarah Everard. He is yet to be sentenced.

[2] The vigil on 13 March 2021 was held in defiance of a police ban of gatherings under the COVID-19 lockdown. An event to remember Sarah was initially proposed by Reclaim the Streets but was cancelled after police refused a permit and a bid to the High Court to allow an exception to the COVID-19 ban on gatherings failed. Despite this, hundreds of women gathered on Clapham Common, close to where Sarah was last seen alive, to lay flowers and hold a minute's silence. During the event, police intervened to stop speeches to the crowd assembled and made a number of arrests. Police were criticized by members of the public, journalists and politicians for the use of excessive force and unnecessary arrests. Images of police forcibly removing women from an assembly called to remember a woman murdered by a police officer led to widespread condemnation and were shared widely online and in the media. The willingness of police to repress an event that constituted a visible objection to men's violence against women was widely seen to be a public relations disaster for the Metropolitan Police despite them being exonerated by Her Majesty's Inspectorate of Constabulary and Fire & Rescue Services (HMICFRS).

3    The organizations involved in the production of this report were: Centre for Women's Justice, the End Violence Against Women coalition, Imkaan and Rape Crisis England & Wales.

4    Mark Kennedy was an undercover police officer who infiltrated dozens of protest groups under the alias Mark Stone between 2003 and 2011. The *Guardian* newspaper first revealed his identity and the story of his undercover deployments in January 2011. The controversy that followed related not just to his infiltration of anti-racist, anarchist and environmental groups but to the way that his case exposed wider practices of political policing in Britain. Kennedy's case in particular exposed the tactic of duping women into sexual relationships (subsequently shown to be a widespread behaviour of undercover police) and the revelations about his role led to the collapse of the prosecution case in a trial of a group of environmental activists in 2011 (Lewis and Evans, 2011). Details of Kennedy's deployment led to further revelations about the work of the secretive National Public Order Intelligence Unit and the longer history of undercover policing from the 1960s. The full details of this case and many others, as well as the aspects of the history of the secret police that came to light following Kennedy's case, is contained in Evans and Lewis (2013).

## References

Amir, M. (1971) *Patterns in Forcible Rape*, Chicago: Chicago University Press.

Bertrand, M. (1969) 'Self-image and delinquency: A contribution to the study of female criminality and women's image', *Acta Criminologica*, 2(1): 71–144.

Bland, L. (1985) 'In the name of protection: The policing of women in the First World War' in J. Brophy and C. Smart (eds) *Women in Law: Explorations in Law, Family and Sexuality*, London: Routledge and Kegan Paul, pp 23–49.

Brophy, J. and Smart, C. (1985) *Women in Law: Explorations in Law, Family and Sexuality*, London: Routledge and Kegan Paul.

Brownmiller, S. (1975) *Against Our Will: Men, Women, and Rape*, New York: Simon & Schuster.

Brucato, B. (2021) 'Policing race and racing police: The origin of U.S. American police in slave patrols', *Social Justice*, 47(3/4): 115–36.

Cain, M. (1989) *Growing Up Good: Policing the Behaviour of Girls in Europe*, London: SAGE.

Carlen, P. (1983) *Women's Imprisonment: A Study in Social Control*, London: Routledge.

Cashmore, E. and McLaughlin, E. (1991) *Out of Order?: Policing Black People*, London: Routledge.

Centre for Women's Justice, End Violence Against Women Coalition, Imkaan and Rape Crisis England & Wales (2020) *The Decriminalisation of Rape: Why the Justice System is Failing Rape Survivors and What Needs to Change*, London: Centre for Women's Justice, End Violence Against Women Coalition, Imkaan and Rape Crisis England & Wales. Available at: https://www.endviolenceagainstwomen.org.uk/wp-content/uploads/C-Decriminalisation-of-Rape-Report-CWJ-EVAW-IMKAAN-RCEW-NOV-2020.pdf [accessed 15 July 2021].

Chadwick, K. and Little, C. (1987) 'The criminalisation of women' in P. Scraton (ed) *Law, Order and the Authoritarian State*, Milton Keynes: Open University Press, pp 254–78.

Chigwada, R. (1991) 'The policing of Black women' in E. Cashmore and E. McLaughlin (eds) *Out of Order? Policing Black People*, London: Routledge, pp 134–50.

Correia, D. and Wall, T. (2018) *Police: A Field Guide*, London: Verso.

Cunneen, C. (2001) *Conflict, Politics and Crime: Aboriginal Communities and Police*, Sydney: Allen & Unwin.

Dobash, R.E. and Dobash, R. (1979) *Violence against Wives: A Case against the Patriarchy*, New York: Free Press.

Dobash, R.P., Dobash, R.E. and Gutteridge, S. (1986) *The Imprisonment of Women*, Oxford: Blackwell.

Dunhill, C. (1989) *The Boys in Blue: Women's Challenge to the Police*, London: Virago Press.

Edwards, S. (1989a) *Policing 'Domestic' Violence: Women, the Law and the State*, London: SAGE.

Edwards, S. (1989b) 'Protecting the honour of innocent men' in C. Dunhill (ed) *The Boys in Blue: Women's Challenge to the Police*, London: Virago Press, pp 193–204.

Evans, R. (2021a) 'Cops joked about sexual relationships with women, inquiry told', *The Guardian*, [online] 7 May, available at: https://www.theg uardian.com/uk-news/2021/may/07/spy-cops-joked-about-sexual-relati onships-with-women-inquiry-told [accessed 15 July 2021].

Evans, R. (2021b) 'Woman deceived by spy cop sees relationship as rape, inquiry hears', *The Guardian*, [online] 10 May, available at: https://www. theguardian.com/uk-news/2021/may/10/woman-deceived-by-spy-cop-sees-relationship-as-inquiry-hears [accessed 15 July 2021].

Evans, R. and Lewis, P. (2013) *Undercover: The True Story of Britain's Secret Police*, London: Faber & Faber.

Farrell, A. (1992) *Crime, Class and Corruption: The Politics of the Police*, London: Bookmarks.

Gilroy, P. (1987) *'There Ain't No Black in the Union Jack': The Cultural Politics of Race and Nation*, London: Hutchinson.

Graham-Harrison, E. (2021) 'Police clash with mourners at Sarah Everard vigil in London', *The Guardian*, [online] 13 March, available at: https:// www.theguardian.com/uk-news/2021/mar/13/as-the-sun-set-they-came-in-solidarity-and-to-pay-tribute-to-sarah-everard [accessed 27 June 2021].

Grierson, J. (2016) 'Hundreds of police in England and Wales accused of sexual abuse', *The Guardian*, [online] 8 December, available at: https:// www.theguardian.com/uk-news/2016/dec/08/hundreds-police-officers-accused-sex-abuse-inquiry-finds [accessed 27 June 2021].

Hague, G., Harwin, N., McMinn, K., Rubens, J. and Taylor, M. (1989) 'Women's Aid: Policing male violence in the home' in C. Dunhill (ed) *The Boys in Blue: Women's Challenge to the Police*, London: Virago Press, pp 23–37.

Hall, S. (1980) *Drifting into a Law and Order Society*, London: The Cobden Trust.

Hanmer, J. (1989) 'Women and policing in Britain' in J. Hanmer, J. Radford and E. Stanko (eds) *Women, Policing, and Male Violence: International Perspectives*, London: Routledge, pp 90–124.

Hanmer, J. and Itzin, C. (2001) *Home Truths About Domestic Violence: Feminist Influences on Policy and Practice: A Reader*, London: Routledge.

Hanmer, J. and Maynard, M. (1987) *Women, Violence and Social Control*, Basingstoke: Macmillan.

Hanmer, J., Radford, J. and Stanko, E. (1989a) 'Policing men's violence: An introduction' in J. Hanmer, J. Radford, and E. Stanko (eds) *Women, Policing, and Male Violence: International Perspectives*, London: Routledge, pp 1–12.

Hanmer, J., Radford, J. and Stanko, E. (1989b) 'Improving policing for women: The way forward' in J. Hanmer, J. Radford, and E. Stanko (eds) *Women, Policing, and Male Violence: International Perspectives*, London: Routledge, pp 185–201.

Heaven, O. and Mars, M. (1989) 'Black women targeted' in C. Dunhill (ed) *The Boys in Blue: Women's Challenge to the Police*, London: Virago Press, pp 232–42.

Heidensohn, F. (1968) 'The deviance of women: A critique and an enquiry', *British Journal of Sociology*, 19(2): 160–75.

Heidensohn, F. (1985) *Women and Crime*, Basingstoke: Macmillan.

Heidensohn, F. (1995) *Women in Control? The Role of Women in Law Enforcement*, Oxford: Oxford University Press.

HMICFRS (2019) *PEEL spotlight report – shining a light on betrayal: Abuse of position for a sexual purpose*, [online] available at: https://www.justiceinspec torates.gov.uk/hmicfrs/publications/shining-a-light-on-betrayal-abuse-of-position-for-a-sexual-purpose/ [accessed 22 June 2022].

HMICFRS (2021) *An Inspection of the Metropolitan Police Service's Policing of a Vigil Held in Commemoration of Sarah Everard*, [online] available at: https://www.justiceinspectorates.gov.uk/hmicfrs/publications/an-inspection-of-the-metropolitan-police-services-policing-of-a-vigil-held-in-commem oration-of-sarah-everard/ [accessed 27 June 2021].

Howell, P. (2011) *Geographies of Regulation: Policing Prostitution in Nineteenth Century Britain and the Empire*, Cambridge: Cambridge University Press.

Hutter, B. and Williams, G. (1981) *Controlling Women: The Normal and the Deviant*, London: Croom Helm.

Johnson, R. (1989) 'Greenham women: The control of protest' in C. Dunhill (ed) *The Boys in Blue: Women's Challenge to the Police*, London: Virago Press, pp 166–76.

Klein, D. (1973) 'The etiology of female crime: A review of the literature', *Issues in Criminology*, 8(2): 3–29.

Kringen, A.L. (2014) 'Scholarship on women and policing: Trends and policy implications', *Feminist Criminology*, 9(4): 367–81.

Laville, S. (2012) 'Revealed: The scale of sexual abuse by police officers', *The Guardian*, [online] 29 June, available at: https://www.theguardian.com/uk/2012/jun/29/guardian-investigation-abuse-power-police [accessed 27 June 2021].

Laville, S. (2015) 'Professionals blamed Oxfordshire girls for their sexual abuse, report finds', *The Guardian*, [online] 3 March, available at: https://www.theguardian.com/society/2015/mar/03/professionals-blamed-oxfordshire-girls-for-their-sexual-abuse-report-finds [accessed 27 June 2021].

Laville, S. (2016) 'The police are still ignoring sexual abuse by officers: It's time for zero tolerance', *The Guardian*, [online] 8 December, available at: https://www.theguardian.com/commentisfree/2016/dec/08/police-sexually-abuse-victims-zero-tolerance [accessed 27 June 2021].

Lee, J.A. (1981) 'Some structural aspects of police deviance in relations with minority groups' in C. Shearing (ed) *Organizational Police Deviance*, Toronto: Butterworth, pp 49–82.

Lewis, P. and Evans, R. (2011) 'Activists walk free as undercover officer prompts collapse of case', *The Guardian*, [online] 10 January, available at: https://www.theguardian.com/environment/2011/jan/10/activists-undercover-officer-mark-kennedy [accessed 27 June 2021].

Lewis, P., Evans, R. and Pollak, S. (2013) 'Trauma of spy's girlfriend: "Like being raped by the state"', *The Guardian*, [online] 24 June, available at: https://www.theguardian.com/uk/2013/jun/24/undercover-police-spy-girlfriend-child [accessed 27 June 2021].

Mason, G. (2002) *The Spectacle of Violence: Homophobia, Gender, and Knowledge*, London: Routledge.

McAuley, C. (1989) 'Nationalist women and the RUC' in C. Dunhill (ed) *The Boys in Blue: Women's Challenge to the Police*, London: Virago Press, pp 133–48.

McCann, K. (1985) 'Battered women and the law: The limits of the legislation' in J. Brophy and C. Smart (eds) *Women in Law: Explorations in Law, Family and Sexuality*, London: Routledge and Keegan Paul, pp 71–96.

Monk, H., Gilmore, J. and Jackson W. (2019) 'Gendering pacification: Policing women at anti-fracking protests', *Feminist Review*, 122(1): 64–79.

Morris, A. (1987) *Women, Crime and Criminal Justice*, Oxford: Basil Blackwell.

Natzler, C. (1989) 'Lesbians, policing and the changing law' in C. Dunhill (ed) *The Boys in Blue: Women's Challenge to the Police*, London: Virago Press, pp 149–65.

Neocleous, M. (2000) *The Fabrication of Social Order: A Critical Theory of Police Power*, London: Pluto.

Neocleous, M. (2021) *A Critical Theory of Police Power*, London: Verso.

O'Shea, M. (1989) 'Policing Irish women in Britain' in C. Dunhill (ed) *The Boys in Blue: Women's Challenge to the Police*, London: Virago Press, pp 219–31.

Oppenheim, M. (2019) 'Police accused of "systemic failure" to protect victims of domestic abuse and sexual violence', *The Independent*, [online] 20 March, available at: https://www.independent.co.uk/news/uk/crime/pol ice-super-complaint-domestic-violence-sexual-violence-centre-women-s-justice-a8830366.html [accessed 15 June 2021].

Pizzey, E. (1974) *Scream Quietly or the Neighbours Will Hear*, Harmondsworth: Penguin.

Radford, J. (1987) 'Policing male violence: Policing women' in J. Hanmer and M. Maynard (eds) *Women, Violence and Social Control*, Basingstoke: Macmillan, pp 30–45.

Radford, J. (1989) 'Women and policing: Contradictions old and new' in J. Hanmer, J. Radford and E. Stanko (eds) *Women, Policing, and Male Violence: International Perspectives*, London: Routledge, pp 13–45.

Ramesh, R. (2014) 'Rotherham: A putrid scandal perpetuated by a broken system', *The Guardian*, [online] 26 August, available at: https://www.theg uardian.com/uk-news/2014/aug/26/rotherham-child-sex-exploitation-capital [accessed 23 June 2021].

Reiner, R. (1992) *The Politics of the Police* (second edition), Hemel Hempstead: Harvester Wheatsheaf.

Reiner, R. (2009) 'Police property' in A. Wakefield and J. Fleming (eds) *The SAGE Dictionary of Policing*, London: SAGE, pp 230–2.

Rigakos, G. (2016) *Security/Capital: A General Theory of Pacification*, Edinburgh: Edinburgh University Press.

Ritchie, A.J. (2017) *Invisible No More: Police Violence Against Black Women and Women of Colour*, Boston: Beacon Press.

Russell, D. (1973) *The Politics of Rape*, New York: Macmillan.

Sanders, T. and Laing, M. (2018) *Policing the Sex Industry: Protection, Paternalism and Politics*, Abingdon: Routledge.

Scraton, P. (1985) *The State of the Police*, London: Pluto Press.

Scraton, P. (1987) *Law, Order and the Authoritarian State*, Milton Keynes: Open University Press.

Seigel, M. (2018) 'Violence work: Policing and power', *Race and Class*, 59(4): 15–33.

Shutter, S. (1989) 'Joint Council for the Welfare of Immigrants (JCWI): Women and the immigration law' in C. Dunhill (ed) *The Boys in Blue: Women's Challenge to the Police*, London: Virago Press, pp 243–50.

Smart, C. (1976) *Women, Crime and Criminology: A Feminist Critique*, London: Routledge.

Smart, C. (1989) *Feminism and the Power of Law*, New York: Routledge.

Smart, C. (1995) *Law, Crime and Sexuality: Essays in Feminism*, London: SAGE.

Smart, C. and Smart, B. (1978) *Women, Sexuality and Social Control*, London: Routledge and Kegan Paul.

Stephenson, M. (2021) 'More than 100 women accuse police officers of domestic abuse, alleging "boys club" culture', *Channel 4 News*, [online] 18 May, available at: https://www.channel4.com/news/more-than-100-women-accuse-police-officers-of-domestic-abuse-alleging-boys-club-cult ure [accessed 23 June 2021].

Syal, R. (2013) 'Rochdale sex-grooming gangs able to flourish due to police errors says report', *The Guardian*, [online] 19 December, available at: https://www.theguardian.com/uk-news/2013/dec/19/rochdale-sex-grooming-gangs-police-errors [accessed 23 June 2021].

Walker, A. (2020) 'Prosecute officers, says Greater Manchester abuse whistleblower', *The Guardian*, [online] 14 January, available at: https://www.theguardian.com/uk-news/2020/jan/14/prosecute-officers-says-greater-manchester-abuse-whistleblower [accessed 23 June 2021].

Westmarland, L. (2001) *Gender and Policing: Sex, Power and Police Culture*, Cullompton: Willan.

Wolfe-Robinson, M. and Dodd, V. (2021) 'Institutional misogyny "erodes women's trust in UK police"', *The Guardian*, [online] 16 March, available at: https://www.theguardian.com/uk-news/2021/mar/16/institutional-misogyny-erodes-womens-trust-in-uk-police [accessed 15 July 2021].

Worrall, A. (1989) *Offending Women: Female Lawbreakers and the Criminal Justice System*, London: Routledge.

# 7

# Sanctuary as Social Justice: A Feminist Critique

*Victoria Canning*

## Introduction: sanctuary and gendered subjugation

The concept of sanctuary is complex and – where seeking asylum is concerned – deeply embedded in political ideologies. In a legal sense, it is most contemporarily linked with the 1951 Convention Relating to the Status of Refugees and its 1967 Protocol, if not also a tool to control non-refugee related migration. That one might be subjected to or fear persecution and be provided sanctuary from a state outside of one's own is a reality entrenched in post-Second World War rights discourse and humanitarianism. In the face of persecution, sanctuary in this sense arguably forms an ideological cornerstone for the fundamental right to life (Article 2, European Convention on Human Rights). Sanctuary therefore remains a contested term, with multiple meanings contemporarily and historically (see Rabben, 2016). For the purposes of this chapter, however, the concept of sanctuary should be understood as a spatialized form of safety, whereby previous subjections to or threats of harm are alleviated, and where one can live free from further harm in the present.

Setting this as a conceptual backdrop, this chapter outlines ways in which the reality of sanctuary is perforated for women seeking asylum in Britain. Women generally comprise two-thirds of the number of people seeking asylum in the UK at any given time (Baillot and Connelly, 2018). Although there is no definitive dataset to evidence the percentage of women who are survivors of sexual violence, refugee women are recognized as having disproportionately experienced high levels of gendered and sexualized abuse (Baillot et al, 2014; Girma et al, 2014; Emejulu and Bassel, 2017). This may be historic abuse during conflict, in camps or asylum centres, at various points of migration, or while in the asylum system itself (Canning, 2014, 2017; Baillot and Connelly, 2018).

Although not prescriptive, survivors of gendered and sexualized violence or sexual torture can experience this as a continuum, or as one-off events from variable social actors (such as militaristic violence, by partners, in detention or by border agents or smugglers; see Kelly, 1988; Canning, 2016, 2017). As one social worker supporting women's and families cases in the North West of England summarized:

'A lot of the women that I represented certainly had experienced gendered forms of persecution. Whether it was rape in the context of war, civil war usually, or FGM [female genital mutilation] or that they were escaping, or sometimes forced marriage. Sometimes they were escaping honour killings, sometimes they were escaping horrendous domestic violence, which was compounded obviously by the attitude of the authorities.'

This statement links to the gaps in justice highlighted across other chapters in this edited collection in relation to accessing justice – social or criminal. This is echoed in the context of mainstream criminology, which has for a long time neglected to give adequate space for the intersectional realities lived by migrant women and the precarious relationship with the state. Given that women generally face significant barriers to prosecution or conviction against domestic or sexual abusers in criminal justice systems which are considered to be somewhat functional, as in the UK (Downes et al, 2014) and that this is compounded for migrant women (Sisters Uncut, 2016; Emejulu and Bassel, 2017), then the prospect of investigating historic abuses in any other global region is clearly diminished. In any case, and as the focus on trafficking highlights towards the end of this chapter, interventions from criminal justice systems are not necessarily reflective of humanitarian interventions, or indeed woman-centred forms of social justice. Again, these gaps in justice are overlooked in mainstream criminology, which often instead focuses on the perceived effectiveness of the application of law, rather than the exacerbated levels of surveillance and controls trafficked women can experience through state-centric approaches to trafficking (also conflated regularly with smuggling, as discussed later).

This chapter draws on reflections from a decade of activist participation and ethnography with women seeking asylum in the North West of England (2008–18);[1] interviews with sexual violence counsellors, psychologists, social workers, medical doctors and general practitioners including a two-year project funded by the Economic and Social Research Council (ESRC) (2016–18); and oral histories with women seeking asylum. Overall, the ESRC project incorporates 74 in-depth semi-structured interviews with psychologists, support workers, border agents, refugee rights activists and other such social actors working with people seeking asylum in Britain, Denmark and Sweden. Twenty of these are in Britain, supplemented with over 500 hours of ethnographic activist research with women seeking asylum during this period. For the purposes of this chapter, only data from Britain is included so as to facilitate an in-depth, rigorous case study approach (see Flyvbjerg, 2006).

## Asylum as a Kafkaesque trial

'It is not necessary to accept everything as true, one must only accept it as necessary' (Kafka, 1955 [1925]). In many cases, seeking asylum in the United Kingdom is a long and arduous feat. In 2019, almost 17,000 people waited longer than six months for an initial decision on their claim for refugee status (Bulman, 2019). The share of asylum applications receiving an initial decision within six months fell vastly from 73 per cent in 2012 to 25 per cent in 2018 (Walsh, 2019). It is worth noting that this is usually only a first step in the system, which is often followed by appeal hearings, long waiting times and lengthy refusal letters.

Two key aspects require a form of testimony towards the beginning of the process: the screening interview and, shortly after, the substantive interview. The former is brief and requires an applicant to outline the *key* reasons why they are applying for refugee status. The latter requires an in-depth examination of all reasons relating to persecution and fear of persecution, including the events leading up to leaving one's country of origin. It is arguably at this point that the asylum system begins to mirror aspects of the criminal justice system. Indeed, as Baillot et al argue: 'Although the asylum system and the Criminal Justice System operate in very different contexts and are governed by distinctive probative and procedural rules ... some of the problematic assumptions that beleaguer the CJS in relation to rape investigation and prosecution are also manifest in the asylum state' (2014: 106). Although Baillot et al are referring specifically to rape investigations, the ways in which interviews proceed do so in a similar way to cross-examination. The person is asked why they applied for asylum, and are commonly asked the same question in various ways. This is to determine if the testimony – the person's story – is likely to be true. Formally, the threshold of proof is much lower in asylum cases than in criminal procedures, but the objective remains the same: to determine 'credibility'. The outcome is confusion: women either consider it a way of 'tripping them up', or an indicator that they should find different ways to say the same thing (see Smith, 2004; Canning, 2019). The former develops mistrust, the latter has potential for testimony to be doubted if the story deviates at all from the original (see Canning, 2014, 2017). This quagmire of questions often proves exhausting. Substantive interviews regularly last for hours: only recently a woman from Syria told me she had spent seven hours, with only one break, outlining her reasons for requiring refugee status.

From a feminist perspective, there are two obvious concerns here. First, as key feminist literatures and key trauma literatures have long addressed, shame, silence and stigma place significant barriers on the disclosure of the kinds of abuses that are disproportionately experienced by women. Discussing sexual violence, torture and sexual torture usually requires some level of trust (Kelly, 1988; Westmarland and Alderson, 2013). That survivors of sexualized violence or torture are required to disclose such abuse – potentially against their own autonomy – is an uncomfortable reality. Second, and importantly, not disclosing such abuse in the first interview and then going on to discuss such violations in the second interview can reduce credibility (Montgomery and Foldsprang, 2005; Bögner et al, 2010). As one asylum women's support officer in England highlighted, "especially with gender issues, there's so much then that ends up being not communicated in the interview. And unfortunately actually ends up being used against claimants in the decisions that they're actually given".

Since 'credibility is also at the heart of the vast majority of contested rape claims, the question of credibility in asylum applications that involve rape may, therefore, be doubly significant' (Baillot et al, 2014: 106; see also the parallels in Smith, 2018), the parallels in feminist concerns regarding sexual violence in the criminal justice SYSTEM begin to merge with those in relation to the asylum system. This issue is well established in criminology, but these parallels often go unnoticed or unexplored. Likewise, the failures were not lost on a refugee women's advocacy officer, who argued that "when you compare the criminal justice system with the asylum system, it might not be perfect the criminal justice system, but things have been recognized and put in place over the years to mitigate some of that; whereas it just hasn't happened in the asylum system" (Women's refugee support worker, Scotland, 2017). The Kafkaesque trial for the right to refugee status then leaves those seeking asylum as temporal outliers: 'asylum seekers', with all the suspicions that come with this term: unworthy of a fully human status until proven persecuted.

## The trial continues

To reiterate, a significant number of people wait longer than six months for an initial decision. This period is one of reduced autonomy. To summarize:

'[W]hen you're an asylum seeker you're not in control of your own life. The Home Office decides where you live, they decide how much money you get, they decide where you can and can't go, they pretty much delineate where your children go to school and most importantly, they decide whether you can stay in the country or not.' (Refugee women's support worker)

The longest period of time spent in the British asylum system now stands at over 20 years – the longest I know personally stands at 15 years. Importantly, this temporal phase is not only restricted by hostile policies and – for some – poverty, but the inability to plan for one's future until refugee status is granted and persecution proven. People seeking asylum receive approximately £37.75 per week to buy food, toiletries and other necessities. The capacity to travel is reduced, as people can seldom afford to go anywhere, and the use of stop and searches on public transport as a means to identify illegalized migrants makes people reluctant to travel while their claims are under review – effectively disrupting support networks or access to counselling or specialist services. People are required to register weekly or monthly at Home Office reporting centres. At the time of writing (2020), this had been suspended due to the COVID-19 pandemic and the risks inherent in face to face contact. Considering that some people are "terrified, they're terrified of being picked up from the Home Office", as one refugee sexual violence counsellor highlighted, since people can be detained while registering, then this may be a welcome relief in regulation for some.

It is here that the asylum trial becomes more reflective of a criminal justice process, with all the stresses attached. This includes for some (see Right to Remain, 2020) the right to appeal a rejection, thus taking the case through to a First Tier Tribunal. If the claim is again rejected, in some circumstances one may move to the Upper Tribunal or Judicial Review (see Canning, 2019: 10). In combination, the Immigration Acts of 2014 and 2016 facilitated the reduction in the right to appeal against asylum decisions in certain cases. One immediate effect of this was a 14 per cent fall in asylum appeals between 2015 and 2016 (from 14,242 to 12,235, see Home Office, 2017). Reductions to Legal Aid have also left people with substantial legal bills – participants in this research received bills amounting to over £2,300. Considering that almost 50 per cent of all appeals are upheld once reviewed, this is likely to mean that people who would have been granted status or whose claims have been incorrectly reviewed will not have an opportunity to do so.[2]

For anyone unfamiliar with such legal processes, the experience is daunting and fraught with uncertainty. Cases may be adjourned or rescheduled at the last minute, causing exasperation and distress as people set temporal goalposts and prepare for court. As a barrister and member of the Queen's Council indicated:

Canning:     How do your clients feel when they're going to court, when they're going to the tribunal or court of appeal or anywhere that's a kind of formal …?

QC:          I think they experience it as really stressful almost *without exception.*

Similarly, one refugee counsellor who regularly attends courts with clients noted, "I'm fine but they are terrified. I haven't taken anybody in that isn't scared stiff." Indeed, I recall a time in Immigration Court when the partner of the appellant almost fainted. On seeing their physical distress, I whispered "It will be OK", only to have the presiding judge threaten that any further 'intervention' from supporters would result in adjournment. The power of law is indeed embedded not only through the structures, but in the micro-level aggressions that exude power and the physical experience of the embodiment of the British judiciary. The alternative to appeal is, however, detention and deportation.

## Immigration detention: transcending the boundaries of criminal justice

As this chapter shows thus far, there are many aspects of the process of seeking asylum which mirror procedures in the criminal justice system. An (understandably) increasingly central focus within criminology, it is important to note that immigration detention bears little actual relation to the criminal justice process: it is an administrative procedure, not a criminal one.

Until the COVID-19 pandemic, the United Kingdom had long had one of the largest immigration detention estates in Europe, holding around 4,000 people in confinement on any given day, in total a fairly static average of around 27,000 people are detained each year (Silverman and Griffiths, 2018). Although this reduced to around 10,000 post-pandemic, people are held in one of the country's six Immigration Removal Centres (IRCs) or Short Term Holding Facilities. Around 47 per cent of all those held under immigration powers have sought asylum at some point (Silverman and Griffiths, 2018). Unlike Denmark and Sweden, there is currently no time limit for detaining people. The majority of detainees are men, with one facility – IRC Yarl's Wood – functioning as a women's facility until 2020, which also held families in a separate wing and which came under significant security for individual and institutional violence.

As Girma et al (2014) noted in depth, immigration detention carries specifically gendered implications for women. Concerns outlined by one barrister echoed these gendered implications:

'[L]ooking at gender discrimination in immigration detention because there is a serious problem, for example, in Yarl's Wood of having all male staff and also lack of provision of sanitary equipment and sanitary towels to women who are held at Yarl's Wood. And many of these women are victims of sexual abuse and torture and so the idea that they are handled every day in detention when they are literally imprisoned by male guards is very, very problematic and it's really traumatising them on a daily basis.'

Moreover, as I was told by a national refugee women's organization coordinator:

'[D]etention for anyone is harmful, being locked up and deprived of your liberty, particularly when you've fled traumatic experiences and then you come to another country for your protection. Being locked up is incredibly harmful for anyone but in detention, for instance, there are particular experiences that women are disproportionately subject to. So one end of that spectrum is sexual abuse and exploitation in detention but also the kind of intrusions into women's privacy and dignity, women who very often experience forms of gender-based sexual violence in their countries of origin, then they come to the UK and in detention they find themselves being put on suicide watch and being watched by male guards.'

Similarly, the landscape of detention has faced serious national and international criticisms, including instances of sexual violence (Canning, 2014; Lousley and Cope, 2017), deaths in custody (which reached its deadliest year in 2017 with six deaths in IRCs; see Institute of Race Relations, 2017), the continued detention of children, and the leaking of public recordings of staff verbally abusing people detained and under their care (Bhatia and Canning, 2020). These various issues led to subsequent inquiries, most notably the Shaw Review, which made 64 recommendations for change, the follow-up to which indicated significant shortcomings in the implementation of said recommendations (Shaw, 2016, 2018; see Bosworth, 2016, for synopsis). Whilst writing this chapter in 2020, constant calls were made for the release of people during the COVID-19 pandemic, including by lawyers and campaigners, which initially led to the release of more than 300 detainees in March 2020 (Taylor, 2020), and subsequently a significant reduction in the detention estate overall. It remains to be seen, however, if this reduction will last.

For practitioners working as legal representatives in IRCs, there can be frustration around the unclear logic of detention in Britain, particularly in confining clients that they deemed vulnerable and in the psychological harms inherent to detention. As one barrister specializing in immigration detention stated, "unlike prison it's administrative detention, so once you are transferred into an immigration centre you are there just because you're an immigrant and there is no end and the psychological effects that this has on people is extraordinary." Similarly, another barrister indicated the impact of temporal uncertainty, "what clients say all the time, is that it's the not knowing, the indefinite detention is ... it's obviously understandably really, really difficult, it can have huge impacts on people's mental health."

The concept of attaining social justice through the asylum process is also diminished by the scarcity of representation while detained. Discussing the transfer of people from Dungavel IRC in Scotland to IRCs in England, one barrister, a second member of the Queen's Counsel I interviewed suggested that:

'[T]here was a significant difficulty in getting access to lawyers for people who were in detention, even though there's supposed to be a fully functioning duty scheme and everything else, but people are waiting longer than the duty scheme allows before ... because in this new notice of removal window thing you get three working days and then you can be removed but you can't necessarily get access to a lawyer within that removal window of three days.'

What is highlighted here is the potential for people to be removed before they are able to access adequate legal representation, or indeed any representation at all, if they have been moved between Scotland and England. Although immigration detention is not restricted to asylum cases, a clear issue remains – that people may be removed who might otherwise gain refugee status had they been able to access a lawyer. As the coordinator of national refugee women's organization indicated, this can be a reality for some, since "we've worked with lots of people who've been in detention on numerous occasions and then ultimately have ended up getting refugee status" (coordinator of national women's refugee organization). As with other aspects of the Kafkaesque nature of the asylum trial, the potential for actualizing social justice is reduced through the very procedures put in place to enact fair access to sanctuary, and adhere to the objectives of the 1951 Refuge Convention.

## Re-trafficking trafficked women?

As we can see then, patterns emerge which indicate that the Home Office and corporations working in cooperation hold an immense amount of structural power. Bolstered by corporate outsourcing which increasingly enacts controls (including through immigration detention, as discussed in the previous section) the British state still holds obligations of protection towards those in fear of persecution. Indeed, corporate controls and the outsourced administration of social institutions has proliferated in the aftermath of austerity, particularly in England and Wales (see Cooper and Whyte, 2017; Albertson et al, 2020; Bhatia and Canning, 2020). However, it is this contradictory disconnect which perhaps most embodies the capricious nature of contemporary approaches to asylum, and which most mirrors the inconstant and changeable nature of its internal borders (El-Elnany, 2020).

For women in particular, a key example of this is Britain's response to human trafficking, and particularly its absorption into the contemporary buzz term 'modern day slavery'.[3] The concept of slavery is one which can easily motivate people from most political spectrums; that is, that slavery is identifiably a 'bad thing' and, depending on one's political motivations or indeed moral stance, should be eradicated for the safety of those subsumed or indeed the good of collective conscience. However, as Milivojevic (2015: 287) argues, women's journeys and access to safe migration can be greatly hindered by conventional and 'humanitarian' crime control measures which seek – at the surface at least – to protect further abuses, specifically sexual trafficking. At ground level, such endeavours not only force women into dominant narratives of victimhood, but create a smokescreen for increasing securitized, and often more dangerous, border controls.

This argument is made visible through multiple attempts by sectors of the British state to respond to survivors of trafficking, including the National Referral Mechanism and the 2011 strategy set out by then Home Secretary (later Prime Minister) Theresa May:

> The UK has a *good record in tackling human trafficking.* That is something we must build on. Our new strategy for tackling human trafficking has four key aims: international action to stop trafficking happening in the first place; a *stronger border* at home to *stop victims being brought* into the UK; *tougher law enforcement* action to tackle the criminal gangs that orchestrate the crime; and improved identification and care for the victims of trafficking. (May, 2011: 3, emphasis added)

Milovojevic's point is palpably visible here: in order of concern is, first, stopping illegal entry; second, increasing scope for criminalization of traffickers; and lastly, the wellbeing of the victims of trafficking. The message was and remains clear – the security of borders are first and foremost, with humanitarian concern being an afterthought (see also Jobe, 2009).

Although there is limited scope to fully develop a discussion on the complexities of trafficking much further in this chapter, the empirical research has drawn two main concerns. First, the dependence on language and credibility has left trafficked women I have spoken with at a significant disadvantage, contributing in two case examples to their refusals. In one such example (Woman A), the appellant had been trafficked from a country in Asia to a Middle Eastern state at a young age by her step-father. In her claim and during the appeal procedures at court, Woman A flittered between the use of the terms 'father' and 'step-father', an unsurprising issue considering both the language barrier and the fact that he had acted as father before she was even five. In Woman B's case, having moved to the UK from a country in Asia with a visa and living with a family member, she was charged as over-staying. Simultaneously, she was living in domestic servitude and only recognized her status as being trafficked when the family member brought friends to sexually abuse her. She escaped, contacted police, her case was refused, she was detained, and faced subsequent appeal refusals. She had not identified with the terms 'trafficking victim' or 'slavery' and thus the neocolonial linguistic landscape within which she now resided did not fully accept her as such, despite the fundamental reality of her experience of trafficking.

Second, and drawing on arguments made earlier, interviewees raised concerns that the state were not only unresponsive to the wellbeing requirements of survivors of trafficking broadly, and sexual trafficking specifically, but that they both mirrored and inflicted the fundamental structures under which the selling of human bodies or sexualities flourish. People working with women seeking asylum raised concerns that destitution maintains the capacity for making decisions that otherwise women may not make, as one migrant rights coordinator argued: "I would say that the government's trying to create a prostitute class. Not a prostitute class, an under-class, like a Victorian under-class because border controls are forcing women into roles that citizen women would not take, necessarily." Another support worker in the North West of England was concerned that women were "falling off our radar" because poverty was pushing those she was supporting into sex industries: "I don't see them anymore in the city, I don't see them anywhere so where are they?" Likewise, the impacts of the process of seeking asylum were taking its toll on the clients of one social worker in particular, who argued that:

> 'Depressed, suicidal, self-harm, most of the women I'm coming across now it's a huge problem, and I'm concerned now because we have been having a government which was talking about how we can stop trafficking of women, now women who are becoming destitute are thrown into prostitution now for survival.'

Interestingly, this particular respondent pointedly addresses two of the arguments I make about the capricious nature of the British state. First, the system is itself producing and reproducing harmful conditions which affect the mental and emotional wellbeing of the women going through it. Second, while the British government has ramped up discourses on the prevention of the trafficking of women, the structural conditions set by governmental legislators, parliament and politicians, in fact, creates the very conditions of destitution and dependence which can exacerbate the existence of both trafficking and forced prostitution.

This brings me to a final and damning indictment from a woman working with survivors of violence who are seeking asylum, who claimed:

'One thing that the women that had been trafficked for sexual exploitation used to say to me was that they just felt like the Home Office was treating them like the traffickers did, and just moving them from location to location around the country. That they had no control over their life before and they have no control now, and it was just repeating their experiences.'

The Home Office – facilitated by its amorphous relations with corporations enacting its groundwork – are both the reluctant providers of protection, and the inflictors of endemic controls.

## Conclusion: What could social justice look like for women seeking asylum?

As this chapter shows, any current concept of justice is rendered structurally void in the lived realities of women seeking asylum in Britain. For survivors of historic violence or abuse, whether in childhood, during conflict or unrest, or along her migratory route, it is unlikely she will ever have an opportunity to see any forms of justice brought to her abuser(s). During the asylum process, women are disenabled from accessing social justice, since the process is marred with disbelief, challenges to her credibility, and the potential for exploitation or further violence through destitution or forced dependency on partners. Since economic dependency is a key contributor to reductions in women's opportunities to leave violent men, it should come as no surprise that this would be compounded for any women whose future in a country is inextricably tied to a family or partner's claim for asylum, or indeed on spousal visas.

The very structures of the asylum system are inherently gendered, and it is this that I wish to emphasize here. Drawing from a statement by a social worker in the North West of England, who had worked navigating the cases of hundreds of women and families seeking asylum over a ten year period, synopsized that:

'The asylum system in the UK has been designed as an anti-women and children system, because those are the groups that are marginalized within the system. Now, why I say so, I will give you an example of the Immigration Act 2016. The Home Office is talking about cutting off support for families, those applications for support have been declined, and who are going to be 99 per cent of those people? Children and women. Men who are single, they can move on, they can just move in with another partner if they get somebody else, but for women and children they are exposed to schools, they are exposed to healthcare, they are exposed to social services. So if a mother cannot take her children to school what happens next? Social services get involved, when social services are involved, what is the law now? Social services have got a duty to inform the Home Office about the families they are dealing with. So this is the dilemma we have, we have got women now who are the worst off.'

The gendered harms are herein laid bare.

However, while acknowledging the endemic harms inherent to the asylum system as it currently stands, there have been clear and vocal shifts towards positive change. First, although the Gender Guidelines (UK Visas and Immigration, 2010; Home Office, 2018) have been slow to take hold, there are arguably small positive shifts occurring which more appropriately centralize the needs of women. As the coordinator of a UK-wide organization working on the rights of refugee women highlighted, "it [the Home Office] has done a fair amount of work recently around gender sensitivity in the asylum process, so around things like making sure that there's childcare available in asylum interviews and that women are able to access a female interviewer or interpreter". Second, subsequent reviews of immigration detention have led to recommendations pertaining to structural changes in light of various abuses and 'scandals' (see Bosworth, 2016; Shaw, 2016). Third, the success in the release of more than 300 people from detention during the COVID-19 pandemic of 2020 should act as a reminder that detention is not an inevitability, it is a decision – one that could be made otherwise. It is a timely reminder that it is worth imagining and building towards an asylum system which is not endemically harmful.

Many of these facets for change lie in the need for governmental reorientation which, by all accounts, take time and lead to variable levels of success. However, I conclude with six key considerations or points of action for those of us working on women's right to asylum:[4]

1. *Change the narrative: recognize the asylum system is working as it is supposed to.* As migrants, researchers, activists and NGOs we often optimistically interpret harm in asylum systems as something being broken. We then address these with recommendations to 'fix' them. While this is an important strategy, we also need a broader structural recognition that systems are designed to be difficult – they are working well for their purpose and require sustained structural change.
2. *Centralize intersectionality: recognize border harms impact on people differently.*

Organizations working with migrant groups should ensure that intersectional experiences of border harms are discussed and addressed. For example, men experience disproportionately high rates of detention, and women higher rates of sexual and domestic abuse. Likewise, ableism and transphobia may need specific recognition in, for example, asylum housing/centres.

3. *Create unscheduled time and space.*

Scheduled activities can be a key contributor to personal development. However, it is also important that organizations allow time and space to spend socially without interference. Simply providing refreshments and space is a welcome way for people to get together without the extra pressure of activities. Likewise, be aware that activities need not always be gender-specific – for example offering knitting classes for women might be useful for some, but sometimes comes at the expense of skills such language classes or computing support.

4. *Where possible and appropriate, avoid narrow labels and definitions.*

Some organizations work to standard definitions of – for example – 'torture' or 'refugee'. While there can be benefits to this, these can also have gendered or intersectional impacts on who is recognized as tortured, or leave gaps in support for various migrant groups. It may be worth organizations being led by the demographics accessing them rather than by narrow legal definitions.

5. *Speak with people, not for people.*

For grassroots, migrant-led organizations, this is an already central facet of resistance. Mutual aid is a key strength of sustained resistance – solidarity is always welcome but it should not come at the cost of the voices of people most affected by borders. Likewise, ensure organizations are enabling dialogue, but do not exploit people for stories or painful histories – this can in itself compound harm.

6. *Make reforms and recommendations, but move towards wholesale change.*

In a time of ever restricting borders, we should aim for and celebrate minor changes that improve the lives and wellbeing of people harmed by border controls. However, some practices are inherently harmful, and structurally racist. Immigration detention, for example, may be less painful for a short time than an indefinite one, but it still exists as a mechanism of racialized controls which do not belong in a progressive, anti-racist society.

This list is far from exhaustive, and only a starting point for attaining localized change in the face of endemic and increasingly harmful border controls. However, in the spirit of feminist activism, centralizing sanctuary – real sanctuary – beyond the harms of the state is a first step to enacting and enabling a move away from the trials of asylum, and towards the utopian objectives of a feminist social justice.

## Notes

[1] For a full interactive outline of the asylum system in the UK, please see the online version of the *Right to Remain Asylum Navigation Board* (Canning and Matthews, 2018). You can access the full board – which outlines all the key steps of the system – here: https://rightt oremain.org.uk/asylum-navigation-board/?fbclid=IwAR0tw1NlhNim8tEgaGUZtbBDC AhV9wdwGVtYROMCND5OpjJHGiT1-flm_d8 [accessed 9 April 2020].

[2] The Acts also created an environment within which people seeking asylum are less able to access housing and healthcare (see Canning, 2017).

[3] The Modern Slavery Act 2015 is presented as an 'Act to make provision about slavery, servitude and forced or compulsory labour and about human trafficking, including provision for the protection of victims; to make provision for an Independent Anti-slavery Commissioner; and for connected purposes' (Modern Slavery Act, 2015).

[4] These ideas have developed from empirical research, as well as informal discussions with women seeking asylum and with practitioners and service providers. They were first presented at the IRISH centre at Birmingham University in January 2020, and the Centre for Refugee Studies at Oxford University in February 2020. Many thanks to Catherine Briddick and Nando Sigona for invitations to engage on these ideas.

## References

Albertson, K., Corcoran, M. and Philips, J. (2020) 'Introduction' in K. Albertson, M. Corcoran and J. Philips (eds) *Marketisation and Privatisation in Criminal Justice*, Bristol: Bristol University Press, pp 1–12.

Baillot, H. and Connelly, E. (2018) *Women Seeking Asylum: Safe from Violence in the UK?* Available at: http://www.asaproject.org/uploads/Safe_from_violence_in_the_UK._ASAP-RC_report_.pdf [accessed 9 April 2020].

Baillot, H., Cowan, S. and Munro, V.E. (2014). 'Reason to disbelieve: Evaluating the rape claims of women seeking asylum in the UK', *International Journal of Law in Context*, 10(1): 105–39.

Bhatia, M. and Canning, V. (2020) 'Misery as business: How immigration detention became a cash-cow in Britain's borders' in K. Albertson, M. Corcoran and J. Philips (eds) *Marketisation and Privatisation in Criminal Justice*, Bristol: Bristol University Press, pp 262–77.

Bögner, D., Brewin, C. and Herlihy, J. (2010) 'Refugees' experiences of Home Office interviews: A qualitative study on the disclosure of sensitive personal information', *Journal of Ethnic Migration Studies*, 36(3): 519–35.

Bosworth, M. (2016) 'Immigration detention under review (again)', *Border Criminologies*, Blog, available at: https://www.law.ox.ac.uk/research-subj ect-groups/centre-criminology/centreborder-criminologies/blog/2016/ 01/immigration [accessed 11 January 2019].

Bulman, M. (2019) 'Nearly 17,000 asylum seekers waiting more than six months to get a decision', *The Independent*, [online] 22 August, available at: https://www.independent.co.uk/news/uk/home-news/asylum-seek ers-waiting-times-home-office-immigration-a9075256.html [accessed 6 April 2020].

Canning, V. (2014) 'International conflict, sexual violence and asylum policy: Merseyside as a case study', *Critical Social Policy*, 34(1): 23–45.

Canning, V. (2016) 'Unsilencing sexual torture: Responses to refugees and asylum seekers in Denmark', *British Journal of Criminology*, 56(3): 438–56.

Canning, V. (2017) *Gendered Harm and Structural Violence in the British Asylum System*, Oxon: Routledge.

Canning, V. (2019) *Reimagining Refugee Rights: Addressing Asylum Harms in Britain, Denmark and Sweden*, Bristol: Migration Mobilities Bristol, available at: http://www.statewatch.org/news/2019/mar/uk-dk-se-reimagining-refugee-rights-asylum-harms-3-19.pdf [accessed 9 April 2020].

Canning, V. and Matthews, L. (2018) *Right to Remain Asylum Navigation Board*, London: Calverts Cooperative.

Cooper, V. and Whyte, D. (2017) 'Introduction' in V. Cooper and D. Whyte (eds) *The Violence of Austerity*, London: Pluto Press, pp 1–34.

Downes, J., Kelly, L. and Westmarland, N. (2014) 'Ethics in violence and abuse research: A positive empowerment approach', *Sociological Research Online*, 19(2), pp 29–41.

El-Enany, N. (2020) *Bordering Britain: Law, Race and Empire*, Manchester: Manchester University Press.

Emejulu, A. and Bassel, L. (2017) 'Women of colour's anti-austerity activism' in V. Cooper and D. Whyte (eds) *The Violence of Austerity*, London: Pluto Press, pp 117–23.

Flyvbjerg, B. (2006) 'Five misunderstandings about case study research', *Qualitative Inquiry*, 12(2): 219–45.

Girma, M., Radice, S., Tsangarides, N. and Walter, N. (2014) *Detained: Women Asylum Seekers Locked Up in the UK*, London: Women for Refugee Women.

Home Office (2017) *National Statistics: Asylum*, [online] available at: https://www.gov.uk/government/publications/immigration-statistics-october-to-december-2016/asylum [accessed 19 July 2019].

Home Office (2018) *Gender Issues in the Asylum Claim*, [online] available at: https://assets.publishing.service.gov.uk/government/uploads/system/uploads/attachment_data/file/699703/gender-issues-in-the-asylum-claim-v3.pdf [accessed 19 March 2019].

Institute of Race Relations (2017) 'The deadliest year in immigration detention', [online] available at: http://www.irr.org.uk/news/2017-the-deadliest-year-in-immigration-detention/ [accessed 11 January 2019].

Jobe, A. (2009) 'Accessing help and services: Trafficking survivor's experiences in the United Kingdom' in L. Dresdner and L. Peterson (eds) *(Re)Interpretations: The Shapes of Justice in Women's Experience*, Cambridge: Cambridge Scholars Press, pp 164–80.

Kafka, F. (1955 [1925]) *The Trial*, London: Penguin Books.

Kelly, L. (1988) *Surviving Sexual Violence*, Minneapolis: University of Minnesota Press.

Lousley, G. and Cope, S. (2017) *We are Still Here: The Continued Detention of Women Seeking Asylum in Yarl's Wood*, London: Women for Refugee Women.

May, T. (2011) 'Human trafficking: The government's strategy', [online] available at: https://www.gov.uk/government/publications/human-trafficking-strategy [accessed 16 January 2019].

Milivojevic, S. (2015) 'Stopped in the traffic, not stopping the traffic: Gender, asylum and anti-trafficking interventions in Serbia' in S. Pickering and J. Ham (eds) *The Routledge Handbook on Crime and International Migration*, Oxon: Routledge, pp 287–301.

Modern Slavery Act (2015) [online] available at: http://www.legislation.gov.uk/ukpga/2015/30/contents/enacted [accessed 16 January 2019].

Montgomery, E. and Foldspring, A. (2005) 'Predictors of authorities' decision to grant asylum in Denmark', *Journal of Refugee Studies*, 18(4): 454–67.

Rabben, L. (2016) *Sanctuary and Asylum: A Social and Political History*, Washington, DC: University of Washington Press.

Right to Remain (2020) *Right to Remain Asylum Navigation Board Online*, [online] available at: https://righttoremain.org.uk/asylum-navigation-board/?fbclid=IwAR0tw1NlhNim8tEgaGUZtbBDCAhV9wdwGVtYROMCND5OpjJHGiT1-flm_d8 [accessed 9 April 2020].

Shaw, S. (2016) *Review into the Welfare in Detention of Vulnerable Persons*, [online] available at: https://assets.publishing.service.gov.uk/government/uploads/system/uploads/attachment_data/file/490782/52532_Shaw_Review_Accessible.pdf [accessed 15 February 2019].

Shaw, S. (2018) *Welfare in Detention of Vulnerable Persons Review: Progress Report*, [online] available at: https://www.gov.uk/government/publications/welfare-in-detention-of-vulnerable-persons-review-progress-report [accessed 15 February 2019].

Silverman, S.J. and Griffiths, M.E.B. (2018) 'Immigration detention in the UK', *Migration Observatory Briefing*, Compas, University of Oxford, [online] available at: https://migrationobservatory.ox.ac.uk/resources/briefings/immigration-detention-in-the-uk/ [accessed 8 June 2020].

Sisters Uncut (2016) 'Migrant women and domestic violence', [online] available at: http://www.sistersuncut.org/2016/09/14/no-sister-is-illegal-migrant-women-and-domestic-violence/ [accessed 8 June 2020].

Smith, E. (2004) *Right First Time? Home Office Asylum Interviewing and Reasons for Refusal Letters*, London: Medical Foundation for the Care of Victims of Torture.

Smith, O. (2018) *Rape Trials in England and Wales: Observing Justice and Rethinking Rape Myths*, Basingstoke: Palgrave.

Taylor, D. (2020) 'Coronavirus: Call to release UK immigration detainees', *The Guardian*, 14 March.

UK Visas and Immigration (2010) *Gender Issues in Asylum Claims*, [online] available at: https://www.gov.uk/government/publications/gender-issue-in-the-asylum-claim-process [accessed 16 June 2020].

Walsh, P. (2019) 'Migration to the UK: Asylum and resettled refugees', *Migration Observatory Oxford*, [online] available at: https://migrationobse rvatory.ox.ac.uk/wp-content/uploads/2019/11/Briefing-Migration-to-the-UK-Asylum-and-Resettled-Refugees.pdf [accessed 6 April 2020].

Westmarland, N. and Alderson, S. (2013) 'The health, mental health and wellbeing benefits of Rape Crisis counselling', *Journal of Interpersonal Violence*, 28(170): 3265–82.

PART III

# The Criminal Justice System and Feminist Praxis

# 8

# Constructing a Feminist Desistance: Resisting Responsibilization

*Úna Barr and Emily Luise Hart*

## Introduction

Desistance theory, which examines how and why people stop offending, has occupied an increasingly central position in criminological discourse over the past 30 years. More recently, criminal justice policy and practice have witnessed a shift towards the uncritical proliferation of desistance (Gov. uk, 2019; Carr, 2021), which, in turn, has taken an uncritical examination of 'crime' and 'offending' (Graham and McNeill, 2018). While desistance theory was conceptualized around the experiences of White men (Gålnander, 2019), more recent examinations of the operation of desistance have explored women's experiences (Rodermond et al, 2016; Hart, 2017a; Österman, 2018; Barr, 2019, Gålnander, 2019). Nonetheless, criminology's focus on desistance theory is illustrative of its phallocentric occupation and this chapter will discuss the implications of this wilful acceptance in criminal justice policy and practice on the experiences of criminalized women. The chapter goes on to consider an alternative anti-carceral, intersectional feminist way forward which directly challenges the current ineffective theory, policy and practice which dominates not only state responses, but also criminology.

Women's experiences are subjugated within all areas of criminal justice and criminology. Where they are considered, their experiences are presented as support for traditional perspectives and (neo)liberal reform with emphasis on individual change and responsibilization (Hart, 2017a; Elfleet, 2021). While there has been a relatively recent move to focus on the relational (rather than individualized) aspects of desistance, at least within the literature and some more critical desistance research (Weaver, 2019), what is missing is a truly structural, intersectional feminist analysis. As Anette Ballinger discusses in

Chapter 2 of this collection, feminist epistemology is necessary to uncover and rebuild discourses about the reality of women's experiences and the gendered social order. It is also crucial that this feminism is grounded in abolitionist thinking and this chapter will argue that intersectional anti-carceral feminist desistance approaches must pave the way forward for both critical criminology and feminist praxis.

This chapter presents three key areas for consideration in building a feminist desistance. First, this chapter will critique the drive of desistance praxis which has perpetually encouraged offenders to (re)enter and engage with 'conventional society' and develop and maintain social bonds that will support desistance trajectories. This chapter will question what 'conventional society' might look like (Graham and McNeill, 2018), particularly for criminalized women, and argue that it is imbued with responsibilization and stigma and that 're/integration' (Carlen, 2012; Graham and McNeill, 2018) is often not possible, nor desired. Second, a discussion will examine the implications of desistance research and theory on state discourse around supporting desistance. We argue that a concentration on agentic, individualized desistance, as well as uncritical promotion of relational desistance, has resulted in state support for responsiblized criminalized individuals making changes to their own lives, in the absence of robust structural support mechanisms. This has a disproportionate impact on women, but is relevant to all criminalized people. As van Ginneken and Hart have argued, 'the desistance process may differ for offenders who face challenges specific to their sentence, history or circumstances' (2017: 5). Criminalized women, as examined in this chapter, may have experienced a roster of similar harms and trauma, including poverty, violence, abuse and discrimination, and these circumstances often do not disappear when desistance attempts are made. An ever-increasing responsibilizing discourse from the state sidelines, yet entrenches, these shared and individual harms. Third, this chapter will outline how the bulk of desistance literature has not critiqued the role of the prison, nor the wider aspects of the criminal justice system in creating social harm, beyond contributing to, or standing as a barrier to, desistance from crime. The complex gendered pains and long-term consequences for women prisoners need to be examined through a feminist, and ultimately abolitionist, lens in order to fully understand the damage women's involvement in criminal justice has, particularly during a time of carceral expansion and recent government policy to expand the women's prison estate (Gov.uk, 2021). We conclude the chapter by putting forward our vision for anti-carceral, intersectional feminist desistance research, theory, policy and practice.

## Conventional society

Central to much desistance research, theory, policy and practice is the idea that it is important that desisters maintain, or develop, bonds to conventional society. This is particularly salient in the 'social bonds' literature, emerging from Sampson and Laub (1993; Laub and Sampson, 2003) but is also present in more recent desistance literature. McNeill (2016) for example, proposed a notion of tertiary desistance following primary (act desistance) and secondary (identity desistance) (Maruna and Farrall, 2004). Tertiary desistance is related to shifts in belonging to a moral and political community. Graham and McNeill (2018) note this involves not only the compliance with the law involved in primary desistance, and the generativity involved in secondary desistance, but also being a 'recipient of social goods' (Graham and McNeill, 2018: 436). While McNeill (2016) and Graham and McNeill (2018) argue that, particularly within punitive societies, there are structural barriers to achieving this sense of belonging, particularly when there is discrimination and exclusion experienced by the criminalized individual related to greater and greater post-punishment disqualification, this analysis misses the experiences of inequality and exclusion involved in the lives of criminalized women (and men) pre-, during and post-punishment.

It is important to consider the relationship with 'conventional society' that any potentially desisting cohort examined in the desistance research has. As noted by Nugent and Schinkel (2016), some of the most cited desistance research is based on particular groups who are more likely to experience the welcoming arms of conventional society. Aresti et al (2010), for example, base their research on men who were university students or had secured a conventional career, while Maruna's seminal study recruited either those 'actively persisting' or 'successfully "going straight"' (2001: 48), the latter likely to be those, by definition, with an amount of social capital unlikely to be present in the lives of criminalized women. While Nugent and Schinkel, on the other hand, base their research about the difficulties maintaining desistance on two cohorts – young people, including one young woman, with a short criminal career, and men on licence after a long period of incarceration – the particular *gendered* pains of desistance have not been examined.

A focus on an ostensibly apolitical 'conventional society' within much of the male-focused desistance literature misses a critical analysis of how the combined forces of patriarchy, neoliberalism and neocolonialism work intersectionally to produce a 'conventional society' which is hostile to criminalized women. It is well known that before coming into contact with the criminal justice system, criminalized women are likely to be victims of gender-based violence and childhood abuse, and are likely to be in poverty. Black and brown women are over-criminalized. Women in prison are five times more likely to experience poor mental health than those in the general population. They are often in prison for non-violent offences, are separated from their children while in prison, often far away from home, and once released, two in five are homeless (Women in Prison, 2021). Before leaving prison, women have the desire to 'go straight', but lack the social, cultural, economic and symbolic capital to be able to do so (Hart, 2017a). A focus on *belonging* in society also ignores the role of the state in producing and upholding gendered and social inequalities, including and beyond post-punishment disqualification. When women are victims of gendered violence, including rape and sexual violence, they are unlikely to receive justice within a misogynistic criminal justice system. As revealed in an *Observer* investigation (Townsend and Jayanetti, 2021), police officers have been involved in a long list of sexual misconduct allegations, including 594 allegations against the Met alone from 2012 to 2018. Indeed, in the beginning of Spring 2021, allegations of sexual misconduct among police officers were so abundant that it led MP Harriet Harman to conclude that the 'system fails women and protects men' (Townsend and Jayanetti, 2021). Beyond the violence of the criminal justice system, women, and women's community groups, are disproportionately likely to be suffering from the violence of austerity (Mansfield and Cooper, 2017) and from the ongoing devastation caused by the inadequate state response to the COVID-19 pandemic, which has seen a disproportionate loss in women's jobs and an increase in unpaid caring roles, while gendered violence including femicide is on the rise (European Commission, 2021). 'Conventional society' for criminalized women is not a welcoming place.

It is perhaps obvious, but also pertinent to note that the intersectional subjugations experienced by criminalized women as they attempt to desist in conventional society can result in barriers to desistance from crime. In her cross-national comparison of English and Swedish criminalized women's experiences of desistance, Linnéa Österman (2018) notes that English women experienced more 'pathway luggage' (challenging issues and experiences in the woman's biography that link to her pathway into crime) in their 'desistance journey' and less formal support. However, negligence or failure by social services was universal but nuanced – English women largely experienced inaction while Swedish women were failed by the nature of the action which was institutionalized, compulsory or medicalized from early on. This finding suggests that bonds to conventional society are affected by structural inequalities in a range of societies. Österman argues that while there is a prominent focus in the desistance literature on the transformative effects of employment, there is less of a focus on the experience of a lack of access to a liveable income, which was found to be particularly prominent in the English data. This is particularly a feature in England where the 'working poor' are a salient reality in late capitalism with their experiences linked to zero-hours contracts, anti-welfare commonsense (Jensen and Tyler, 2015), austerity and, more recently, the disproportionate impact of COVID-19. Österman identifies a 'survival narrative' for those on low/no income which included resorting to sex work. Depression and unprocessed trauma were common cross-national experiences which were experienced as barriers to change. Yet there were differences in the cohorts. Österman found there were myriad 'structural ladders' present in the Swedish data, so much so that one participant (Eva) noted that 'so many doors exist … an array of fantastic back up' (Osterman, 2018: 122), including conversation therapy, residential rehabilitation, access to free psychologist support including support centres, sexologists and drug support centres, probation, counsellors, drugs-, finance- and housing-support counselling. Österman found that, within the Swedish data, the notion of human support built on trusting relationships, safety and legitimacy was key. Within the English narratives, however, structural support only ever emerged in conversation when women referred to its absence. While supportive family relationships provided valuable 'scaffolding' for the women, intimate relationships more often acted as a barrier to the women's routes out of offending. These issues surrounded abuse, a gendered caregiving narrative where women were assumed to be able to support desisting men (discussed further later in this section), and issues in relation to childcare. Above all, Österman noted a distinct lack of agency and 'choice' in the English women's narratives and noted that they experienced a significantly higher number of, and intensity of, barriers to desistance than the Swedish women. As Grundetjern and Miller (2019) note, this can lead women to continued offending in places where they can achieve empowerment, for example by drug dealing. This was also a finding of Barr and Christian's (2019) research, where women found empowerment and escape from abusive relationships within their drug dealing. As argued by Grundetjern and Miller (2019: 431): 'If the "replacement self" on offer to women is one that ties them to gendered constraints, women who find empowerment in their offending may be understandably resistant to such change.' It is fair to conclude, therefore, that the inequalities and marginalizations experienced by women in conventional society can stand as barriers to their desistance. Why criminalized women would want to form bonds to unequal and marginalizing societies should also be questioned.

One trope of the desistance literature is the often uncritically presented 'professional ex' or generative actor who seeks to redeem themselves, often through taking on voluntary positions (Maruna, 2001; McNeill and Weaver, 2010). This is a central feature of secondary or 'identity desistance' (Maruna and Farrall, 2004). Not only is the conventional society to which the criminalized individual is 'giving back' to left uncritiqued, but the unpaid work itself is presented in a normative fashion. This masks the embedding of inequalities created by neoliberalism, patriarchy, neocolonialism, heteronormativity, ableism and other structures which stigmatize and other particular groups, including criminalized women, in conventional society. It also masks the individualistic, responsibilized ideology which promotes unpaid work (for some). While the benefits of voluntary working are well known, and indeed were expounded upon by the research participants in Barr (2019), there is a real and present danger that the policy message is that criminalized individuals – and women in particular, who are already disadvantaged by the burden of unpaid care work and further stigmatized by their 'double deviance' – should be encouraged to take on unpaid positions to 'give back' to the society that they 'wronged'.

Notably, Nugent and Schinkel (2016) found that their one young woman respondent was more determined and, indeed, more successful in her 'relational' attempt at desistance, particularly by repairing bonds with her family, corresponding with previous desistance research on girls (Barry, 2006, 2010). Yet, stigma can be gendered in the experiences of criminalized women, and when women are victims. This can result in both poor relationship experiences and a denial of victimhood (Rutter and Barr, 2021). Shame and stigma can affect women's relational networks, particularly where criminalized women are seen as doubly deviant (Worrall, 1990). Gålnander (2020) notes that women in his desistance study employed concealment as a stigma management tool, something which he noted created a barrier to generativity and ultimately to achieving the relational desistance which they desired. Gålnander (2020) also contends that reintegrative shaming (Braithwaite, 1989) may not be useful, nor indeed possible for criminalized women. Gålnander (2020: 1317) concludes that relational, tertiary desistance should be 'conceptualized more in terms of the importance for desisters to gain social recognition as "normal" or be included in mainstream society, and with less focus on recognition of change, from something "bad" into something "better"'. Imogen Tyler (2020) has explored the particularly gendered experiences of stigma, noting that stigma is not a neutral sociological experience, but something which is tied closely to systems of power. Indeed, Tyler traces the etymological origins of stigma to the branding of slaves, branking (gagging) of women in public spaces, and penal tattooing, which she relates to 21st-century online (and offline) misogynist vitriol and threats of violence. Tyler discusses a long history of gendered penal stigma, arguing that 'the history of racial capitalism cannot be separated from regimes of patriarchy – stigma power functions intersectionally' (2020: 82–3). Therefore, rather than criminalized women being encouraged to be seen as 'normal' within mainstream (patriarchal, neoliberal, neocolonial) society, what is more important is a critical analysis of, and resistance to, the structures of patriarchal racial capitalism that provide the backdrop to their experiences of stigma which surrounds their victimization, criminalization and desistance.

Further, regarding relational desistance, Nugent and Schinkel (2016) note their young men respondents' reliance on girlfriends to maintain their desistance, indicating the additional burden of care shouldered by women, often criminalized themselves. In Barr's (2019) research, evidence of criminalized women supporting their male partners' desistance was also present. As Halsey and Deegan (2015) argue, these women are a highly marginalized and often traumatized group. Criminalized women are often responsibilized to desist themselves, while living with the expectation that they will support other's (the men in their lives') desistance. There are further gendered aspects to relational desistance. As contended by Barr and Christian (2019), any consideration of criminalized women's desistance which does not consider gendered violence is incomplete. As already noted, women who enter the criminal justice system are likely to have experienced childhood abuse. Criminalized women are likely to have experienced domestic abuse from a current or former partner. Indeed, women who successfully present as desisting can be simultaneously in abusive, violent and controlling relationships which encourage this desistance from crime (Barr and Christian, 2019). The enduring consistency of experiences of violence within the criminal justice system with experiences of violence outside the criminal justice system, *some of which present as a move away from crime*, calls into question the impact of uncritical relational desistance theory and its promotion in policy and practice. Intersectional anti-carceral feminist praxis is required both to support desistance from crime and desistance from harm (Barr, 2019) more generally.

By considering the realities of 'conventional society' in the lives of criminalized and desisting women, the promotion of connections to such a society within understandings of desistance can certainly be called into question. Österman (2018) sets out the numerous barriers to desistance experienced by criminalized women in conventional society in England and Sweden, characterized by a lack of social support and agency, in-work poverty, abuse and trauma. Women are unlikely to receive the 'social goods' (McNeill, 2016; Graham and McNeill, 2018) involved in tertiary desistance. Yet it is not only where desistance is not forthcoming that criminalized women face the harms of conventional society. In the taking on of the generative roles espoused by the mechanisms of secondary desistance, women are often encouraged/coerced into unpaid voluntary work, something which is particularly jarring in the age of in-work poverty and within the contexts of women already overrepresented in unpaid caring positions.

Stigma, as Tyler (2020) has persuasively argued, should be viewed as a concept imbued with, and emerging from, the structural forces of patriarchal racialized capitalism. When stigma is contested in the lives of criminalized women, rather than a promotion of women to be included as 'normal' within mainstream society, it is the very structural forces which inform mainstream society which therefore require resistance. The patriarchal contexts which surround relational desistance are further overlooked by traditional (male- and agentic-focused) desistance theorists where abusive relationships are not considered. Indeed these relationships can often quantitatively produce a period of desistance (Barr and Christian, 2019).

Women are further marginalized by desistance literature when they are promoted as the – figuratively and literally – supporting character to men's desistance journeys. These arguments have concluded that conventional society is structured by hetero-patriarchy, neoliberalism and neocolonialism, which create harm for criminalized women. At times this harm may even promote desistance, certainly the non-desistance-curtailing harm is overlooked and disregarded by the bulk of desistance theorists. In addition, the harm of desistance theory which promotes (neo-)liberal reform and individualized responsibilization within criminal justice policy and practice must be recognized and contested. In the following section, we consider the state's understanding of desistance, particularly in contrast to intersectional feminist understandings of the experiences of criminalized women as they attempt to desist.

## Implications of desistance research on state policy and practice

Desistance research has no doubt had an influence on current criminal justice policy and practice (Carr, 2021). The prison and probation service have produced guidance on desistance on their website (Gov.uk, 2019). The website is a good indication of hegemonic state understandings of desistance theory. This guidance appears to be influenced by a number of key desistance studies (McNeill et al, 2012; Maruna, 2017; Maruna and Mann, 2019) and the work of charity organizations (CLINKS, 2013; Terry and Cardwell, 2015) as well as research by the National Offender Management System and the Scottish Justice Directorate. There is no indication as to why these particular studies are included on the website and although this chapter does not have the scope to examine in detail each of the documents linked on the website, a brief consideration here is illuminating in determining the state's understanding of desistance.

The Revolving Doors Agency report (Terry and Cardwell, 2015) brings together a meta-analysis on desistance from offending, recovery from mental illness and recovery from substance misuse. As the authors note, desistance requires maintenance over time 'in the face of stigma, anxiety and fear, barriers to opportunities and social exclusion' (p 5). Rather than finding that success is found in resistance to these structural barriers, in support and love, the finding is that what is important are 'personal skills and capabilities, support networks, self-confidence and location' (p 5). The authors particularly highlight the 'crucial role of agency and subjectivity' (p 6). This is certainly a convenient conclusion for the state. The later finding that '[e]liminating discrimination, stigma and inequality will support people's journeys of recovery and desistance' (p 19) is less embraced by the government's advice on the website.

Maruna and Mann's (2019) research meanwhile concludes that the experiences of successful desistance cohorts 'suggest that people are more likely to desist when they have strong ties to family and community, employment that fulfils them, recognition of their worth from others, feelings of hope and self-efficacy, and a sense of meaning and purpose in their lives' (p 7). Maruna and Mann point to both the importance of social supports and structures as well as individuals' identity, sense of self and patterns of thought. The government advice seems to particularly be focused on the latter conclusions.

Similarly, Maruna's (2017) argument, presented on the government's website, that desistance should be seen as a 'social movement', with attention given to the structural obstacles in the way of a 'desistance-informed' future, is largely not reflected in the government's advice. Instead, the argument that desistance is different from rehabilitation-focused research and practice, seems to have been seized upon by the state to place a focus on responsibilized individuals (and responsibilized close partners/family members/friends) making changes to their lives, in the absence of any input from the state. This wilful ignorance of the centrality of powerful structures having influence on criminalization, victimization and desistance in more critical desistance research (Hart, 2017b), alongside a particular reading of the well-cited male-focused traditional studies, to the benefit of an agentic focus, has produced an individualized responsibilization narrative in the government's advice.

The desistance advice on the website does not contain a list of state resources for financial, housing, employment, education, mental health or refuge support. While education, housing and employment are presented as desistance supporting, these are presented as individualized 'routes out'. There is no 'array of fantastic backup' presented, as Österman's participant, Eva found in Sweden (2018: 122). The government advice instead adopts a responsibilizing narrative both for the desisting individual and their supporting friend, partner or relative who is seeking out the advice. On the whole, the advice appears to take a 'responsibilizing-relational', social bonds perspective in the encouragement of desistance ('encourage pro-social recreational activities so they can meet people with similar interests and develop positive support networks'). The meaning of 'pro-social' here is ambiguous. There is a theme of individualized (neoliberal) self-empowerment running through the advice ('support them to develop the things that help them to move away from crime' and 'build a positive, collaborative relationship communicating respect and encouraging self-respect') while also noting the importance of alternative identities such as 'student, employee or parent'. There are key traditional cognitive desistance findings (Burnett and Maruna, 2004) and advice presented, for example around the role of hope ('convey a belief in them and a sense of hope and optimism about how they can live a better life and about their future'). Generativity is also presented in an uncritical fashion ('help them to recognize what they can give to others, or contribute to their community') while there is no recognition of the abusive interpersonal relationships and trauma criminalized people, and women in particular, are likely to have experienced, nor an indication as to why they might experience a lack of hope. Interestingly, there *is* a recognition of the role of stigma in a criminalized individual's life and 'desistance journey' ('having a criminal record carries a huge stigma and limits opportunities for success and reinforcing this stigma isn't helpful'). However, there is a vacuity of awareness of the role of the state and intersecting powerful systems which create this stigma. As Tyler (2020) would argue, there is a purposeful lack of recognition of the role of stigma power. The final advice around what not to do to support desistance is not to tell the potential desister 'you have given up on them'. Of course, this final, scaremongering, piece of advice has particular implications for the women supporting men's desistance, as well as family and friends supporting criminalized women's desistance, with a dearth of structural support. The take-home message of the government's guidance on desistance is that this is a 'journey' which can, and should, be supported by well-meaning family and friends but is ultimately an individual crusade, with the responsibility for desistance placed clearly and completely away from the state. Meanwhile, within the advice is a clear picture of an ideal responsibilized individual – a 'family man/ good mother' who contributes to society by their involvement in both paid work and 'generative' (free) labour. Not only does this uncritically favour a heteronormative 'good capitalist', this advice also does not examine the structural barriers, stigma power, inequality and processes of exclusion which can stand in the way of desistance.

This policy focus on individualism and the neoliberal discourse of responsibilization is not a new direction when it comes to the state's understanding of criminalized women's experiences. This language is also reflected in the 2007 Corston Report (Corston, 2007), the Female Offenders Strategy (Ministry of Justice, 2018) and the Farmer Report (Farmer, 2019) into the importance of strengthening female offenders' family and other relationships to prevent reoffending and reduce intergenerational crime (Booth et al, 2018; Elfleet, 2021; Rutter and Barr, 2021). Within each of these policy documents is a particular (neo)liberal 'feminist' understanding of 'empowerment' and a promotion of resilience. As Elfleet (2021) has argued, this is omnipresent in the day-to-day practice of Women's Centres set up in the aftermath of the Corston Report (2007). Although these documents do not explicitly refer to desistance theory, it is no doubt that a particular understanding of desistance has been, and will continue to be, politically useful in securing support for the notion of individualized change and (neo)liberal reform. Within the summary of evidence on reducing reoffending (Ministry of Justice, 2013) that supported the since widely condemned Transforming Rehabilitation agenda which led to the short-lived privatization of probation, was a section, however, summarizing desistance theory and research. In particular the evidence presented included the importance of maturity, family and relationships, sobriety, employment, hope and motivation, having something to give to others, having a place within a social group, not having a criminal identity, and being believed in. Again the focus on individualized change is clear. Desistance research and theory has had a clear impact on criminal justice policy, practice and advice (Carr, 2021). As argued by Weaver (2019: 653), 'interpretations, in policy and practice, of desistance processes are prone to being over-simplified, generalized, decontextualized and individualistic'. The hegemonic understanding of desistance is influenced by male-focused, individualized theory which has had a clear impact on responsibilization discourse. In the final section, we examine the alternative opportunities presented by an anti-carceral, intersectional feminist approach to desistance theory.

## An anti-carceral, intersectional feminist approach

This final section will argue how the bulk of desistance literature has failed to engage with any meaningful critique of the role of the prison or the wider harmful elements of the criminal justice system, beyond outlining how the carceral state broadly contributes to or stands as a barrier to desistance from crime. An anti-carceral, feminist desistance must engage with abolitionist rather than reformist approaches to prison and incarceration. The complex gendered pains and long-term consequences for women prisoners need to be examined through a feminist but also ultimately an abolitionist lens in order to fully understand the damage women's involvement in criminal justice has, particularly during a time of carceral expansion and recent government policy to expand the women's prison estate (Gov.uk, 2021).

The issues surrounding women's prisons and women offenders' experience of custody are crucial here. The gendered pains of custody and the consequences for desistance and women's well-being more widely, is not to be underestimated. This is not a new statement – Crewe et al (2017) have detailed the particular gendered pains of imprisonment, noting both that 'the pains and problems of long-term imprisonment were experienced with significantly greater severity by the women than the men' (p 1365) and that women's experiences of pain in prison while serving long sentences should be understood in the context of life-course experiences of abuse and trauma. Despite repeated highlighting of gendered abuses, pains, injustices and traumas as a result of prison (Carlen, 1998; see also Chapter 10 in this volume) in particular, but also probation and criminal justice based responses more widely, little has changed in relation to policy development or practice when working with women offenders. The outcomes-driven nature of funding streams for work with offenders and the way in which this lends itself to more individualized interventions that can 'evidence' results has created a self-perpetuating cycle where one process bolsters the other.

Research with a more critical edge has demonstrated problems around resettlement, reoffending and desistance during and following a custodial sentence. Research into women prisoners has found that a responsibilization agenda that permeates the prison has a detrimental impact on prisoners' ability to prepare and plan for release (Hart, 2017a). Also, Carlton and Segrave (2013) provide a series of critical essays documenting the struggles women face post-release internationally. Prison can also delay maturation (Liebling and Maruna, 2005), weaken bonds between the prisoner and society (Condry et al, 2016) and render prisoners detached from the routines that need to be established when in the community (Schinkel and McNeill, 2016). More critical research by Sered (2021) into women formerly incarcerated on long-term sentences in Massachusetts has argued that conventional measures of recidivism and desistance have undervalued the importance of macro barriers such as housing and employment and focused on individual choice. This is despite these 'choices' being constrained by said structural issues and the vulnerable and marginalized nature of women caught up in the criminal justice system. Desistance researchers and penal reformers have certainly argued for a reduced reliance on custodial sanctions (McNeill and Weaver, 2007; Hough et al, 2012). However, the reformist trajectory of desistance research and criminal justice practice has led to the continued notion that prison could work under certain circumstances. As stated, this notion is bolstered by policy developments that mean prisons (like probation) are increasingly judged on their reoffending rates and outcomes.

As Olufemi (2020: 111) has argued, '[p]rison provides an individualistic response to harm – it locates the problem in the body of the "bad" person rather than connecting patterns of harm to the conditions in which we live'. These connecting patterns of harm are felt particularly acutely by women offenders. It is important, therefore, to understand these pains of imprisonment and patterns of harm as reproductions of abuse in the narratives of criminalized women. The focus and drive of future desistance studies on and around women must therefore be abolitionist in nature and any desistance study which is not abolitionist can therefore ultimately not be feminist. Reformism in desistance research has also led to the stagnation of more imaginative, radical and abolitionist policy and practice. Calls for the abolition of women's prisons should not be a niche or radical proposal when most women (72 per cent) in 2020 who entered prison under sentence did so for committing a non-violent offence (Ministry of Justice, 2021). This reformism and previous governments' failures to take radical action, is now being exacerbated by the current British Conservative government's ideologically driven funding cuts to welfare service provision flanked by their ongoing programme of prison building and carceral expansion (Gov. uk, 2021). The potential for penal policy around decarceration for women and the now long-held belief that prison-based solutions are harmful for women and their families is currently in tatters following the Conservative government's decision to spend £150 million on building 500 more prison places for women.

These are imminent and worrying plans being proposed and carried out by the government in regard to women and trans prisoners that need to be resisted as a matter of urgency. Hart (2017b) has previously argued for a 'critical desistance' approach, grounded in the abolition of prisons and punishment, rather than the reform of a system that seems to restrain desistance trajectories. The suggested framework for developing a 'critical desistance' has multiple components, including the need to engage with wider political and abolitionist movements and forms of social resistance. This is particularly important for an intersectional feminist desistance approach which must locate and ground desistance and anti-carceral based research within social movements and campaigning. There is much work to be done and carceral expansion is being actively resisted by networks of grassroots groups such as Community Action on Prison Expansion (CAPE, 2021).

It is crucial therefore that feminist desistance researchers work to find routes out of and away from women's imprisonment that are abolitionist in nature, that instead engage with community and transformative justice based solutions. Such research should also work to stop the abusive violence that permeates institutional and domestic spheres without relying on the harmful and violent carceral answers to solve problems. Currently the majority of existing desistance theory and criminal justice practice are incompatible with intersectional feminist theory and epistemology, which rejects neoliberal and carceral solutions and is incompatible with an abolitionist model of critical desistance (Hart, 2017b). Instead of continued research into how to encourage and foster resilience in women, feminist desistance researchers need to be working to change the systems that are making these women vulnerable.

## Conclusion

Grounded in the experiences of White men, desistance research and theory has avoided a truly structural intersectional analysis. Stigma-power has been described by Imogen Tyler (2020: 260) as 'the machinery of inequality' and it is clear to see how the uncritical promotion of desistance from crime as a stigma avoidance mechanism can be a source of harm in the lives of criminalized women. When desistance research and theory promote (re-)engagement with conventional society, the inequalities and subjugations experienced by particular groups, including women, are obfuscated. Capitalism, colonialism and patriarchal conditions particularly intersect to ensure that criminalized women are not supported to desist in conventional society. Encouraging desistance from crime for criminalized women, and the partners they are expected to support, while ignoring the abuse, racism and poverty criminalized people and their families face, is an additional source of harm.

It is important that we challenge responsibilizing, individualized desistance discourse, particularly when it is adopted by the state. Hegemonic understandings of desistance can and do have harmful implications for the lives of women drawn into the criminal justice system, their families and friends, as well as those outside it. Responsibilization is often fully integrated into the application of traditional desistance theories and therefore also becomes the end product, leading to a focus on the presence or absence of agency and resilience in women. Victimhood is erased by neoliberalism when the ideal neoliberal subject 'is one who faces adversity and makes the best of all situations' (Phipps, 2014: 34). Desistance theory and practice must challenge this individualized discourse.

While the role of the state is minimized in the promotion of an individualistic approach to desistance research and theory, the nature of neoliberalism and the role of the carceral state is promoted in desistance research and theory which advocates for the use of the (often reformed) prison, probation or part-privatized criminal justice service. An opposing feminist body of work is well-versed in the harms of the criminal justice system for women (Taylor, 2018; McNaul, 2021). This is particularly salient at the time of writing (July 2021) with the recent announcement of 500 new prison places for women in England. Yet, there is perhaps room for hope in the renationalization of the probation service and, particularly, in the increased anti-carceral element to feminist activism. With this context in mind, we put forward a framework for an intersectional, anti-carceral feminist desistance:

1. Desistance theory, policy and practice must call for the immediate abolition of women's prisons and, in particular, the expansion of the women's prison estate requires swift resistance. Imprisonment is antithetical to desistance, but further to this is associated with a number of significant harms. The focus requires a shift therefore to community resilience and transformative justice (McNaul, 2021) models of desistance.
2. Key to an abolitionist desistance-focused future is wider welfare-based interventions and structural changes that crucially do not serve to maintain the existing systems. The punitive tendencies of the state under contemporary neoliberalism utilize divisive means to maintain legitimacy for the system. The introduction therefore of non-reformist reforms (Hart et al, 2020) such as the removal of criminal records (as barriers to employment); decoupling of drugs from the criminal justice system; decent quality social housing for all; safe spaces for women and

children; truly accessible mental health support; fairly paid and unionized employment and access to universal education needs to be promoted.

3. Structural gendered inequalities shape women's experiences of criminalization, victimization and desistance. An intersectional anti-carceral feminist desistance means resistance to all forms of gendered violence – at the interpersonal level, at the cultural level, and the level which is state sanctioned. As Sisters Uncut have recently argued:

> What could lessen the likelihood of our experiencing violence … are things such as radical and comprehensive sex education, expansive notions of gender, the abolition of exploitative work practices that condone and encourage abuse, properly funded domestic violence services, scaled-up community intervention, robust accountability processes, and a system of benefits that enables people to live comfortably so that they can escape abuse if they need to. (Sisters Uncut, 2021)

4. As alluded to in this chapter, empowerment and structural support must not be linked to traditional and heteronormative models of gender and must also be trans-inclusive. Desistance research and policy has given weight to a heteronormative agenda and this should be resisted at all turns.

5. Desistance theory, policy and practice must account for and value women's lived experiences. Listening to women and their often erratic subjective experiences must inform desistance theory, policy and practice. Evidence (Hart, 2017a; Barr, 2019) shows the issues women need to deal with to avoid a continued disrupted and traumatic future life and it is not a desire to be seen as 'normal' or to be accepted by some flawed notion of society.

Intersectional feminist approaches to desistance that consider structural and systemic inequalities, which can stand as barriers to desistance from both crime and harm, illuminate the possibilities of an anti-carceral feminism and abolitionist futures. This shift in focus to community empowerment, the resisting of heteronomative, neoliberal understandings of the good life, a trans-inclusive approach and ultimately resisting individual responsibilization has the potential to make real changes to work and support with the vulnerable women and their families that are currently damaged by the extreme criminal justice related harms but crucially this framework can inform and alter existing desistance praxis.

## References

Aresti, A., Eatough, V. and Brooks-Gordon, B. (2010) 'Doing time after time: An interpretative phenomenological analysis of reformed ex-prisoners' experiences of self-change, identity and career opportunities', *Psychology, Crime & Law*, 16(3): 169–90.

Barr, Ú. (2019) *Desisting Sisters: Gender, Power and Desistance in the Criminal (In)Justice System*, London: Palgrave Macmillan.

Barr, Ú. and Christian, N. (2019) 'A qualitative investigation into the impact of domestic abuse on women's desistance', *Probation Journal*, 66(4): 416–33.

Barry, M. (2006) *Youth Offending in Transition: The Search for Social Recognition*, London: Routledge.

Barry, M. (2010) 'Youth transitions: From offending to desistance', *Journal of Youth Studies*, 13(1): 121–36.

Booth, N., Masson, I. and Baldwin, L. (2018) 'Promises, promises: Can the Female Offender Strategy deliver?' *Probation Journal*, 65(4): 429–38.

Braithwaite, J. (1989) *Crime, Shame and Reintegration*, New York: Cambridge University Press.

Burnett, R. and Maruna, S. (2004) 'So "prison works," does it? The criminal careers of 130 men released from prison under Home Secretary Michael Howard', *Howard Journal of Criminal Justice*, 43(4): 390–404.

Carlen, P. (1998) *Sledgehammer: Women's Imprisonment at the Millennium*, London: Macmillan.

Carlen, P. (2012) 'Against rehabilitation: For reparative justice: 22nd Eve Saville Memorial Lecture', [online] available at: https://www.crimeandjustice.org.uk/resources/against-rehabilitation-reparative-justice [accessed 25 May 2021].

Carlton, B. and Segrave, M. (eds) (2013) *Women Exiting Prison: Critical Essays on Gender, Post-Release Support and Survival*, Oxon: Routledge.

Carr, N. (2021) 'Critical perspectives on desistance', *Probation Journal*, 68(2): 141–5.

Clinks (2013) 'Introducing desistance: A guide for voluntary, community and social enterprise (VCSE) sector organisations', [online] available at: http://www.clinks.org/sites/default/files/null/Introducing%20Desistance%20-%20August%202013.pdf [accessed 25 May 2021].

Community Action on Prison Expansion (CAPE) (2021) [Online] available at: https://cape-campaign.org/ [accessed 30 July 2021].

Condry, R., Kotova, A. and Minson, S. (2016) 'Social injustice and collateral damage: The families and children of prisoners' in Y. Jewkes, J. Bennett and B. Crewe (eds) *The Handbook on Prisons*, London: Routledge, pp 622–40.

Corston, J. (2007) *A Review of Women with Particular Vulnerabilities in the Criminal Justice System*, London: Home Office.

Crewe, B., Hulley, S. and Wright, S. (2017) 'The gendered pains of life imprisonment', *The British Journal of Criminology*, 57(6): 1359–78.

Elfleet, H. (2021) 'Neoliberal feminised governmentality: The role and function of a post Corston Report (2007) Women's Centre in the North-West of England', *British Journal of Community Justice*, 16(2): 1–22.

European Commission (2021) *2021 Report on Gender Equality in the EU*, [online] available at: https://ec.europa.eu/info/sites/default/files/aid_development_cooperation_fundamental_rights/annual_report_ge_2021_printable_en_0.pdf [accessed 25 May 2021].

Farmer, L. (2019) *The Importance of Strengthening Female Offenders' Family and other Relationships to Prevent Reoffending and Reduce Intergenerational Crime*, London: Ministry of Justice.

Gålnander, R. (2019) 'Being willing but not able: Echoes of intimate partner violence as a hindrance in women's desistance from crime', *Journal of Developmental and Life-Course Criminology*, 5(3): 437–60.

Gålnander, R. (2020) '"Shark in the fish tank": Secrets and stigma in relational desistance from crime', *British Journal of Criminology*, 60(5): 1302–19.

Gov.uk (2019) 'Desistance', [online] available at: https://www.gov.uk/guidance/desistance [accessed 25 May 2021].

Gov.uk (2021) 'Extra funding for organisations that steer women away from crime', [online] available at: https://www.gov.uk/government/news/extra-funding-for-organisations-that-steer-women-away-from-crime [accessed 25 June 2021].

Graham, H. and McNeill, F. (2018) 'Desistance: Envisioning futures' in P. Carlen and L.A. França (eds) *Alternative Criminologies*, Abingdon: Routledge, pp 443–51.

Grundetjern, H. and Miller, J. (2019) 'It's not just the drugs that are difficult to quit: Women's drug dealing as a source of empowerment and its implications for crime persistence', *British Journal of Criminology*, 59(2): 416–34.

Halsey, M. and Deegan, S. (2015) '"Picking up the pieces": Female significant others in the lives of young (ex)incarcerated males', *Criminology & Criminal Justice*, 15(2): 131–51.

Hart, E.L. (2017a) 'Women prisoners and the drive for desistance: Capital and responsibilization as a barrier to change', *Women & Criminal Justice*, 27(3): 151–69.

Hart, E.L. (2017b) 'Prisoners post release: The need for a critical desistance' in E.L. Hart and E.F.J.C. van Ginneken (eds) *New Perspectives on Desistance: Theoretical and Empirical Developments*, London: Palgrave Macmillan, pp 267–88.

Hart, E.L., Greener, J. and Moth, R. (eds) (2020) *Resist the Punitive State: Grassroots Struggles Across Welfare, Housing, Education and Prisons*, London: Pluto.

Hough, M., Farrall, S. and McNeill, F. (2012) *Intelligent Justice: Balancing the Effects of Community Sentences and Custody*, London: Howard League for Penal Reform.

Jensen, T. and Tyler, I. (2015) '"Benefits broods": The cultural and political crafting of anti-welfare commonsense', *Critical Social Policy*, 35(4): 470–91.

Laub, J.H. and Sampson, R.J. (2003) *Shared Beginnings, Divergent Lives: Delinquent Boys to Age 70*, Cambridge, MA: Harvard University Press.

Liebling, A. and Maruna, S. (eds) (2005) *The Effects of Imprisonment*, Cullompton: Willan.

Mansfield, M. and Cooper, V. (2017) 'The failure to protect women in the criminal justice system' in V. Cooper and D. Whyte (eds) *The Violence of Austerity*, London: Pluto Press, pp 188–94.

Maruna, S. (2001) *Making Good: How Ex-Convicts Reform and Rebuild Their Lives*, Washington, DC: American Psychological Association.

Maruna, S. (2017) 'Desistance as a social movement', *Irish Probation Journal*, 14(1): 5–16.

Maruna, S. and Farrall, S. (2004) 'Desistance from crime: A theoretical reformulation', *Kölner Zeitschrift für Soziologie und Sozialpsychologie*, 43: 171–94.

Maruna, S. and Mann, R. (2019) *Reconciling 'Desistance' and 'What Works'*, [online] available at: https://www.justiceinspectorates.gov.uk/hmiprobat ion/wp-content/uploads/sites/5/2019/02/Academic-Insights-Maruna-and-Mann-Feb-19-final.pdf [accessed 25 May 2021].

McNaul, G. (2021) 'Contextualising violence: An anti-carceral feminist approach' in R. Killean, E. Dowds and A.M. McAlinden (eds) *Sexual Violence on Trial: Local and Comparative Perspectives*, London: Routledge, pp 213–28.

McNeill, F. (2016) 'Desistance and criminal justice in Scotland' in H. Croall, G. Mooney and M. Munro (eds) *Crime, Justice and Society in Scotland*, London: Routledge, pp 200–16.

McNeill, F. and Weaver, B. (2007) *Giving Up Crime: Directions for Policy*, Edinburgh: Scottish Consortium on Crime and Criminal Justice.

McNeill, F. and Weaver, B. (2010) *Changing Lives? Desistance Research and Offender Management*, SCCJR Project Report; No.03/2010.

McNeill, F., Farrall, S., Lightowler, C. and Maruna, S. (2012) *How and Why People Stop Offending: Discovering Desistance*, Glasgow: Institute for Research and Innovation in Social Services.

Ministry of Justice (2013) *Transforming Rehabilitation: A Summary of Evidence on Reducing Reoffending*, London: HMSO.

Ministry of Justice (2018) *Female Offender Strategy*, London: HMSO.

Ministry of Justice (2021) *Offender Management Statistics Quarterly, October to December 2020*, London: Ministry of Justice.

Nugent, B and Schinkel, M. (2016) 'The pains of desistance', *Criminology & Criminal Justice*, 16(5): 568–84.

Olufemi, L. (2020) *Feminism Interrupted: Disrupting Power*, London: Pluto Press.

Österman, L. (2018) *Penal Cultures and Female Desistance*, New York: Routledge.

Phipps, A. (2014) *The Politics of the Body: Gender in a Neoliberal and Neoconservative Age*, Cambridge: Polity Press.

Rodermond, E., Kruttschnitt, C., Slotboom, A.M. and Bijleveld, C.C. (2016) 'Female desistance: A review of the literature', *European Journal of Criminology*, 13(1): 3–28.

Rutter, N. and Barr, Ú. (2021) 'Being a "good woman": Stigma, relationships and desistance', *Probation Journal*, 68(2): 166–85.

Sampson, R.J. and Laub, J.H. (1993) *Crime in the Making: Pathways and Turning Points through Life*, Cambridge, MA: Harvard University Press.

Schinkel, M. and McNeill, F. (2016) 'Prisons and desistance' in Y. Jewkes, J. Bennett and B. Crewe (eds) *The Handbook on Prisons*, London: Routledge, pp 607–21.

Sered, S.S. (2021) 'Beyond recidivism and desistance', *Feminist Criminology*, 16(2): 165–90.

Sisters Uncut (2021) 'Policing is the crisis', *New Socialist*, [online] available at: http://newsocialist.org.uk/transmissions/policing-is-the-crisis/ [accessed 14 July 2021].

Taylor, C. (2018) 'Anti-carceral feminism and sexual assault: A defense', *Social Philosophy Today*, 34: 29–49.

Terry, L. and Cardwell, V. (2015) *'Understanding the whole person': The First in a Series of Literature Reviews on Severe and Multiple Disadvantage*, London: Revolving Doors Agency.

Townsend, M. and Jayanetti, C. (2021) 'Revealed: The grim list of sex abuse claims against Metropolitan police', *The Observer*, [online] 20 March, available at: https://www.theguardian.com/uk-news/2021/mar/20/revealed-the-grim-list-of-sex-abuse-claims-against-metropolitan-police [accessed 24 March 2021].

Tyler, I. (2020) *Stigma: The Machinery of Inequality*, London: Zed Books.

Van Ginneken, E.F.J.C. and Hart, E.L. (2017) 'Introduction' in E.L. Hart and E.F.J.C. van Ginneken (eds) *New Perspectives on Desistance: Theoretical and Empirical Developments*, London: Palgrave Macmillan, pp 1–10.

Weaver, B. (2019) 'Understanding desistance: A critical review of theories of desistance', *Psychology, Crime & Law*, 25(6): 641–58.

Women in Prison (2021) 'Key facts', [online] available at: https://www.womeninprison.org.uk/campaigns/key-facts [accessed 24 August 2021].

Worrall, A. (1990) *Offending Women: Female Lawbreakers and the CJS*, London: Routledge.

# 9

# Improving Police Responses to Sexual Abuse Offences against British South Asian Women

*Aisha K. Gill*

## Introduction

Over the last few years, the number of sexual offences reported to the police in England and Wales has steadily grown, with consistent increases in every quarterly analysis since March 2013 (Harrison and Gill, 2018). Factors such as the secrecy that often surrounds abusive situations, the shame felt by victims, the chance of not being believed and the low likelihood of prosecution (let alone conviction) mean that few victims come forward. It is widely recognized that crime statistics significantly underestimate the scale of the problem, and this issue is compounded in South Asian communities because they have especially low rates of sexual abuse reporting.

   This limited representation of the true scale of sexual abuse (because so few victims come forward) applies to all British regions and communities. However, this chapter attempts to contribute to a small literature base by focusing on the low level of sexual abuse reporting from South Asian women, and particularly on how four British police force areas currently respond to sexual abuse incidents where the victim belongs to the British South Asian community. Factoring in relevant literature suggesting that aspects of policing may still suffer from institutional racism, the chapter explores what happens when gender is also a factor in police handling of sexual abuse cases/reports. In this context, it considers why British South Asian women do not report sexual abuse to the police and considers what more can be done to encourage increased reporting in this, and other Black and racially minoritized communities.

# Intersectional feminist analysis of sexual abuse in South Asian communities

Debates about intersections have a long history in the UK, and have taken place specifically in gender studies, race and ethnic studies, and cultural and diaspora studies. These debates have challenged the invisibility of Black people and the absence of theoretical/analytical frameworks that can account for how intersecting social divisions such as class and race affect different groups within particular contexts (Day and Gill, 2020). According to Brah and Phoenix (2004), a person's multiple identities are neither discrete nor explicit, but inseparable: each identity has its own unique, related form of oppression or dominance that alters when it intersects with another identity – for example, minority women face the differing oppressions that stem from being women and from being an ethnic minority. The common and important thread linking these assertions is the idea that in order to understand gendered violence, we must consider social and cultural difference, and have the tools to explain this in ways that do not simply reproduce stereotypical representations of Black and racially minoritized women's subjectivity or everyday experiences of their cultures and communities.

Gender has enjoyed a significant and sustained level of engagement in the British criminological community, and this is reflected in criminal justice policies. However, notwithstanding some exceptions, British criminology is yet to incorporate intersectional frameworks, with 'race' in particular being conspicuously absent (Parmar, 2017; Day and Gill, 2020). In 2016, the UK Ministry of Justice published findings of a review into ethnic minority involvement in the justice system. It concluded that a statistically significant difference exists between the experiences of Black and racially minoritized women and those of White women at the arrest, charging and prosecution stages for a range of crimes/reports (that is, not just sexual abuse), and that Black and racially minoritized women are more likely to receive custodial sentences on conviction (Uhrig, 2016).

Feminism has always recognized the role played by different forms of power, and the interplay between these forms (Yuval-Davis, 2010). This understanding has led some feminists to explore how issues of violence that disproportionately affect Black and racially minoritized, refugee women and girls are often treated as separate (and somehow different) from violence against women (VAW) across the rest of British society (Gill and Begum, 2022). There are two pertinent areas in the current literature: the relationship between the police and Black and racially minoritized communities, and why women in general, and British South Asian women in particular, fail to report sexual abuse.

## Police attitudes towards Black and racially minoritized survivors/victims

To date, most of the literature on race and policing has focused on issues such as stop and search policy, arrest, racial stereotyping, and disparity in sentencing and prison populations (Kochel et al, 2011). However, little literature has addressed how the police work with female abuse victims from Black and racially minoritized communities – that is, the intersectionality between policing, race and gender. The relationship between the police and Black and racially minoritized victims – particularly, for this study, South Asian women – is therefore fundamental, but the small number of previous studies on this subject have largely focused on domestic rather than sexual violence (Choudry, 1996). For example, Belur (2008: 427) argues that Asian domestic violence survivors 'suffer a double disadvantage – first, inadequate services provided by the police to victims of domestic violence in general, and second, current policing arrangements [which] are unable to cater to their differing needs on account of their ethnicity'. Mama highlights three major areas of concern for Black women: (1) their reluctance to ask the police for help; (2) the abusive attitudes displayed towards them by the police; and (3) police reluctance to fully enforce the law (Mama, 1989, cited in Belur, 2008). Further, Brown (2000, cited in Belur, 2008) argues that many male police officers view domestic violence as 'rubbish' work, believing that such 'emotional labour' should be carried out by female officers (Belur, 2008: 429). In short, there is a basic lack of trust and confidence in the police regarding how they will deal with South Asian women; Belur claims this is due to a 'combination of possible intentional discrimination on the part of some officers and unwitting racism on the part of the majority' (Belur, 2008: 430).

## Underreporting of rape

In their study of South Asian immigrant women in Toronto, Ahmad et al (2009: 613) found that delayed help-seeking was common, with the dominant reasons being 'social stigma, rigid gender roles, marriage obligations, expected silence, loss of social support after migration, limited knowledge about available resources and myths about partner abuse' (Ahmad et al, 2009: 613). Other reasons include economic dependency on the perpetrator, fears of deportation (Lee and Hadeed, 2009; Mirza, 2016) and the cultural concepts of honour and shame (Gill, 2004). In her study, Anitha (2011: 1276) explains how South Asian women were reticent to speak out about sexual abuse due to 'their understanding of dominant moral codes within their community, which seldom blamed men for their abuse and for fear of being disbelieved or the shame a disclosure would bring on *themselves*' (emphasis in original).

Other research has explored why victims of various ethnicities withdraw from the criminal justice process once a report has been made. One Home Office report highlights that the two most cited reasons for this are that victims do not wish to go through a court hearing, and/or just want to move on (Feist et al, 2007). Other contributory factors include whether the victim has been injured, the victim–offender relationship and the police area in which the offence was committed, with some police areas more successful than others at reducing the likelihood of a victim withdrawing (Feist et al, 2007). Hohl and Stanko (2015: 327) state that trust between the police and the victim is easily lost when officers 'communicate disbelief and disrespect or when the victim loses faith in the police' to investigate. This further underscores the significance of issues of trust and confidence in the police.

## Methodology

This research had two aims: first, to discover why British South Asian victims do not report sexual abuse; and second, to evaluate what more could be done to encourage increased reporting. Data collection for the project took place between May 2013 and June 2015. The larger study adopted a mixed-methods approach involving focus groups and semi-structured interviews with women living in British South Asian communities: two in the Midlands, one in the north of England and one in the south. Focus groups were used in the belief that they would attract English-speaking and non-English-speaking participants and encourage participation from women who may have been reluctant to be interviewed on their own, or who might otherwise have felt they did not have anything relevant to say (see Gill and Harrison, 2019). In total, approximately 85 women participated in these sessions. Not all of them spoke – however, given the extreme sensitivity of the subject matter, some lack of participation was understandable and expected, and justified the use of larger-than-normal groups. While some women spoke more than others, no individuals dominated any of the discussions. The four groups had a varied mixture of women in terms of age, generation, ethnic origin (Pakistani, Indian and Bangladeshi) and whether or not they had been born in the UK, arrived with their spouse or entered on spousal visas. To supplement these general opinions garnered from the focus groups, 13 British South Asian sexual abuse survivors (Gill and Harrison, 2019), 13 non-government organizations (NGOs) working with sexual abuse survivors, and 13 other professionals from criminal justice agencies and government departments were interviewed.[1]

Data from the police were collected through interviews with nine police officers from four police areas, all of which had relatively high South Asian populations; the analysis here focuses mainly on these nine interviews. To supplement these responses, one chief prosecutor, one senior civil servant (responsible for protecting vulnerable adults and children) and one policy officer were also interviewed. While acknowledging that this small scoping study cannot be considered to fully represent the views of the police in general, it does offer a snapshot of the views held by a few relevant professionals at a specific time. To ensure confidentiality, police areas and ranks are not reported (see Harrison and Gill, 2018).

## British South Asian women's underreporting of sexual abuse

From the outset, this study was predicated on the assumption that significant numbers of British South Asian women do not report sexual abuse to the police. Therefore, our first task was to collate data to test this supposition and evaluate its accuracy. Government reports and statistics did not prove helpful, as while offenders' race is recorded in these documents, victims' ethnic backgrounds are not. Consequently, the conclusions presented here rely largely on evidence from police officers and focus group participants. While this may raise questions of validity, our findings do support those of other, similar studies (Lee and Hadeed, 2009). During the focus group sessions, participants were asked whether they thought women from their communities would report sexual abuse either to family, friends or the police. The majority emphatically answered 'no' in reference to the police. The correctness of this opinion was also supported by the answers received from the 13 interviewed survivors – while most (12/13) reported their abuse to either family or friends, only two involved the police.

The police interviews revealed a similar picture, with a general consensus that reports of sexual abuse from British South Asian women were rare. One officer noted "very little reporting within domestic relationships" in · their area, and described recording from Pakistani, Bangladeshi and Indian communities as "negligible". Another said they did not "think a lot of people come forward from South Asian communities" and that sexual abuse was "massively underreported". This belief was also shared by other officers, who spoke of "less referrals from the South Asian community"; one officer described sexual abuse within British South Asian communities as a "blind spot". Despite this dearth of reporting, all officers noted that sexual abuse was occurring within the South Asian communities in their area. One officer summarized the situation: "It's as prevalent as it is with any other community." Another argued: "We know it happens. It happens in the family, it happens online, it happens in institutions, places of worship, it happens in the street. ... I have no doubt that it is as prevalent in Asian communities as it is in any other." This indicates that the premise of this research – that British South Asian women are unlikely to report sexual abuse, especially to the police – is correct. For example, the assumption of much British criminology and criminal justice policy that gender is the primary axis of marginalization is not limited to the sexual violence field: it is also seen in relation to women's imprisonment and the policing of drugs, mental health, homelessness and sex work (Tompkins and Neale, 2018).

## Reasons for underreporting

Having established that a problem existed, the study's next step was to discover the reasons why. Focus group discussions revealed that the reasons lay largely in the women's perceptions of the police, which aligns with the trust and confidence issues cited in the literature and discussed earlier in this chapter. The women's perceptions centred on three areas: (1) who the police were; (2) misunderstandings of culture and cultural needs; and (3) trust.

One of the commonest viewpoints held by the focus group members was that the police would all be men. Although the police in England and Wales do not represent the general population in terms of gender or race, police officers are not all men and, interestingly, eight of the nine officers interviewed were female. In the year to March 2016, 28.6 per cent of all officers in the UK were female, and 31.2 per cent of all new recruits to the force were female. In the same period, 5.9 per cent of all officers were Black and minority ethnic, with 12.1 per cent Black and minority ethnic representation among new recruits (Home Office, 2016). Nevertheless, participants understood why many female victims would assume the police were men: "I can understand that they see men. The police are mainly men; it's all men in their family, so that's what they expect."

Another reporting barrier the focus groups cited was the belief that the police did not understand British South Asian culture. This perception was tested by asking officers why they thought underreporting from this community was so prevalent. Many appreciated that a number of factors were likely at work. However, in contrast to the women's perceptions, the officers cited culture as *the* most prevalent factor influencing underreporting. One officer said they thought that "for certain communities, including the Asian [ones], their culture, their tight-knit family background – almost the Victorian ethos – is their Achilles' heel". Another said: "It is a culture of silence. … They'll never say anything."

While it is important to acknowledge the role honour and shame play in controlling women's lives and motivating violence, understanding honour-based violence/abuse (HBV/A) and other harmful 'traditional' forms of violence as inherently *cultural* practices remains problematic for victims/survivors of such crimes and for wider responses to VAW. As 'honour' is a broad and all-encompassing term that covers 'an entire codex of concepts and behaviours' (Gill, 2004), the violations that may trigger violence are wide-ranging. However, in the context of HBV/A in classically neo-patriarchal societies, common 'dishonourable' or 'shameful' behaviours that may prompt violence include staying out late, wearing makeup, wearing 'Westernized' clothing, wanting to leave an abusive husband, refusing an arranged marriage, and dating and socializing with someone outside the community (Papp, 2010). Ultimately, irrespective of their specific behaviour, the victims/survivors of HBV/A – including 'honour' killings – are women believed to have deviated from the moral code and thus undermined the family's honour (Jiwani and Hoodfar, 2012). All the police officers interviewed recognized the existence and importance of honour and shame as key factors behind women's failure to report sexual abuse. One officer explained how "issues of honour and shame clearly play a part ... [they] are ingrained deeply in the South Asian communities particularly ... [and] are significant barriers". Another believed that the issue of honour is so deeply entrenched that mothers think, "My reputation – the reputation of my family – is dependent on not reporting this matter." Other officers acknowledged the threat of shame:

> 'I've actively seen where a female is ... married into a family [and] her whole support system is being catered [to] by that family. The shame that you'll bring on them is immeasurable. "Don't do it" I think is perhaps what they are being told. Their culture is about shame and dishonour and it's shameful even [to] talk to the police, let alone describe what's happened to them.'

Many police officers in this study recognized that the significance of family and community in British South Asian culture prevented some victims from reporting abuse. One commented that British South Asians often "keep it within the family" and that "very strong family ties" led to some victims' reluctance to pursue criminal convictions. This reluctance was also coupled with a concern that if they put pen to paper, they would become instrumental in convicting their husband or uncle or second cousin. As one (South Asian) officer put it:

> 'It is just expected, particularly the pressure from our parents, [that] even though we might not want to follow [it], the pressure from the wider family [is that we should] deal with things ourselves and [that] we don't need to do it the British way, which would be, say, through the police.'

Consequently, many officers believed that family pressure was one reason why many victims who had initially reported incidents to the police later retracted their statements:

'So we have a girl who reports at school that she's been raped and sexually assaulted for many years by her father. Mum knew about it and, in fact, was party to it. Mum and Dad get arrested. Child gets placed with another family member ... when we go back the next day to do further work, because she's already given a video interview that night disclosing horrendous incidents of assault over many years, family members have been round to that address and spoken to that child who is now saying she wants to retract. She's been approached at school by other family members and told to retract. ... She's been pressurized into saying it should be kept within the family; it's too shameful to be brought outside [to a police officer].'

Such findings mirror the work of Yoshioka et al (2003), who found that where South Asian women disclosed abuse to brothers and fathers, they were often advised to stay in marriages and keep the matter within the family. The previous quote also offers insight into the control – noted by many officers – that British South Asian families have over women. This mirrors the findings of Lee and Hadeed (2009). One officer stated: "They've got no support network; they perhaps haven't got a job; they haven't got any finances that they can rely on and so what husband says, and what husband's family says, goes." Another officer referred to the "real 1950s views around it. I think that's very much in play in South Asian communities, coupled with the fact that they are often so reliant on their sole provider and their families for support, they are not going to say anything".

Another problem for some British South Asian females was an inability to access support – many victims simply do not know where to find it. As one officer put it:

'There'll be families, won't there, who are ostracized and don't know how to. ... They can't just pick up the phone can they? They might not be allowed out of the house. They might not know how to tell somebody; [they] just don't know where to go and where to seek that advice from.'

Fear of the consequences of going against family wishes and reporting sexual abuse to the police may be another reason why British South Asian victims choose silence. As one officer pointed out, speaking up can result in "physical risk – and so why would she [report]? Why would she put herself at even greater risk?" Another officer described what they saw as the difference between White British and British South Asian communities:

'The distinction I make and it might not necessarily be right, but people tend to fall out over matters within the White British community, or what you might call it, but don't tend to take any retribution, in my experience. Whereas I tend to find there is a very real live threat of retribution within the South Asian community.'

Retribution of this kind can include ostracism from family and the community, disadvantaged marital prospects or, at the other end of the spectrum, forced marriage and HBV (Gill, 2004). Pressure can come from the wider community as well as the family. One officer recounted a case where the offender's family knocked on the door of the victim's family and said, "Tell your daughter … not to carry on. You know this will be sorted within our community."

## Understanding cultural needs

In addition to believing the police would not understand South Asian culture, the focus group members also thought the police would not understand their needs. Lack of culturally and linguistically appropriate services, language barriers and being unfamiliar with legal rights have all previously been cited as reasons why South Asian women do not report abuse (Belur, 2008; Lee and Hadeed, 2009; Anitha, 2011); consequently, this response from the women was not unexpected. However, the police interviewed for this study did display some awareness of these issues. For example, a few officers cited language – victims' inability to speak English and disinclination to use sexual terms because of modesty – as another potential barrier to adequate reporting. Modesty is especially pertinent given the women's perceptions that all police are male. While two of the studied police areas had officers able to translate, even these areas acknowledged that they could not cater for the numerous languages and dialects used in their regions. All four areas had access to a national language line, although, as one officer explained, an impersonal telephone voice was ineffective in establishing trust and rapport – two factors that have been cited as important in encouraging contact with the police.

Another officer saw the need to use sexual vocabulary as a limiting factor when it came to progressing with a prosecution and giving evidence in court. While they recognized that retelling a sexual crime is incredibly difficult for any victim, they thought it could be more difficult for British South Asian victims because "[y]ou've got the added complications of what the family are thinking and all the associated risk that goes with it". Yet another impediment for some British South Asian victims who do not speak English is that there are no equivalent words in Urdu or Punjabi for 'rape'. While an English speaker can walk into a police station and tell the officer at the front desk (who might be a man) that she has been raped, women who do not speak English are faced with the prospect of having to tell this first-line officer the intricate details of what has happened to them without being able to use a specific word to explain it. When modesty and shame preclude the telling of such a story, non-reporting may become the preferred option.

Trust and lack of confidence were reported as the final factors preventing reporting; these are also prevalent issues in the general policing of Black and racially minoritized communities. All the police interviewed were aware of such perceptions, although did not always accept that they could have contributed to causing them. For example, one officer thought it was often difficult to ascertain whether this mistrust was a result of "British policing" or limited "confidence in policing from Pakistan and Bangladesh". According to this same officer, this lack of faith in the police could also be caused by a particular view of them implanted in the victims' minds by their families. If so, it is possible to detect a link between this issue of trust and the element of control – but it is also possible that such views were a product of general distrust towards the police felt by the South Asian community at large. Trust and confidence must be earned, and it is interesting that the police who participated in this study were aware of the need to be concerned not only with the facts and figures of sexual abuse reporting, but also with the need to build trust and confidence with British South Asian women.

To test the perceptions of the focus groups, it was important to create a picture of how complaints were dealt with when British South Asian victims of sexual abuse did come forward. This testing of perceptions and reality was necessary to ascertain whether current police practices had to change, or whether there was simply a need to disseminate police practices more widely to British South Asian communities. The interview questions for this part of the study focused on three areas: (1) whether there was specific police provision for British South Asian victims; (2) whether there had been any recent changes in practice; and (3) what training was available to enhance police understanding of relevant cultural issues. While some noteworthy information was gathered, it features unverified accounts of police practice, and it was unlikely that 'horror stories' were going to be shared.

When officers were asked what services were specifically available for women from the British South Asian community, many initially said there was no distinct provision, especially regarding the initial call. They took the view that, at this stage, the emphasis was on securing and preserving evidence and determining what was necessary in terms of the victim's health and wellbeing on a more practical level. However, as the case progressed, the victim's specific needs were considered. For example, in all four police areas, if a female officer was asked for, attempts were made to secure one; in some areas, this extended to providing a British South Asian female officer. However, all areas noted that it was not always possible to meet such requests, especially when it was a "response officer who made the initial house call". Further, two of the four police areas realized that some victims might actually prefer to talk to a White officer because of fears that their story might otherwise get back to their community. This assumption, which displays a good general awareness of the reservations held by some British South Asian women, was based on the concern that the cultural beliefs of some South Asian police officers were stronger than "their job vocational duties". To keep reports as confidential as possible, the officers in one area made a point of putting as little information as they could on any police computer that could be accessed by all police staff. Importantly, as one officer stated, "[it is] imperative that we listen to the victim and her needs and try to accommodate them as best as we can". In other cases, officers were well informed about third-sector agencies in their locality that could potentially help complainants, including independent sexual violence advisors (ISVA) and NGOs working to support victims of sexual abuse.

Many of the officers also showed a good level of cultural understanding regarding the ongoing risks to which some of these women might be subject. For example, it was understood that most of the reported offences were domestic: "We [therefore] have to be mindful of the fact that because they quite often know their attacker, the risk factors ... can be heightened." Risk factors to British South Asian women included the potential for further violence and HBV. Consequently, officers had to be mindful of the victim's home environment and consider the potential consequences for the victim following the reporting of an offence, asking themselves questions such as: "What checks and measures have been put in place for her? Do we take her out and put her into secure accommodation? Is there an HBV risk? Could they attempt to intimidate her?" One officer voiced similar concerns:

'If you've got somebody from a South Asian community, then I'd certainly think "Is there an HBV risk here?" but also "What risk does the perpetrator continue to pose to that victim?" Whether it's through further domestic assaults, whether it's through sexual assaults, whether it's through intimidation. There could be a lot of things, whether it's through family trying to dissuade the victim from speaking with police or continuing with the complaint.'

Another officer noted the potential for intimidation and future violence when they explained the specific provisions their area had for British South Asian victims. When interviewing the complainant, they would always ensure that the suspect's family were not in the room – their primary aim was to speak to the victim alone, except when a friend or an officially employed interpreter was present to provide specific support. Risk assessments would also be made on an ongoing basis, with every provision put in place to try to protect the complainant.

## Recent improvements to police practice

All four police areas shared the perception that much had changed over the past few years regarding police practice, officer demographics and cultural understandings in relation to sexual abuse cases involving Black and racially minoritized survivors. One officer explained that their unit was now 65 per cent women, which was useful for all female sexual abuse victims/survivors; another described how they had gained cultural awareness of the Sikh faith and the Gurdwara from a newly appointed ISVA based at the police station full time. Nonetheless, the police interviewees were aware that much more work needed to be done:

> 'To come into contact with somebody from the South Asian community, you've got a whole raft of learning to do, very quickly, which probably isn't going to happen. … You are likely to lose your victim quicker than you are going to learn about that community and [then there's] all of the added pressure on top of the – "I've been raped" – you know, the family issues and the HBV concerns – so, as [name of police force], I think we are very good at it. As a police force [in the] UK, I think we are better at it than we used to be and I am sure there are forces doing it better than others [and] forces that do it worse, but I think collectively we have still got a lot of learning to do.'

Other officers, especially those who worked to support British South Asian women, talked about improved relationships with NGOs. They remarked that in the past, there was a sense that neither group really understood what the other actually did, but that these barriers were now beginning to dissolve. One officer attributed this change to a slight increase they had seen in reporting from British South Asian victims/survivors. They felt that NGOs were now better able to correctly state what the police would do if a sexual abuse report was made to them. The officer saw it as important for all agencies involved in a sexual abuse case to "work that step closer, in order that we know what each other's business is … so that we can pass that message to the victim". This increase in partnership working is a factor that also benefits other sexual abuse victims, regardless of race or gender.

Another officer was using social media (Twitter) to try to remove obstacles between the police and the community by informing residents exactly what they could expect if they made a sexual abuse complaint. This officer also shared the profiles of the staff who would be working with community members, an important step in dispelling the perception that all officers are men. However, this endeavour was not specifically aimed at the South Asian community and shows how the police are trying to encourage more sexual abuse victims in general to come forward and, through this, prevent a cycle of persistent victimization. While specific policies may be required for specific groups, if some operational and tactical activities benefit all sexual abuse victims, this can only be positive and impactful on a much greater level. Initiatives such as this are also more likely to be implemented nationally if they can be seen as benefiting the majority rather than just the minority.

Technology was used in a similar way by another area that provides information on its website about how sexual abuse victims can be supported. Again, this was not aimed at British South Asian women specifically, but offered information about historical abuse, relevant support services, persistent victimization and what to do if English was not an individual's first language. Importantly, this information also took into account the fact that the person may be in a domestic relationship with their attacker and face physical and mental fears and consequences. Rather than having specific information for specific ethnic groupings, this area was ensuring that its information was broad enough to meet the cultural needs of as many communities as possible.

More specific to South Asian survivors, another area was working with mosques and the British South Asian community to promote the fact that sexual abuse is unacceptable, and to let women know that if they reported it to the police, their complaint would be taken seriously and acted upon. This same area had made increasing reporting from British South Asian women one of its annual priorities. Clearly, then, the police officers interviewed recognized that cultural and linguistic understanding was perhaps more important than the gender and/or race of the police officer, a factor Belur (2008) has previously identified.

It is widely known that understanding a community comes from either being part of it or from instruction. Although some of the officers interviewed were British South Asian, the vast majority were not; and while all the police officers in this study demonstrated some awareness of cultural issues, only one of the four policing areas had a sound cultural training process in place. Given that all four areas had high South Asian populations, this finding demonstrates a failure on the part of the criminal justice system. When asked about the specific training officers would receive, an officer from the first area said: "They will have had diversity training, but it's going to be pretty basic ... it's not going to be in depth." An officer from the second area explained, "there's obviously diversity training that they do as part of their initial course, but that's about it if I'm honest". Officers from a third area stated:

Officer 1:     We used to get diversity training. Does that still happen? I don't even know if it still happens.

Officer 2:      I think you get it when you join but I don't think you
… have to keep redoing it. Once you've had your initial
kind of training, that's it really though, isn't it?

Organized cultural diversity training in these three areas was thus nonexistent. Although the interviewed officers did display a good level of cultural understanding, this knowledge was thought to be connected to individual motivation rather than being the outcome of a force or national edict. In fact, one of the officers confirmed that gaining cultural understanding was up to officers themselves: "It's down to individual officers. … Some might understand the concepts better than others."

When asked whether more training was required, particularly in terms of South Asian culture, one officer agreed: "I think that's the bit that we miss. … You get a little bit [in diversity training] but you won't get a great deal." Another accepted that "we probably do need to invest more for that [good] level of understanding".

But the fourth area was different. It was not only providing in-depth training, but also trying to share this best practice with other neighbouring forces. The impetus for and emphasis on cultural training had come from the bottom up, again emphasizing the element of personal endeavour. One officer explained that she had undertaken a lot of cultural awareness more broadly, reading books and reports, while another pointed to knowledge gained from being practically involved with the issues that typically arose during these sorts of cases: "It has been hands-on and wanting to know. And we want to know." These officers had initially arranged for an NGO that supports British South Asian victims to speak to their colleagues and fully explain the concepts of honour, shame and HBV/A; officers freely acknowledged that general diversity training "wouldn't help with HBV". This initial NGO training was then replicated internally and provided to all front-line officers to ensure that they would know what signs to look for when going into women's homes and that were aware of the cultural 'dos and don'ts'. When asked why this level and breadth of training was important, one officer explained that it was impossible to work with British South Asian women unless such issues were understood. For example, during training, officers learnt that interviewing a complainant at home may be counterproductive, especially if she was living with her husband's family. They were also made aware of risks such as forced marriage and the signs that it may be about to take place, such as a girl's continued absence from school.

While all the officers interviewed seemed to possess this knowledge, many from the other three areas also recognized that realistically, it was unlikely that the first-response officer would have this depth of understanding. Given that the behaviour of the first-line officer is a factor that may determine whether or not a British South Asian woman continues with police involvement, it is imperative to improve the cultural knowledge of the police at all levels.

## Taking responsibility for more effective policing

To provide more effective policing and, consequently, stronger protection for British South Asian women, all police participants acknowledged that some level of change was required. However, when asked whose responsibility it was to make this change, many cited others apart from themselves. One believed the responsibility lay with the British South Asian community:

> 'It's got to start there and if it's religious, it's got to start with imams coming out and saying: "This should not be tolerated." It's then got to start with the communities themselves. … I think then … it's got to be law enforcement agencies, police, CPS [Crown Prosecution Service], [the] judiciary. It's got to be health, doctors and its then – almost that cherry on the icing – support from the third-sector agencies.'

Another officer reiterated this view: "The people in the temples, Gurdwaras and mosques and the people in local. … They're the ones that could be doing a great deal more."

The civil servant interviewed also mentioned the role and influence of faith groups – but, interestingly and in direct contrast to the criminal justice responses, he thought the ultimate responsibility lay with the police:

> 'I still see it as police … the police have to take responsibility for working out who are the right supporting mechanisms, because we're talking about crimes and their core business is crime. So I'm quite clear [that] they can't see this as being a sort of community-led process. I think they and other people like me definitely have a role in trying to work out ways of empowering people to do that from within communities, but [the police] have to be the trigger.'

Police officers were also asked whether they thought they should be doing more to try to dispel some of the perceptions they knew British South Asian women held about them. In particular, they were asked whether they thought they could do more outreach work in the community to try to effect this change. Some said they were already working with schools and getting involved in training, but the vast majority did not see community education as their job. One argued that "at the end of the day, we're police officers". Another agreed: "Why does it always have to be police?" Yet others said: "That's not what I'm paid to do" and "[o]ther agencies are quite happy to let us do their job for them. There's got to be community workers.

There's social workers. There's the schools, you know. It's not always down to police. We're struggling enough".

These responses indicate a lack of clarity and consensus in terms of who should lead and be responsible for change. Until this issue is resolved, it will serve as a stumbling block to reform. It is also a disappointing and deficient response considering that the police do have to take some responsibility for the tensions that exist between themselves and Black and racially minoritized communities.

## Conclusion

An intersectional feminist approach is key to understanding how social and cultural difference affects gendered violence and its handling by police, particularly in relation to Black and racially minoritized women. The policing of Black and racially minoritized communities has been marked by institutional racism, over-policing and under-protection. Few studies have explored the intersectionality of race, gender and policing and how it may contribute to low reporting of sexual abuse on the part of Black and racially minoritized women, and intersectional frameworks remain notably absent in British criminology. Although small, this study contributes to the existing literature by examining policing practice in response to British South Asian women who have suffered sexual abuse, using an intersectional feminist approach to consider how police responses to these crimes can be improved. Comparing these findings to those of Belur (2008), it appears that some positive changes have occurred in this sphere, including increased numbers of female and Black and racially minoritized officers and individual efforts to improve responses on the part of some committed officers. However, although these measures are welcome, they are not necessarily the answer to better policing in this area. Rather, policy must focus on improving cultural and linguistic understanding across the entire force nationwide, which will more effectively tackle the reasons for British South Asian women's culture of silence and thus help combat gendered injustice. This can be achieved by sharing exemplary working practices and using community multi-agency forums. Initially, such forums should be led by the police, but all agencies should take an active part in providing better education and awareness-raising programmes and establishing a network of advocates. This level of police involvement may also help officers enhance working relationships with the British South Asian community; the benefits of such efforts should reach other Black and racially minoritized communities, too. Support services must play a role in addressing the specific socio-cultural and intersectional context of sexual violence in British South Asian communities.

This study highlights some of the intersectional problems associated with taking a non-gendered approach to sexual abuse. Sexual violence in

South Asian communities remains one form of oppression among many for numerous victims/survivors; failure to take account of these various oppressions places such survivors at further risk and compounds the justice system's failure to protect them. By adopting a critical approach that centres sexual abuse survivors' needs, partnerships between criminal justice bodies have the potential to establish an intersectional pathway to safety that offers genuine empowerment to end *all* forms of oppression and sexual violence against *all* survivors. This feminist intervention in criminal justice – a multi-layered, intersectional and integrated approach – will require involving the broader community in combatting the causes of sexual violence, empowering survivors to speak out and enabling the justice system to meet their unique needs.

## Note

[1] It is important to refer to these women as sexual abuse survivors rather than victims, as this conveys a sense of strength and hope. It also acknowledges that despite the stereotypical and colonial production of South Asian women as in need of being saved by others (Razack, 2004), there are some who are willing to stand up and fight against patriarchal/male violence from within their own communities (Patel and Bard, 2010).

## References

Ahmad, F., Driver, N., McNally, M. and Stewart, D. (2009) 'Why doesn't she seek help for partner abuse? An exploratory study with South Asian immigrant women', *Social Science & Medicine*, 69(4): 613–22.

Anitha, S. (2011) 'Legislating gender inequalities: The nature and patterns of domestic violence experienced by South Asian women with insecure immigration status in the United Kingdom', *Violence against Women*, 17(10): 1260–85.

Belur, J. (2008) 'Is policing domestic violence institutionally racist? A case study of South Asian women', *Policing and Society*, 18(4): 426–44.

Brah, A. and Phoenix, A. (2004) 'Ain't I a woman? Revisiting intersectionality', *Journal of International Women's Studies*, 5(3): 74–87.

Choudry, S. (1996) *Pakistani Women's Experience of Domestic Violence in Great Britain*, London: Home Office, Research Findings No 43.

Day, A.S. and Gill, A.K. (2020) 'An intersectional approach to improving the efficacy of partnerships between women's organisations and the criminal justice system in relation to domestic violence', *British Journal of Criminology*, 60(4): 830–50.

Feist, A., Ashe, J., Lawrence, J., McPhee, D. and Wilson, R. (2007) *Investigating and Detecting Recorded Offences of Rape*, Home Office Online Report 18/07, London: Home Office.

Gill, A.K. (2004) 'Voicing the silent fear: South Asian women's experiences of domestic violence', *The Howard Journal of Criminal Justice*, 3(5): 465–83.

Gill, A.K. and Begum, H. (eds) (2022) *Child Sexual Abuse in Black and Minoritised Communities: Improving Legal, Policy and Practical Responses*, London: Palgrave.

Gill, A.K. and Harrison, K. (2019) '"I am talking about it because I want to stop it": An exploration of child sexual abuse and sexual violence against women in Britain's South Asian communities', *British Journal of Criminology*, 59(3): 511–29.

Harrison, K. and Gill, A.K. (2018) 'Breaking down barriers: Increasing sexual abuse reporting rates in British South Asian communities', *British Journal of Criminology*, 58(2): 273–90.

Hohl, K. and Stanko, E. (2015) 'Complaints of rape and the criminal justice system: Fresh evidence on the attrition problem in England and Wales', *European Journal of Criminology*, 12(3): 324–41.

Home Office (2016) *Police Workforce, England and Wales, 31 March 2016*, Statistical Bulletin 05/16, London: Home Office.

Jiwani, Y. and Hoodfar, H. (2012) 'Should we call it "honour killing"? No. It's a false distancing of ourselves from a too-common crime: the murders of females', *The Montreal Gazette*, [online] available at: https://www.pressreader.com/canada/montreal-gazette/20120131/281831460623735 [accessed 13 July 2021].

Kochel, T., Wilson, D. and Mastrofski, S. (2011) 'Effect of suspect race on officers' arrest decisions', *Criminology*, 49(2): 473–512.

Lee, Y. and Hadeed, L. (2009) 'Intimate partner violence among Asian immigrant communities', *Trauma, Violence & Abuse*, 10(2): 143–70.

Mirza, M. (2016) 'The UK government's conflicting agenda and "harmful" immigration policies: Shaping South Asian women's experiences of abuse and "exit"', *Critical Social Policy*, 36(4): 592–609.

Papp, A. (2010) *Culturally Driven Violence against Women: A Growing Problem in Canada's Immigrant Communities*, Frontier Centre for Public Policy, FCPP Policy Series No. 92.

Parmar, A. (2017) 'Intersectionality, British criminology and race: Are we there yet?', *Theoretical Criminology*, 21(1): 35–45.

Patel, P. and Bard, J. (2010) 'From multiculturalism to multifaithism: A panel debate', *Studies in Ethnicity and Nationalism*, 10(2): 310–14.

Razack, S. (2004) 'Imperilled Muslim women, dangerous Muslim men and civilised Europeans: Legal and social responses to forced marriages', *Feminist Legal Studies*, 12(2): 129–74.

Tompkins, C., and Neale, J. (2018) 'Delivering trauma-informed treatment in a women-only residential rehabilitation service: Qualitative study', *Drugs: Education, Prevention and Policy*, 25(1): 47–55.

Uhrig, N. (2016) *Black, Asian and Minority Ethnic Disproportionality in the Criminal Justice System in England and Wales*, Ministry of Justice, London: Ministry of Justice.

Yoshioka, M., Gilbert, L., El-Bassel, N. and Baig-Amin, M. (2003) 'Social support and disclosure of abuse: Comparing South Asian, African American and Hispanic battered women', *Journal of Family Violence*, 18(3): 171–80.

Yuval-Davis, N. (2010) 'Theorizing identity: Beyond the "us" and "them" dichotomy', *Patterns of Prejudice*, 44(3): 261–80.

# 10

# Traumatizing the Traumatized: Self-Harm and Death in Women's Prisons in England and Wales

*Kym Atkinson, Helen Monk and Joe Sim*

## Introduction

> Women who end up in prison are among the most powerless and disadvantaged in our society, largely due to traumatic life experiences such as sexual and physical abuse, mental and physical ill health, racism and discrimination, underpinned by poverty and inequality. (INQUEST, 2019)

The dominant discourses surrounding self-harm and death in women's prisons, disseminated through an interlinking, deeply patriarchal, network of state, media, liberal reform groups and academic power structures, have socially constructed a particular 'truth' through portraying these profoundly social phenomena in individualistic, pathological terms either as a 'cry for help', a result of 'unfortunate' bureaucratic failure or a combination of both. This chapter is concerned with utilizing feminist methodology and theory to critique this dominant 'truth' and to illustrate how such apparently 'deviant' behaviour can be understood not as a cry *for* help but as a rage *against* the specific pain that women prisoners experience through being exposed to psychologically withering prison regimes. These regimes reflect, reinforce and reproduce the decimating experiences that the majority of women in prison also encounter on the outside.

The chapter is divided into four parts.[1] First, it provides a critical overview of the data concerning self-harm and deaths in women's prisons. Second, it considers how a feminist epistemology, built on 'feminist praxis', can be used to 'unsilence' the voices of women in prison, and their families, and place their experiences directly at the centre of knowledge production (Stanley, 1990). This praxis is not simply about focusing on what kind of knowledge is being produced but, crucially, Stanley asks, what is this knowledge for? For her, '[s]uccinctly the point is to change the world, not only to study it' (Stanley, 1990: 15). Third, it develops a feminist, theoretical perspective in order to critically conceptualize the nature of life and death in women's prisons. Finally, the chapter outlines a number of feminist-based strategies and interventions for the prevention and elimination of self-harm and deaths in prisons. These strategies can also contribute to the radical transformation in, and eventual abolition of, a pain-inducing institution which has been endlessly critiqued for its abject failure to live up to its own self-serving rhetoric for the last 200 years (Foucault, 1979).

## Gender, self-harm and death

Self-harm and death, and the *potential* for self-harm and death, stalk the prison. This means that *all* prisoners, not the 'pathological' few, are at risk at any point during their sentence. In 2015, there were:

> [T]en times more self-inflicted deaths per 1000 people in custody than there were suicides per 1000 people in the community. Men in prison were six times more likely to take their own life than men in the community, and women in prison were 24 times more likely to take their own life than women in the community. (National Audit Office, 2017: 15)

According to the charity INQUEST, between 2012 and April 2022, there were 97 deaths in women's prisons, 36 of which were self-inflicted. Six transgender women killed themselves in men's prisons between 2013 and 2018 (Inquest.org.uk, 2021).

In 2018/19, 11 women died in prison, up from eight in the previous year. Three of these deaths were self-inflicted. The remaining five resulted from 'natural' causes (Prisons and Probation Ombudsman, 2019: 57). However, the idea of a 'natural' death in prison is extremely problematic, given the operationalization of power inside. For INQUEST, 'no death in prison is natural' as the 'failure to treat prisoners with decency, humanity and compassion is a "consistent feature" of deaths [inside]' (INQUEST, cited in Sim, 2019).

In mid-October 2019, Caria Hart became the 109th woman to die since 2007, the year when the Corston Report called for radical change in women's prisons and the criminal justice response more generally (Taylor,

2019). Caria's death followed the death of a newborn baby in September 2019 in the privately run Bronzefeld prison, Europe's largest female prison. The baby's mother had given birth overnight when she was alone in her cell. Over the previous two years, there had been another four cases where women had 'given birth in distressing and potentially unsafe circumstances, including one woman who gave birth in her cell and another who was left in labour at night-time supported only by another pregnant prisoner' (Devlin and Taylor, 2019).

According to the charity Women in Prison:

> This is not the first time a tragedy like this has happened, and it certainly won't be the last without urgent action. The government can't even tell us how many women in prison are pregnant and how many babies are born in prison. At the very least they need to publish this data, but the real question is why pregnant mothers are in prisons at all. (Women in Prison, cited in Devlin and Taylor, 2019)

In January 2016, Sarah Reed suffered a 'harrowing' death in Holloway (INQUEST, 2019: 10). Sarah's death provides a chilling case study of the harms that prison can do to women who have already been harmed, traumatized and numbed by their pre-prison experiences. Her baby daughter had died suddenly in 2003. She and her partner were told to find an undertaker and to take a taxi home, along with the baby's dead body. The desperately callous response to the death of her child seriously impacted on Sarah's mental health. In 2012, she was beaten so severely by a male police officer (who was given a community service order and sacked from the force) that two of her ribs were broken. Three years later:

> The convergence and intersectionality of Sarah's race, gender and mental health vulnerability combined in a vortex of race discrimination and institutional indifference. In late 2015, while in a secure mental health ward, Sarah claimed that an elderly male patient tried to sexually assault her. She defended herself, was restrained and subsequently arrested, and on 14 October was placed on remand, at the direction of the magistrate, solely for the purposes of obtaining psychiatric reports assessing her fitness to plead. (Jasper, 2017)

In prison:

> She was sleepless, hallucinating, chanting, and without the medication she had relied on for years. Much of her behaviour was interpreted by prison staff as a discipline issue. Sarah was put on a basic regime and denied visits from family and lawyers, despite her right to visits as

a remand prisoner. Sarah was put on 'four man unlock' and a screen was placed before her cell door. Sarah was found lying in her bed with a tight ligature around her neck and could not be resuscitated. The jury at the inquest concluded that unacceptable delays in psychiatric assessment, inadequate treatment for her high levels of distress, and the failure of prison psychiatrists to manage Sarah's medication contributed to her death. Marilyn, Sarah's mother, believed Sarah was a victim of collective failure of those involved in her care. (INQUEST, 2019: 10)

Between September 2019 and September 2020, there were 58,870 incidents of self-harm in male and female prisons (Ministry of Justice, 2021: 1). This amounted to 161 each day. Self-harm is highly gendered. In the three months to September 2020, 'there were 14,167 self-harm incidents, *up* 9% on the previous quarter, comprising a 5% *increase* in male establishments and a 24% *increase* in female establishments' (Ministry of Justice, 2021: 1, emphasis in original):

> The rate of incidents, which takes population size into account, was 595 incidents per 1,000 prisoners in the male estate in the 12 months to September 2020, down 6% from 635 incidents per 1,000 prisoners in the 12 months to September 2019. *The rate of incidents in female establishments was far higher, and increased by 18%, from 3,016 in the previous 12 months to 3,557 in the latest 12 months.* (Ministry of Justice, 2021: 4, emphasis added)

According to the Chief Inspector of Prisons, the lockdown generated by COVID-19 had resulted in incidents of self-harm increasing to 'unprecedented levels for women' (HM Inspectorate of Prisons, 2021: 11). And when they do self-harm, women prisoners can experience further punishment:

> [r]epressive prison regimes impose punishments on women for self-harming. Suicidal women are often segregated and isolated, facing long hours locked up in cells. Inadequate drug detoxification, failing healthcare and lack of therapeutic strategies all contribute to the systemic neglect of women's physical and mental health. (Coles, cited in INQUEST, 2019: 8)

Death also follows women when they have been released. In 2018/19, according to the Ministry of Justice, '[t]here were 1,093 deaths of offenders in the community in England and Wales ... up 13% from 964 deaths in 2017/18' (Ministry of Justice, 2019: 3). One hundred and forty seven of these deaths involved women, 13 per cent of all deaths for the year: '[t]he main cause of female deaths … was self-inflicted (34%), followed by deaths from natural causes (22%). In 2017/18, the highest proportion of female deaths were due to natural causes (33%)' (Ministry of Justice, 2019: 5–6).

However, like prisons, the idea of a 'natural' death in the community is also problematic. Women are released 'with just £46, a plastic bag, nowhere to live and the threat of a return to custody if they miss their probation appointment' (Prison Reform Trust, 2020). In other words, 'they continue to be governed by practices that worsen their marginalisation' (Kendall, 2013: 48). Psychologically, their subjectivities are also constrained 'by a risk management discourse that defines them as being perpetually at risk of reoffending, and psy-science practices (such as psychology, psychiatry and social work) that construct them as being psychologically, behaviourally, morally and cognitively flawed' (Kendall, 2013: 48). Women, therefore, experience specific forms of 'social death' inside and outside of the prison (Price, 2015) which are generated by their structural location on the bottom rung of a gendered ladder of power which generates a 'lifetime experience of harm' (Pantazis, 2004: 215).

Death for women extends across the criminal justice system. This is graphically illustrated by women killed by men who were under probation supervision. In the case of Quyen Ngoc Nguyen, the inquest jury found that the system for public protection was 'dysfunctional' and that she was unlawfully killed (INQUEST, nda). The failure by the West Midlands Police and the National Probation Service to take action in Lisa Skidmore's case also contributed to her homicide. Her killer had indicated to these services that he was a risk. Despite this, as Deborah Coles of INQUEST noted:

> The shocking death of Lisa Skidmore was preventable and the direct result of a failing criminal justice system. Warnings about physical and sexual violence to women were ignored by both the probation and the police service. This inquest has performed a vital function of enabling proper public scrutiny and identifying systemic failings. This must result in real change. *This is not an isolated case and until violence against women is taken seriously by authorities the deaths will continue.* This cannot be allowed to happen. (INQUEST, ndb, emphasis added)

## A feminist methodology of self-harm and death

Over the past four decades, feminist-based, grassroots, activist organizations and charities – Women in Prison, Women in Special Hospitals and INQUEST – have been pivotal in creating a space for the experiences and the voices of women detained in different state institutions to be recognized and heard. No longer hidden in the desolate shadows of these institutions, they have been reclaimed as full, agentic human beings who give meaning to their lives *and* deaths. The process of acknowledging these experiences, and hearing these voices, as well as the experiences and voices of their families, has been crucial because *not* being heard in itself can be understood as a form of trauma-inducing injustice (Stauffer, 2015). In working with bereaved families, INQUEST has sought to:

> make visible the women behind the statistics and the structural issues behind their criminalisation and imprisonment. We seek to show the human face of this pernicious social problem, because so many of these deaths are preventable. They raise profound concerns about human rights violations – not only the failure to provide a safe and dignified environment, but also the failure to act to prevent further deaths, an aspiration that unites all bereaved families. (INQUEST, 2019: 4)

There are two further issues to consider. First, the interventions made by grassroots, activist organizations, and the feminist epistemology which underpins their work, have challenged the state's definition of reality – its 'truth' – regarding the social harms the prison engenders which have been masked, hidden and shrouded in a blanket of secrecy. While this blanket has not been totally shredded, it has been severely torn by these groups. This has been done through highlighting the psychologically decimating experiences of women detained in state institutions, as well as the traumatic experiences of their families, to indict the often-mendacious definition of reality propagated by the state, its media acolytes and the politically expedient policies of politicians.

These interventions have generated alternative, critical bodies of knowledge from below. In Foucauldian terms, this process can be understood as 'the insurrection of subjugated knowledges' (Foucault, 2003: 7). This insurrection from below has revealed a very different penal and social reality for women far removed from the state's dominant definition of that same reality. As Carol Smart has noted, it is important to recognize 'the significance of knowledge as power. … Knowledge is not something extra … like the icing on a cake, but is synonymous with power, politics and action' (Smart, 1995: 216).

Second, these organizations have resisted being incorporated into the regressive machinery of the state and the abject supplication and snake oil professionalization of support services that goes with this incorporation. In refusing to be both 'defined in' and 'defined out' by the state, and in refusing to use official discourse – such as INQUEST's use of the term 'self-inflicted death' rather than 'suicide' – these groups have carved out a transformative ideological and material space and avoided the pitfall of incorporation, a process which has historically and consistently undermined the prospects for radically changing the immense, and unaccountable, power of the prison to punish (Mathiesen, 1980; Sim, 2009).

In contrast, the often-uncritical support given to therapeutically based interventions and specific programmes for women in prison individualize and responsibilize them and, consequently, distract attention away from the structural issues confronting them, both inside and outside, which decimate their lives. In that sense, the liberal emphasis on the rehabilitation, reform and reintegration of former prisoners back into 'normal' society is fallacious in that, as Pat Carlen has argued, it fails to consider the structural issues facing former prisoners:

> [R]e-integration, re-settlement or re-entry are often used instead of re-habilitation. Yet all of these terms, with their English prefix 're', imply that the law breakers or ex-prisoners, who are to be 're-habilitated'/'re-integrated'/'re-settled' or 're-stored', previously occupied a social state or status to which it is desirable they should be returned. Not so. The majority of prisoners worldwide have, prior to their imprisonment, usually been so economically and/or socially disadvantaged that they have nothing to which they can be advantageously rehabilitated. (Carlen, cited in Sim, 2014: 21)

## Theorizing self-harm and death

If women in prison experience their lives as bleak and stunted – what Lisa Stevenson calls the 'poverty and pain of the "now"' (Stevenson, 2014: 147) – then, following her argument, self-harm and self-inflicted deaths can be understood as a 'response to a future devoid of surprise'. In a fundamental sense, therefore, death and self-harm 'answer[s] in one temporality a question that cannot be posed in another: what if the future cannot redeem the present?' (Stevenson, 2014: 147). Similarly, Jill Stauffer has pointed out that if individuals, 'because of abuse or neglect' are denied the human relationships 'necessary for self-formation' then this will impact on their psychological capacity 'to take on the present moment freely'. This she terms 'ethical loneliness' (Stauffer, 2015: 26).

These profound insights can be used to critically analyse the haunting nature of self-harm and self-inflicted deaths in women's prisons. Women prisoners live their lives – or rather attempt to eke out an existence – second by punitive second, in the psychological wasteland of the prison. Each day is predictable and routinized in a system of *'constrained choice'*, a concept which captures 'the limited choices available to many marginalised women' who then experience 'cumulative disadvantage rooted in historical and structural forms of inequality that produce oppression, trauma and subsequent harm ... the pathways and choices that bring women to prison continue to shape their lives inside' (Owen et al, 2017: 5, emphasis in original).

Ex-prisoners are also confronted by the prospect of a future 'devoid of surprise', built on an iron network of intersecting, patriarchal power which, due to its inevitable predictability, is also incapable of 'redeem[ing] the present' (Stevenson, 2014: 147). As already noted, this includes homelessness, poverty and unemployment. Additionally, there is the eternal threat, and direct experience of, male violence,[2] racist, homophobic and transphobic harms and systemic, unrelenting attacks on their self-esteem underpinned by the remorseless reinforcement of their lack of worth as human beings. The unyielding ache of living wounded lives in soul-crunching conditions outside of the prison do not provide the conditions for positive self-validation, irrespective of the programmes of normalization the women are exposed to inside which emphasize raising individual self-esteem and promoting personal self-worth. As Lynne Haney has noted, programmes for women inside and outside of prisons are based on encouraging a sense of 'dependency', changing 'dangerous desires' and 'replicating a process of disentitlement' (Haney, 2010: 208–9). In short, they are about 'the therapeutics of neoliberalism' (Haney, 2010: 225).

According to Stauffer, feeling insecure can be understood as 'the trauma of loss of safety. In particular, it is the loss of the sense the lucky among us have that other human beings will treat us as human beings rather than as objects to be disposed of or abused at will' (Stauffer, 2015: 27). Additionally, the behaviour of women in prison should be understood not as a pathological response to a benevolent, empowering, gender-neutral environment but as a *rational* attempt at 'managing trauma symptoms' (Owen et al, 2017: 64). In that sense:

> Drug use, self-harm, defiance, and other negative behaviors exhibited by women inmates may be better understood as trauma-survival behaviors that alleviate deep sensory distress, rather than a blatant disregard for the institutional rules. Common correctional routines or practices can worsen or alleviate the sensory distress that accompanies trauma. ... In the absence of alternatives and living in a climate of fear, [some] behaviors offer a sense of control and psychological and physiological relief. (Benedict, cited in Owen et al, 2017: 64–5)

Making these links is crucial for challenging the discourse of pathological determinism enveloping women who self-harm or who die in prison – a discourse which is supported by an intersecting, destructive network of patriarchal power dominated by 'judges of [female] normality' (Foucault, 1979: 304) – as well lifting the cloak of invisibility and blanket of silence thrown over self-harm and self-inflicted deaths by the state. In short, the traumas women experience on the outside are reinforced and intensified by different state institutions – particularly criminal justice and state welfare institutions – with which they come into contact and which, despite the efforts of some staff who try to work humanely and empathically with them, ultimately reproduce systemic patterns and processes of gendered injustice and inequality.

Given this, self-harm and self-inflicted death can be understood as *rational* responses to intolerable, dehumanizing experiences, both inside and outside of prisons. Following Liz Stanley and Sue Wise, this behaviour involves women 'actively *constructing*, as well as interpreting, the social processes and social relations which constitute their everyday [penal] realities' (Stanley and Wise, 1990: 34, emphasis in original).

The women's prison experiences can be linked dialectically to broader, structural processes of gender subordination. It is *these* ferocious processes which are pathologically dehumanizing. It is *not* the women's individual psychologies. They are caught in the pliers of this subordination which denies them their full humanity and reduces them to the belittled, spectral status of abandoned beings which can have a profound impact on their psychological wellbeing. According to Stauffer, '[b]eing abandoned by those who have the power to help produces a loneliness more profound than simple isolation' (Stauffer, 2015: 5). As a place of punishment, and as one element in the continuum of pain that the women experience, often for the majority of their lives, the prison, in its present form, cannot fulfil their profound yearning to be free of feeling abandoned, and the dissolution of the self that flows from this. In practice, these feelings are endlessly reproduced and reinforced. Like acid, this continuum corrodes the desire for a stable and meaningful sense of self the women might aspire to, and desire.

Self-harm and deaths can, therefore, be understood as emanating from the jarring dislocations detonated in the subjectivities of women in prison, and in the outside world. These immensely harmful dislocations are deeply social in their origin and are generated by highly gendered micro and macro structures of patriarchal and fratriarchal power operating in, and through, the discourses, policies and practices of deeply masculinized, state institutions (Remy, 1990; Connell, 1994). Individually, they are toxic; together they are deadly.

## A feminist reckoning with the state

How can the destructive processes of patriarchal domination and subordination which provide the context for self-harm and deaths in women's prisons be contested and overturned? The final part of this chapter considers this question. It explores a number of feminist-based interventions and strategies designed to radically transform women's prisons and the wider culture and politics of patriarchal power structures within which prisons operate and, to which, as 'insignia of [gendered] power' they provide legitimacy (Tokarezuk, 2019: 248).

First, the binary divide between women in prison and women on the outside needs to be confronted. Binaries reinforce socially constructed differences, obfuscate communalities and isolate bodies and minds. In challenging these binaries, the material *similarities* between incarcerated women and women on the outside should be recognized, particularly in terms of the intertwined relationship between harm, protection and safety. For INQUEST, building strategies which respond to these issues, and which link the outside and the inside, should be the starting point for thinking about radically transforming both social spheres:

> Many women in prison have experienced sexual and physical abuse, violence and trauma and have been failed by multiple agencies. There is no clear demarcating line between women as defendants and women as victims or complainants. Self-harm, violence and death experienced by women in custody forms part of a continuum of violence that usually starts in the community and follows them into, and back out of, prison. *Within this framework, INQUEST perceives imprisonment as a form of state sanctioned violence against women, and part of a cycle of harm that too often leads to trauma, injury and death.* The use of punishment and imprisonment is the result of a lack of political will to take seriously violence against women across society. The imprisonment of women is a matter for everyone – feminists and social justice campaigners alike. Those fighting for gender equality and justice must take seriously the plight of women in prison. (INQUEST, 2018: 19, emphasis added)

INQUEST's argument that prison should be conceptualized as 'a form of state-sanctioned violence against women' has been reflected by anti-carceral feminists and, in particular, the need to develop a 'broad and layered understanding of "violence against women" that encompassed the structural violence of social inequalities, the violence of state institutions and agents, and interpersonal forms of violence, including rape, battering and sexual coercion' (Thuma, 2019: 2).

Second, the links between the macro and the micro exercise of patriarchal power raise significant questions about how safety and protection can be operationalized in the 21st century. For Lena Palacios, it is important to 'reconceptualise safety in ways that address harm while resisting the vigilantism of "call out culture" and permanent exile as solutions' (cited in Brown, 2020: 78). This would involve putting into practice strategies which ensure safety and protection while directly confronting the question of social harm. In turn, this requires moving beyond 'individualised notions of protection, safety, and by extension safe space' and moving towards a position where 'safety is collective rather than individualised'. This position 'requires an analysis of who or what constitutes a threat and why, and a recognition that those forces maintain their might by being in flux. And among the most transformative visions are those driven less by a fixed goal of safety than by ... freedom' (Palacios, cited in Brown, 2020: 78). According to Emily Thuma (2019: 157), what is needed is 'an antiviolence praxis rooted in an intersectional analysis of oppression'.

Third, as anti-carceral feminists have argued, the prison is a highly gendered, *state* institution (Thuma, 2019). To paraphrase Nicola Lacey, it is a site of '[gender] ordering practices' (Lacey, cited in Coleman and Sim, 2000: 629). As noted, Raewyn Connell has argued that 'the state is *historically* patriarchal, patriarchal as a matter of concrete social practices. ... State structures are effectively controlled by men; and they operate with a massive bias towards heterosexual men's interests' (Connell, 1994: 163, emphasis in original). In the context of the role played by these institutions in reproducing a deeply unequal, highly gendered, capitalist, social order, she has asked if 'a feminist state [was] conceivable' (Connell, 1994: 165). In order to build institutional structures which are, in theory, policy and practice, *feminist*, then the contemporary state would need to be 'replaced by demilitarisation and participatory democracy' (Connell, 1994: 165). Importantly, this development:

> would be nugatory unless the cultural distinction which reproduces women's exclusion from state power, the distinction between public (masculinized) and private (feminized) were abolished. In one sense that seems to imply an end to the state as such, which is founded on such a distinction. In another sense it suggests an expansion of the realm to which a programme of democratisation would apply. The state would become, so to speak, broader and thinner. (Connell, 1994: 165)

The demand to democratize prisons raises a series of questions about the mechanisms of accountability which need to be developed in order to bring the institution under democratic control, including the state agents working within them, whose often-capricious use of their discretionary powers only adds to the distress of the confined. There is a systemic culture of immunity and impunity which has allowed state agents to avoid responsibility for the abject levels of self-harm and preventable deaths inside. There is an 'accountability void' (Coles and Shaw, nd: 25). How, therefore, can this void be eliminated? And what structures can be put in place so that those responsible are held accountable for women's deaths in prison while simultaneously ensuring that future deaths are prevented and eventually eliminated?

Fourth, these strategies plug into the more general question of abolishing women's prisons. They epitomize the point made earlier in this chapter by Liz Stanley (Stanley, 1990) concerning the relationship between knowledge production and radical social change – in this case, radical, penal change – and can be understood as feminist stepping stones towards the abolition of women's prisons in their current, repressive form. They are examples of 'feminist [penal] praxis' designed both to *prevent* and *eliminate* prison harms and deaths through focusing on safety and protection for women in prison while strategically linking this praxis to wider feminist campaigns around women's safety outside of the prison and, ultimately, contributing to the abolition of women's prisons. This link is crucial in contesting the material and ideological isolation of imprisoned women from mainstream feminist politics, and politics more generally. If fat was, and is, a feminist issue so too are the desperate harms, and ignominious deaths, suffered by women in prison.

In 1990, Pat Carlen argued for the development of a 'woman-wise penology' built on an 'open-ended feminist jurisprudence' as key steps leading eventually to 'the virtual abolition of women's imprisonment' (Carlen, 1990: 9). This abolitionist position avoided the pitfalls of liberal reformism, and challenged the power of the prison, to engage in the centuries-old state strategy of 'carceral clawback' (Carlen, 2002) where threats to its ongoing existence through anything other than self-delusional, snake oil, liberal policy reforms have been derided, delayed and defused before being harmlessly integrated into the system. She concluded:

> The choice is between continuing to squander millions of pounds on prisons or taking bold steps to stop legislators and sentencers seeing the prisons as being the ultimate panacea for all political, social and penal ills. Abolishing women's imprisonment for an experimental period might be one small step towards giving the criminal justice and penal systems the thorough shake-up they so desperately need. (Carlen, 1990: 125)

Fifth, three decades on, Carlen's model for radically decarcerating, and ultimately abolishing, women's prisons, remains visionary. A number of organizations have demanded introducing radical alternatives to women's prisons. In the aftermath of the appalling death of the baby in Bronzefeld prison referred to earlier, Women in Prison called on the government 'to introduce deferred sentencing for pregnant women and urgently prioritise investment in women's centres, social housing, education and health care' (cited in Devlin and Taylor, 2019: 13).

Working closely with the families of the deceased, charities such as INQUEST have also demanded that a range of radical policies based on 'an abolitionist vision and decarceration strategy' should be developed (Carlton and Russell, 2018: 122). These policies would include: creating a Standing Commission on Custodial Deaths with a specific stream on the deaths of women in prison; redirecting resources away from criminal justice to radical alternatives to custody based on social care, welfare housing and health strategies; stopping the prison building programme; reviewing sentencing policy in England and Wales; reviewing the deaths of women post-release; and ensuring that the families of the deceased have access to justice via non-means-tested legal aid (INQUEST, 2018, 2019).

Finally, how can radical alternatives to women's prisons be linked to the rich body of work around feminist conceptualizations of justice? Answering this question means '[c]onnecting criminal justice and institutional justice' and 'reconceptualising justice' through feminist praxis' (Atkinson, 2020: 270, 289). In theoretical, political and practical terms, this would also mean thinking about the meaning of safety for women in the 21st century. As Alison Phipps has argued, safety should not 'reinforce the stigmatisation and alienation of marginalised people' (cited in Atkinson, 2020: 294). Imprisonment is one area in which this is evident, as Richie (2012: 15) notes, for Black women who experience male violence, there are 'perils inherent in relying on intervention strategies … that focus on punishment rather than prevention of violence and that ignore the broader need for redistribution of social power along gender and racial lines'. Therefore, women's safety 'in any institution or community can … be connected to the safety of women more generally' (Atkinson, 2020: 294). In line with this, Kristin Bumiller has called for grassroots feminist organizations to make 'connections to other broadly based anti-violence movements both locally and globally, including those that raise concerns about the state as perpetrators of violence in the form of police brutality, discrimination against immigrants, racism in all aspects of crime enforcement and in foreign wars' (Bumiller, 2008: 164).

These connections illuminate the links between 'intimate partner violence, community violence, state violence, and the harm caused by public policy' (Richie, 2012: 102). This strategy would challenge the isolating alienation that women in prison endure by linking their physical and psychological desolation to the interpersonal and structural politics of women's safety more generally. Given that 'heteropatriarchy kills' (Harris, 2011: 13), no woman in prison is safe, until all women are safe.

## Conclusion

For 200 years, the prison has been a site for delivering punishment and pain to poor and powerless women. In the third decade of the 21st century, it continues to fulfil this historical role. The fact that the present Conservative government (2021) is contemplating building 500 new prison places for women, in the face of the abject failure of the prison to fulfil its official goals, indicates that punishing poor women remains central to the state's strategy of discipline and control. In an age of rampant white-collar, corporate and state criminality, it is not the 'good chaps' who engage in hugely detrimental social harms which often lead to thousands of violent, preventable 'social murders' (Tombs, 2016) who are at the centre of the state's malevolent, punitive gaze. As ever, it is those languishing at the bottom of the ladder of gendered, social inequality, living in a compassionless, neoliberal society, who are punished for being poor, a brutal process which, for women, is compounded by the disproportionate misery inflicted by austerity-driven cuts (Perrons, 2021).

Women in prison are mangled debris who are mercilessly 'churn[ed]' through unforgiving state institutions from an early age in increasingly racialized numbers (Sawyer and Wagner, 2019: 4). Marie Baker, who was sentenced to 24 weeks in prison for begging for 50 pence in the street, provides one vivid, poignant illustration of the will to punish (Sim, 2019). Prosecuting women for the non-payment of television licences, which accounted for 30 per cent of all female prosecutions in 2018, further illustrates the pitiless nature of gendered punishment. According to the BBC, 'the higher number of women prosecuted was due to *"the increased availability of women to answer the door whenever we visit, and the increased likelihood of women to open the door and engage positively"'* (BBC cited in Casey, 2019, emphasis added).

Contemporary women's prisons, like their historical predecessors, are not overflowing with conventionally defined, dangerous individuals. As this chapter has shown, while the vast majority of incarcerated women might not be dangerous to the prison, and the wider society, the prison, and the wider criminal justice and welfare systems, are dangerous to them. Introducing and *enforcing* the feminist-based strategies outlined in this chapter, and abolishing prisons in their present form, is the only viable option if the dangers posed to women in prison are to be alleviated.

This is both a political *and* moral issue. There is a direct obligation on the part of academics, and the wider society, to recognize that 'saying or doing nothing' is not an option as this constitutes 'another harm'. Living in a world where the systemic harms generated by the prison are an everyday occurrence, makes us 'all responsible – to varying degrees – for recovery from and prevention of such harms' (Stauffer, 2015: 28).

This profound insight is something for us all to reflect on, and to take direct and concerted action about, if the next preventable death in women's prisons is to be avoided.

## Notes

[1]    Thanks to Lindsey Metcalf for organizing the 'Shut Up and Write' sessions at Liverpool John Moores University where much of this chapter was written. Thanks also to Úna Barr and Katie Tucker for their helpful comments on an earlier draft of this chapter.

2   Research in Scottish prisons has found that 80 per cent of women in prison had a 'history of significant head injury, with sustained domestic abuse the most likely cause' (Brooks, 2021).

## References

Atkinson, K. (2020) *'An Amplified Space': A Feminist Poststructuralist Analysis of Sexual Violence at University*, unpublished PhD thesis, Liverpool John Moores University.

Brooks, L. (2021) 'Four in five female prisoners in Scotland found to have history of head injury', *The Guardian*, [online] available at: https://www.theguardian.com/society/2021/may/13/four-in-five-female-prisoners-in-scotland-found-to-have-history-of-head-injury [accessed 8 June 2021].

Brown, M. (2020) 'Transformative justice and new abolition in the United States' in P. Carlen and L.A. Franca (eds) *Justice Alternatives*, London: Routledge, pp 73–87.

Bumiller, K. (2008) *In An Abusive State: How Neoliberalism Appropriated the Feminist Movement Against Sexual Violence*, Durham, NC: Duke University Press.

Carlen, P. (1990) *Alternatives to Women's Imprisonment*, Buckingham: Open University Press.

Carlen, P. (2002) 'Carceral clawback: The case of women's imprisonment in Canada', *Punishment and Society*, 4(1): 115–21.

Carlton, B. and Russell, E. (2018) *Resisting Carceral Violence: Women's Imprisonment and the Politics of Abolition*, Basingstoke: Palgrave Macmillan.

Casey, T. (2019) 'Poverty is not a crime: ending imprisonment for debt', Centre for Crime and Justice Studies, October, [online] available at: https://www.crimeandjustice.org.uk/resources/poverty-not-crime-ending-imprisonment-debt [accessed 8 June 2021].

Coleman, R. and Sim, J. (2000) '"You'll never walk alone": CCTV surveillance, order and neo-liberal rule in Liverpool city centre', *The British Journal of Sociology*, 51(4): 623–39.

Coles, D. and Shaw, H. (nd) *Learning from Death in Custody Inquests: A New Framework for Action and Accountability*, London: INQUEST.

Connell, R.W. (1994) 'The state, gender and sexual politics: Theory and appraisal' in H.L. Radtke and H.J. Stam (eds) *Power/Gender: Social Relations in Theory and Practice*, London: SAGE, pp 136–73.

Devlin, H. and Taylor, D. (2019) 'Multiple inquiries ordered into death of baby in UK prison', *The Guardian*, [online] available at: https://www.theguardian.com/uk-news/2019/oct/08/multiple-inquiries-ordered-into-death-of-baby-in-uk-prison [accessed 15 April 2021].

Foucault, M. (1979) *Discipline and Punish: The Birth of the Prison*, Harmondsworth: Peregrine.

Foucault, M. (2003) *Society Must Be Defended*, London: Penguin.

Haney, L.A. (2010) *Offending Women: Power, Punishment and the Regulation of Desire*, Berkeley: University of California Press.

Harris, A. (2011) 'Heteropatriarchy kills: Challenging gender violence in a prison nation', *Journal of Law and Policy*, 37(1): 37–65.

HM Inspectorate of Prisons (2021) *Business Plan 2021–22*, London: HM Inspectorate of Prisons.

INQUEST (nda) *Media Release: Inquest Exposes 'Dysfunctional' System for Public Protection and Concludes Quyen Ngoc Nguyen was Unlawfully Killed*, London: INQUEST.

INQUEST (ndb) *Media Release: Failures of West Midlands Police and National Probation Service Contributed to Homicide of Lisa Skidmore Inquest Finds*, London: INQUEST.

INQUEST (2018) *Dying on the Inside: Examining Deaths in Women's Prisons*, London: INQUEST.

INQUEST (2019) *Still Dying on the Inside: Examining Deaths in Women's Prisons Update*, London: INQUEST.

Inquest.org.uk (2021) *Deaths in Women's Prisons*, [online] available at: https://www.inquest.org.uk/deaths-in-womens-prisons [accessed 27 July 2022].

Jasper, L. (2017) 'Those who failed Sarah Reed must be held to account', *The Guardian*, [online] available at: https://www.theguardian.com/commentisfree/2017/jul/24/sarah-reed-death-avoidable-mental-illness-holloway-prison [accessed 16 April 2021].

Kendall, K. (2013) 'Post-release support for women in England and Wales: The big picture' in B. Carlton and M. Segrave (eds) *Women Exiting Prison: Critical Essays on Gender, Post-Release Support and Survival*, London: Routledge, pp 34–55.

Mathiesen, T. (1980) *Law, Society and Political Action*, London: Academic Press.

Ministry of Justice (2019) *Deaths of Offenders in the Community, England and Wales, 2018/19*, London: Ministry of Justice.

Ministry of Justice (2021) *Safety in Custody Statistics, England and Wales: Deaths in Prison Custody to December 2020 Assaults and Self-harm to September 2020*, London: Ministry of Justice.

National Audit Office (2017) *Mental Health in Prisons*, London: National Audit Office.

Owen, B., Wells, J. and Pollock, J. (2017) *In Search of Safety: Confronting Inequality in Women's Imprisonment*, Oakland: University of California Press.

Pantazis, C. (2004) 'Gendering harm through a life course perspective' in P. Hillyard, C. Pantazis, S. Tombs and D. Gordon (eds) *Beyond Criminology: Taking Harm Seriously*, London: Pluto, pp 192–216.

Perrons, D. (2021) *Is Austerity Gendered?* Cambridge: Polity.

Price, J.M. (2015) *Prison and Social Death*, New Brunswick: Rutgers University Press.

Prison Reform Trust (2020) *New Report Exposes System Failure Condemning 6 out of 10 Women Leaving Prison to Homelessness*, London: Prison Reform Trust.

Prisons and Probation Ombudsman (2019) *Annual Report 2018–19*, CP 175, London: Her Majesty's Stationery Office.

Remy, J. (1990) 'Patriarchy and fratriarchy as forms of androcracy' in J. Hearn and D. Morgan (eds) *Men, Masculinities and Social Theory*, London: Unwin Hyman, pp 43–54.

Richie, B. (2012) *Arrested Justice: Black Women, Violence, and America's Prison Nation*, London: New York University Press.

Sawyer, W. and Wagner, P. (2019) *Mass Incarceration: The Whole Pie 2019*, The Prison Policy Initiative, [online] available at: https://www.prisonpol icy.org/reprts/pie2019.html [accessed 20 June 2019].

Sim, J. (2009) *Punishment and Prisons: Power and the Carceral State*, London: SAGE.

Sim, J. (2014) '"Welcome to the machine": Poverty and punishment in austere times', *Prison Service Journal*, 213: 17–23.

Sim, J. (2019) 'Shredding human beings: Death and self-harm in prisons', Blog, Centre for the Study of Crime, Criminalisation and Social Exclusion, Liverpool John Moores University, [online] available at: https://ccseljmu. wordpress.com/2019/02/15/shredding-human-beings-death-and-self-harm-in-prisons/ [accessed 23 September 2019].

Smart, C. (1995) *Law, Crime and Sexuality: Essays in Feminism*, London: SAGE.

Stanley, L. (1990) 'Feminist praxis and the academic mode of production: An editorial introduction' in L. Stanley (ed) *Feminist Praxis: Research Theory and Epistemology in Feminist Sociology*, London: Routledge, pp 3–19.

Stanley, L. and Wise, S. (1990) 'Method, methodology and epistemology in feminist research processes' in L. Stanley (ed) *Feminist Praxis: Research Theory and Epistemology in Feminist Sociology*, London: Routledge, pp 20–60.

Stauffer, J. (2015) *Ethical Loneliness: The Injustice of Not Being Heard*, New York: Columbia University Press.

Stevenson. L. (2014) *Life Beside Itself: Imagining Care in the Canadian Arctic*, Oakland: University of California Press.

Taylor, D. (2019) 'Inquiry launched into death of woman at Derbyshire prison', *The Guardian*, [online] available at: https://www.theguardian.com/ society/2019/oct/13/inquiry-launched-into-death-of-woman-at-derbysh ire-prison [accessed 15 April 2021].

Thuma, E. (2019) *All Our Trials: Prisons, Policing and the Feminist Fight to End Violence*, Urbana: University of Illinois Press.

Tokarezuk, O. (2019) *Drive Your Plow Over the Bones of the Dead*, London: Fitzcarraldo.

Tombs, S. (2016) *'Better Regulation': Better for Whom?* Briefing 14, London: Centre for Crime and Justice Studies.

# 11

# Sensing Injustice? Defences to Murder

*Adrian Howe*

Othello: 'Good, good, the justice of it pleases; very good.'
Shakespeare, cited in Neill (2006: 196–7)

## Introduction

In December 2015 the South African Supreme Court of Appeal set aside a conviction and sentence for culpable homicide, substituting a verdict of murder.[1] Commenting after the decision, the victim's mother said this:

> Now we've seen that the justice system works. ... This is respect for my daughter and her life also, and respect for women all over this country, because we have too much of this happening and people get away with it. If you do the crime, you have to do the time. I'm not really interested in how much time, but I'm happy with the verdict. I feel better we have justice for her. (June Steenkamp, cited in Allison, 2015)

June Steenkamp was paying tribute to her daughter Reeva, the victim in one of the most-publicized 21st-century intimate partner femicide cases to date. Getting away with it – that's how victims' families invariably describe any verdict less than murder. The justice system 'worked' for June Steenkamp because in her eyes a verdict of murder respected her daughter's life and, by extension, the lives of all South African women. Respect in the first instance but also justice for Reeva: the family had finally got 'justice for her'. Justice is what the families always want. Anything less than a murder conviction is, in their eyes, an injustice.

It's not just the families. For nearly four decades, feminist researchers and anti-violence activists across all Anglophone jurisdictions have condemned a legal status quo in which wife-killers avail themselves of defences, indicatively provocation by sexual infidelity, thereby avoiding a murder conviction and receiving instead verdicts for the lesser, 'second degree' crime of manslaughter and frequently risibly short sentences.[2] Such dispositions in intimate partner femicide cases, feminists claim, fail victims – in a word, they are unjust. Minister for Women and Equalities Harriet Harman spoke for many when, leading the early 21st-century movement to reign in defences to murder in England and Wales, she declared:

> For centuries the law has allowed men to escape a murder charge in domestic homicide cases by blaming the victim. Ending the provocation defence in cases of 'infidelity' is an important law change and will end the culture of excuses. There is no excuse for domestic violence, let alone taking a life. (Harriet Harman, cited in Verkaik, 2008)

It was, she said, 'a terrible thing to lose a sister or a daughter, but to then have her killer blame her and say he is the victim of her infidelity is totally unacceptable. The relatives say "he got away with murder" and they're right' (cited in Hinsliff, 2008). On any feminist reading, men 'getting away' with murdering their women partners and former partners is self-evidently unjust. It follows that a murder conviction is perceived as just, or in any event, as delivering justice to victims.

But could it be that when feminists demand justice for femicide victims they fall into a binary trap of assuming justice to be the self-evident opposite of injustice? This chapter explores that question in relation to feminist advocacy of criminal law reforms that curtail victim-blaming defences to murder. The reforms, now implemented across several Anglophone jurisdictions, were designed to counter a perceived injustice in the criminal justice system's handling of intimate partner femicide cases. Have they had their intended effect of stopping men getting away with murder and, if so, does this deliver justice to victims? Focusing on the English law reforms, I shall argue that this feminist-initiated intervention, one informed by decades of feminist scholarship and mounted against strident opposition from the legal fraternity, has been a largely successful challenge to what the editors of this collection call the endless capacity of the state 'to close things down … and to disentangle the connections we can make within and across the theory-policy-practice nexus' (Introduction, this volume). Rejecting provocation by alleged 'sexual infidelity', historically a wife-killer's best chance of avoiding a murder conviction; winning the parliamentary debates and implementing reforms banning this excuse is, I suggest, feminist praxis at its best. Giving vent to decades of feminist criticism of the operation of the provocation defence in intimate partner femicide cases, this legislative catharsis has demonstrated that law reform, for all its limitations, can be a meaningful part of tackling injustice as a feminist issue if grounded in feminist praxis.

Whether the reforms have delivered justice to victims is, however, a much more complex question. I shall begin by addressing that question before proceeding to an assessment of the efficacy of the feminist-driven UK law reform movement to stop men getting away with murder in intimate partner femicide cases.

## Is injustice self-evident?

To begin with the deceptively straightforward question of justice *versus* injustice: in *The Concept of Injustice*, his critique of over 2,000 years of justice theorists from Plato through to Rawls, Eric Heinze identifies a justice/injustice binarism trap that has precluded them from radically rethinking injustice. Unsettling the age-old assumption that injustice has a straightforward relationship of mutual exclusion with some conceptually prior notion of justice, he argues that injustice cannot be assumed to be the 'sheer negation of justice' (2013: 5). Not that in querying this assumed relationship of mutual exclusion Heinze is advocating the opposite extreme. Rejecting 'the nihilist view' that justice and injustice are 'meaningless or wholly relative concepts', he acknowledges the existence of 'everyday senses in which the binarism seem to work well enough' (2013: 6). While Heinze does not specify the everyday senses he has in mind, he allows that some writers, notably Arendt, Levinas, Primo Levi and others who speak of 'mass' injustices such as genocide, can assume injustice to be 'sufficiently evident' (2013: 42). No justice theory is needed to grasp heinous injustices. It is rather 'our sense of injustice that stakes out the ontologically and conceptually prior moment', a moment from which we 'arguably proceed to theorize about justice' (2013: 42).

But if we were to linger a bit longer in that prior moment staked out by what Heinze, in uncharacteristic universalizing mode, calls 'our sense of injustice', questions arise. What about when injustice might be sensed by some, but is not yet sufficiently evident to others?[3] What about when the very existence of an injustice felt by some might be hotly disputed by others as was the case in the controversy sparked by the feminist-led movement to reform the English law of murder? (Howe, 2013). Surely Heinze allows too much to his chosen theorists when he permits them to assume that heinous injustices like genocide are 'sufficiently self-evident' (2013: 42). Isn't it precisely because mass injustice is not 'sufficiently evident' to enough people, say in Nazi Germany, that it occurs? Can injustice ever be assumed to be 'sufficiently evident', even events deemed to have been heinous by later generations and post-war tribunals?

Heinze would be on stronger ground, and in good company, if he stuck to querying the self-evidence of injustice. Many influential theorists, Derrida, Walter Benjamin and Robert Cover, among others, have argued in a similar vein, querying taken for granted assumptions about justice and by extension, injustice. Reflecting on the violence of law and indeed, the axiomatically violent foundation of all law, they have pronounced the impossibility of doing justice. It is not merely that, as Marianne Constable puts it in *Just Silences: The Limits and Possibilities of Modern Law*, there appears to be 'no necessary connection between law and justice' (2005: 133). The disjunction between law and justice is said to be much deeper than that, some calling it 'the law–justice contradiction' (Valverde, 2002: 85). As Heinze puts it: 'either you can do law, or you can do justice, but you can never do both' because justice in codified form 'necessarily and actively' generates injustice (2013: 9).

Feminist criminologists and law scholars in the business of thinking about how to do justice to victims of men's violence, especially those calling for law reform, have not always paid sufficient attention to this law–justice conundrum – to the fact that there is no necessary connection between law and justice. Take, for example, those of us striving to elevate intimate partner femicide to the category of mass injustice. By invoking the voice of dead victims, claiming to speak for them, aren't we appealing to what Constable calls 'an oft-unnamed justice', implicitly seeking justice for victims while condemning manslaughter sentences for their killers as *ipso facto* unjust? (2005: 46). Here, Heinze comes to the rescue, granting that those with a 'so-called pragmatic bent' who deal with 'specific, concrete problems' and see justice and injustice as straightforward opposites may not need 'a deeper approach' (2013: 2). After all, injustice arises in the context of specific disputes and he certainly agrees that it must be analysed in context. Indeed, context is crucial to Heinze for developing the concept of injustice. That injustice emerges out of broader contexts – social, economic, cultural, ethical and political contexts – might be 'a perfectly familiar idea', but in his view, its consequences for the concept of injustice have been neglected. Not for him a decontextualizing of justice within 'a context of isolated, abstracted ethical reason' that only reinforces 'the binarist assumption' of a straightforward relationship between the 'just' and 'unjust' (2013: 27).

Context also matters profoundly to feminist researchers. For decades feminist criminologists and legal scholars have plotted the vastly different social contexts in which men and women kill each other in intimate partner homicides. Singling out the broader misogynist cultural context of provocation by infidelity femicide cases and their reception in criminal courts, our 'reforming ideas of justice' could well be described as 'hypercontextual' (Larner, 2001: 107). Not that this approach is fully understood by non-feminist commentators. Even one who recognizes feminist jurisprudence, for example, as having 'a long tradition of defending context against abstraction' and 'narrative against rules' adds 'personal judgment against structural constraints' to his characterization of feminist tradition, thereby underselling theoretically informed feminist analysis as merely 'personal' (Manderson and Yachnin, 2010: 210). There is surely no need here to resort to the by now clichéd feminist view that 'the personal is political' to see just how highly politicized the fight for justice for femicide victims has been. The political import of June Steenkamp's post-sentence remarks is clear in the South African context: the murder conviction handed down to her daughter's killer was not only respect and justice for her; it was 'respect for women all over' that country.

## Sensing injustice?

The controversial early 21st-century English reforms that expressly excluded loss of self-control in the new loss of control defence provides a window into conflicting views of what constitutes justice and injustice in a murder trial. More, they highlight the radical space opened up by a feminist intervention that has interrogated how gender has been conceptualized in the law of murder and, in the process, exposed the state's complacent response to victims of intimate partner femicide. For Harriet Harman, who led the reforms banning 'sexual infidelity' as an excuse for murder, the injustice of manslaughter verdicts handed down in provocation by infidelity femicide cases was manifest. Defendants were getting away with murder and Harman was determined to abolish the provocation defence that had enabled wife-killers to get away with murder for centuries:

> This defence is our own version of honour killings and we are going to outlaw it. We have had the discussion, we have had the debate and we have decided and are not going to bow to judicial protests. ... I am determined that women should understand that we won't brook any excuses for domestic violence. (Harman, cited in Hinsliff, 2008)

In short, the defence was, in her view, producing unjust outcomes. Others vigorously opposed the proposed law reforms as they made their way through the parliamentary process (Howe, 2013). *The Times* reported the reform bid under the headline 'An unjust, feminist view of murder' where it was said that a 'trio of feminists' – Harman, Solicitor-General Vera Baird and Justice Minister Maria Eagle – were bent on ensuring that a man who kills his wife for infidelity will be convicted of murder 'straight up':

> No excuses about provocation or loss of control, thank you very much. As Ms Baird put it: 'The days of sexual jealousy as a defence are over'. So much for poor Othello's account of himself as 'one not easily jealous,

but, being wrought, perplex'd in the extreme'. The Moor would get short shrift from Ms Baird. (McDonagh, 2008)

Notwithstanding Harman's reminder that the 'reality' is that '86 per cent of domestic homicides are committed by men, and the victims are their female partners' and that the 'infidelity clause … is overwhelmingly used by men', this commentator got the impression that the reformed law would regard women's violence leniently while viewing men's violence as 'beyond the pale'. Such was 'the feminist take on murder', according to *The Times* reporter. For her, the proposals were 'politically motivated', producing an 'unjust, feminist view of murder' (McDonagh, 2008). Poor Othello and his sexual obsessions, a feminist might respond, do not get short shrift at all in the reforms. As we shall see, they have been subjected to vigorous feminist scrutiny and found wanting.

The question of what counts as justice and what as injustice was also at the heart of Cambridge law professor John Spencer's objections to the reforms. He felt they had the potential for 'grave injustice'. Inasmuch as 'unfaithfulness by a supposedly committed sexual partner is liable to cause deep shock and hurt, and for some of them, quite likely to provoke explosive anger', it was 'outrageous', in his view, that a 'person' who loses self-control and kills must now be convicted of murder (Spencer, 2009). Harman's sense of injustice is staked out in a vastly different ontologically and conceptually prior moment to Spencer's – hers born from feminist outrage at wife-killers' continuing success in evading murder convictions by invoking an historically mandated and culturally inscribed victim-blaming defence; his from outrage at depriving the killer of that very same time-honoured defence. This belief in the self-evidence of one's view of injustice has a universalizing 'we' corollary: a claim to speak authoritatively for others. Harman speaks for victims' families and advocates; Spencer for society at large. There is, however, a crucial difference between their respective speaking positions. Harman's 'we' is authorized by decades of investigative feminist analysis revealing how 'justice' and 'injustice' are positioned in decided femicide cases – justice is delivered to offenders; depriving them of a defence to murder is 'unjust'. Spencer's 'we' is simply self-authorized: everyone, he assumes, agrees that killing while in an explosive provoked anger should not result in a conviction for murder.

The universalizing 'we' and 'our' are pervasive in mainstream criminology and socio-legal studies, including the latter's law and literature wing. In his exploration of the extent to which 'our experience with drama' influences 'our ideas about justice', Larner considers a scene from a play in which a baby gets stoned to death in a pram. He believes 'our sense of outrage, horror and injustice is manifest' here – it's a 'dramatic moment' that evokes 'a sense of injustice' (1998: 3; 1999a: 417). What, though, if the victim is a woman?

Does 'a sense of injustice' and outrage arise there? Apparently not for Larner who in his commentary on Shakespeare's *Othello* has nothing to say about Desdemona's death while maintaining that Othello's suicide 'reknits' society (1999a: 421). Inasmuch as he grants that justice in a democracy is 'worked out most appropriately when it grapples frankly with the inevitable messy claims and counter claims, points of view and pressure of a multifarious society', he might want to consider this feminist counter-claim: a society 'reknit' by a wife-killer's suicide is not one women are likely to feel safe in (1999b: 201).[4]

So much for assuming there's a universal 'sense of injustice'. What about a 'sense of justice'? The injustice perceived by feminists surveying the killing field of intimate partner femicide might be contrasted with the 'sense of justice' that Mihaela Mihai invokes several times in her contribution to the literature on transitional criminal trials. She favours criminal proceedings that affirm 'the value of equal respect and concern for both victims and abusers' (Mihai, 2011: 111). Referencing the Holocaust trials, she insists that the procedural rights of defendants must not get sacrificed by judges more intent on addressing the victims' 'negative emotions of resentment and indignation'. Extolling the merits of 'an inclusive sense of justice' for victims and victimizers, she singles out as exemplary the Eichmann trial where judges disqualified 'unrelated stories' of victims in order to send out a message about 'the value of equal respect' for victimizer and victims. For Mihai then, the scope of 'the sense of justice' covers the procedural rights of defendants (2011: 113, 116). In intimate partner femicide cases – where defendants' procedural rights have trumped victims' rights for centuries – justice seems to go all one way down the well-trodden path of justice for victimizers. Not that this would surprise professor of victimology Jan Van Dijk. Identifying compassion for the vulnerable as a core Christian value and 'victim care' as the 'quintessential operationalization of Christian morality', he suggests that 'one would expect the use of the victim label for persons hurt by crime to have led to an outpouring of compassion for those so labelled'. However, Christian victim care has 'never included the care of victims of crime' (Van Dijk, 2008: 19–21). Moreover: 'The Christian value of forgiveness fundamentally denies the moral right of victims to be angry and seek gratification for their emotional need to see their victimisation avenged. It therefore presents a strong intuitive justification for reducing to an absolute minimum the victim's rights in criminal procedure' (Van Dijk, 2008: 19–21). Challenging that 'intuitive justification' is at the heart of the feminist reform process.

## 'Doing justice' in criminal courts

In *Just Silences*, Constable claims that 'modern law often seems silent as to justice' (2005: 7). Certainly this is true of traditional provocation by sexual infidelity cases. There the term 'injustice' is used as if it were as self-explanatory as justice, while unfailingly favouring defendants, not victims, as worthy recipients of justice. Thus in the 1957 case of *Bullard v R*, Lord Tucker delivering the opinion of the Judicial Committee declared that: 'Every man on trial for murder has the right to have the issue of manslaughter left to the jury if there is any evidence upon which a verdict can be given. To deprive him of this right must of necessity constitute a grave miscarriage of justice.'[5] By describing the provocation defence as a 'right' to a manslaughter verdict, Lord Tucker might seem to have put the argument for the provocation defence at its highest, that is until it is recalled how problematic rights discourse is. Which is the 'higher' right – his to a defence or hers to life? Moreover, it pays to consider the kind of 'evidence' Lord Tucker believes might warrant a manslaughter verdict in an intimate partner femicide case. Historically, that 'evidence' was the victim's 'provocative' behaviour, indicatively her verbosity or alleged adultery. Hence the provocation defence's colloquial name: the 'nagging and shagging' defence. More recently, 'evidence' on which manslaughter verdicts have been returned for killing women partners might be that she did not so much provoke as consent to being killed.

Consider, for example, a 2006 case in which a man killed a woman by strangulation during sex. He claimed it was consensual and the death accidental.[6] At his trial for her murder, his counsel advised him not to run involuntary manslaughter as an alternative to murder. When the jury convicted him of murder he appealed, arguing that the trial judge should have directed the jury as to the possibility of a manslaughter conviction even though the defence had not raised it. Concurring with the decision in *Bullard*, the House of Lords quashed the murder conviction and ordered a re-trial. According to Lord Bingham, the 'interests of justice' are not served if defendants are 'over-convicted' or 'under-convicted', thereby endorsing the view that depriving a defendant of the right to have the issue of manslaughter left to a jury constitutes a grave miscarriage of justice.[7] The word 'justice' appeared in the judgement 37 times, 'injustice' only twice, the question of delivering or doing justice to defendants clearly preoccupying the court. It is notable, however, that when the manslaughter alternative was put before the jury at the second trial, the jury convicted him of murder by 11–1. Two juries then, one given the manslaughter option, one not, saw no injustice in calling the defendant's crime murder.

Consider too the 2001 provocation case of *R v Smith (Morgan)* where Lord Hoffman noted that while 'the general principle is that the same standards of behaviour are expected of everyone', this was not 'a rigid rule':

> It may sometimes have to yield to a more important principle, which is to do justice in the particular case. So the jury may think that

there was some characteristic of the accused, whether temporary or permanent, which affected the degree of control which society could reasonably have expected of *him* and which it would be unjust not to take into account.[8]

Lord Hoffman's view was cited favourably by Lord Scott of Foscate in his dissenting opinion in a 2001 case, an appeal against a conviction for the murder of two women. Lord Scott also cites Lord Steyn's dissenting opinion in the 1978 case of *Luc Thiet Thuan*, yet another intimate partner femicide case, that 'nobody should underestimate the capacity of our law to move forward where necessary, putting an end to demonstrable unfairness exposed by experience'.[9] But what is 'demonstrable unfairness'? To offenders or victims? Lord Scott's position was clear. Standing against any undervaluing of 'the vitality of the common law' which he located in its capacity to widen the provenance of provocative behaviour on the part of victims contributing to their deaths, he was keen to avoid 'doing an injustice' to the appellant in the instant case.[10]

Doing justice to offenders was also a priority in the 1979 case of *Vinagre*, an appeal against sentence in a wife-killing case.[11] In *Vinagre*, the Court of Appeal questioned whether, following the logic of medical evidence about 'Othello Syndrome', it was necessary, 'if justice was to be done', to determine whether there was evidence that the victim, the appellant's wife, had been unfaithful. If so, it was a 'straightforward case of a jealous husband'. If not, the 'Othello Syndrome' could be 'called in aid'. The concept did not appeal to the Court, but as the trial judge had accepted the plea, the Court felt obliged to consider its sentencing implications. It decided that whatever the appellant 'may have been suffering from at the time when he killed his wife', he was no longer suffering from 'the kind of mental imbalance' that would justify a life sentence. It followed that 'justice' demanded that his sentence be reduced to seven years' imprisonment. In *Townsend*, another 1979 case, the 'real question' for the Court of Appeal was whether 'bearing in mind the domestic nature of the offence' – a man's attempted murder of his wife – as contrasted with an armed robbery 'leading to the same result', it was possible to 'take a rather more merciful view than that taken by the trial judge?' The Court decided, without any further explanation, that 'justice would be done in this case' – a case where it was thought the woman might never recover from her shotgun wounds – if they reduced his 15-year sentence by five years.[12]

By contrast, the 2002 *Humes* case, the three femicide cases that precipitated the English reform movement, was an appeal against sentences handed down to men convicted of manslaughter on the ground they were too lenient, that is, unjust.[13] Appealing against sentences of four to seven years on the ground they were too unduly lenient, the Attorney General referred to discrepancy between sentences for manslaughter in provocation by infidelity cases and sentences for other offences of homicide or serious violence. The Court of Appeal was unmoved. The appeals were turned down, promoting the Solicitor General to embark on the reforms abolishing the provocation defence and installing a new defence of loss of control that expressly excluded sexual infidelity as a trigger for loss of control in the face of vigorous opposition from upper echelons of the judiciary on the ground that the reforms themselves were unjust (Howe, 2013).

Has what is perceived as justice and injustice in courts' handling of intimate partner femicide cases shifted in the post-reform era? I have written elsewhere about the controversial 2012 post-reform case of *Clinton*, conjoined appeals by men convicted of murdering wives who had left them.[14] The appeals provided the Court of Appeal with the first opportunity to comment on the new legislation banning infidelity as a trigger for loss of control in the new loss of control defence. The court managed to find a way around the ban. In its view, 'infidelity' taking the form of a wife's departure from a marriage may properly (that is, justly) be taken into consideration for the purposes of the partial defence of loss of control when such behaviour was 'integral to the facts as a whole' (cited in Howe, 2013: 775). Clinton's conviction for murder was overturned. At his second trial he pleaded guilty to murder. But with 'infidelity' still a mitigating factor in sentencing, his minimum sentence was reduced from 26 to 20 years.

The post-*Clinton* cases reveal that while murderous rage over sexual infidelity can still be raised in loss of control and diminished responsibility defences, defendants are today far more likely to be convicted of murder and receive longer sentences than in the pre-reform era. This must surely count as a resounding success for a feminist reform movement determined to stop men getting away with murder (see Howe, 2019a, 2019b). For example, Heather Arthur and Christine Baker were killed by their husbands in Newcastle, England on the same day in May 2013 after discovery of their affairs with other men. Arthur's killer pleaded guilty to manslaughter on the basis of loss of control but was convicted of murder and given a life sentence with a minimum of 18 years. Baker's husband pleaded guilty to murdering his wife. He received a life sentence with a minimum of 13 years, the judge taking into account 'the effect your wife's revelations about the affair and about the details of the relationship will have had on you' (cited in Howe, 2014b). Impliedly, it would be unjust to exclude such a consideration.

Are these outcomes typical of the new order? In my study of men who faced trial in the reform jurisdiction of England and Wales for killing wives, partners or former partners over the five-year period from 1 January 2012 to 31 December 2016, I identified 317 defendants who were charged with murder, 240 (75 per cent) of whom pleaded guilty to that offence or were found guilty by a jury (Howe, 2019a, 2019b). To summarize the study's main findings: there has been a profound shift in law's truth about femicide. Defendants once characterized as impassioned killers deserving of sympathy are now being condemned as irrationally jealous murderers and sentenced to life imprisonment. Of the 240 (75 per cent of those charged) who pleaded guilty to murder or were convicted of murder by a jury, three received a whole life sentence, including two who had killed previous partners. The rest were given life sentences with minimum terms ranging from 11 to 38 years, far longer than sentences handed down prior to the reform. Ninety defendants admitted murder from the start or did so when it became clear during the trial that they had no viable defence. What becomes immediately clear from the guilty pleas is not only that allegations of sexual infidelity are losing their excusatory force, but that these 'red mist' cases can now be more readily identified as departure cases – where the victim was estranged from her male partner, in the process of leaving him or seeking a divorce.

The chances of a man avoiding a murder conviction for killing a woman partner or former partner have diminished substantially. Of the 36 defendants running the new loss of control defence, 27 were found guilty of murder. In one case, that of a husband who killed his wife believing her to be having an affair, the prosecutor told the jury there must be evidence that the defendant had 'excusably lost control'. But the 'plain truth' was that any loss of self-control here was 'borne entirely of anger and jealousy at what he perceived to be his wife's sexual infidelity' (cited in Gye, 2013).[15] The jury agreed. Verdict: murder. Juries also rejected defences for men who strangled former partners for starting a new relationship; who killed them on being told their marriage was over and for one husband who struck her with force 'off-the-scale in its ferocity' during an argument about her request for a divorce (BBC, 2013). One jury was unimpressed with the loss of control defence run by a man who recorded his fatal attack and his final words – 'you lying cow Janee, you're dead' and 'I can't believe you're going straight from me to this guy' recorded on a dictaphone he left under a bed to spy on her. Verdict: murder. Sentencing him to life imprisonment with a 20-year minimum term, the judge explained the new legal status quo thus: one may be 'heartbroken' at a break-up, but the 'failure of a marriage and disappointment at being left for another man is relatively slight mitigation' (Arkell, 2013). It could no longer found a defence.

Other defendants denied all criminal responsibility, some conjuring up increasingly far-fetched scenarios in which they had acted in self-defence. All were convicted of murder. No defendant claiming the fatality was an accident escaped a murder conviction and once again, the context of these killings was a recent or impending separation. One man claimed his former partner had accidently overdosed. The prosecution case was that he had harboured thoughts of a reconciliation but killed her when he saw she had removed all his photos. The judge explained law's new understanding of relationship breakdown's depleted excusatory force: feeling 'hurt and puzzled' when your wife asks for a separation or removes your photos is no excuse for murder. Wanting to 'move on with her life' even if he 'harboured thoughts that there would be some sort of reconciliation' was something a woman was 'entitled to do' (McCarthy, 2014). In the post-reform cases, her newly recognized entitlement is cancelling out his traditional entitlement to a conviction for manslaughter, all of these 'accidental' killers receiving life sentences for murder with minimum terms ranging between 22 and 25 years.

Court dispositions in post-femicide cases suggest that defendants who were once characterized as impassioned killers deserving of sympathy now tend to be condemned as irrationally jealous murderers. In one departure case, the prosecutor told the jury that sexual jealously 'can't excuse an unlawful killing. However humiliated and upset he felt, there was no justification for killing her in broad daylight, and we say this is murder' (Murdermap, 2013). Nor did pleading guilty to murder save another defendant from a long sentence: life with a minimum term of 20 years. The judge regarded the 'considerable emotional strain' he was under as 'significant' but being 'understandably upset' about the relationship ending did not warrant stabbing her 13 times. After all: 'Many men and women have to endure the discovery that the husband, wife or partner is no longer content with the relationship they have. … Many are jealous or unhappy. But what the law cannot and will not permit is the use of violence' (Osuh, 2012).

Juries do sometimes accept loss of control defences, resulting in convictions for manslaughter and sentences ranging from as low as six years, reminiscent of the pre-reform era. Among other troubling cases, a defendant said he 'snapped' when his wife admitted having sex with a lover and was planning to leave him. The jury was told that legally, his claim that his wife had admitted having sex with another man was not a defence to murder. But if they believed she had threatened to leave and that was the trigger for him to snap, they could acquit him of murder. Might someone, the defence asked, who 'realised both the deception he has been subjected to and the fact his life was about to be utterly shattered, snap, as he did?' After three days of deliberation, the jury agreed – killing an unfaithful woman who 'threatened' to leave was not murder (Calderwood, 2016).

There is no space here to elaborate further on the cases. Suffice it to say that analysis of court outcomes for intimate partner killings committed after the period covered by my 2012–16 study reveals the same pattern of failed defence narratives and convictions for murder. Recall that the English reformers claimed they were implementing 'an important law change' that would 'end the culture of excuses' and 'end the injustice of women being killed by their husband then being blamed' and that 'the days of sexual jealousy as a defence are over'. Are those days over? Not quite. Loss of control defences can still succeed. In the post-reform period a few defendants were given sentences for manslaughter of between four to seven years, on a par with the pre-reform sentences that had so outraged families and reformers. Yet while residual jury sympathy for some enraged killers and occasional risibly short sentences remain causes for concern, the feminist-inspired English reform appears to be working to curtail both unfaithfulness and departure as excuses for murder. So many guilty pleas and convictions for murder are testimony to that. The historically mandated provocation by infidelity script followed by so many men in so-called 'crimes of passion' is being exposed as code for a man's murderous rage at being abandoned by a woman who, as criminal courts are increasingly recognizing, is entitled to leave a relationship without fatal consequence. The reform is having its intended effect – men, at least most of them, are no longer 'getting away with it'.

## Justice for victims and their families?

As for victims' families, do they feel they are now getting justice as June Steenkamp did? When the defendant in the infamous pre-reform 'red mist' *Humes* case received a seven-year sentence for manslaughter, the victim's family was outraged. The sentence left the victim's family furious that he was seen as the victim while the actual victim, Madeleine Humes, 'wasn't heard at all' (cited in Hinsliff, 2003). Turning to the post-reform cases, one family was outraged that the jury had cleared the defendant of murder in a case reported under the headline: 'Manslaughter injustice'. Aware that the killer would serve only half of his 18-year term, the victim's son despaired: 'Nine years for a man that's capable of killing someone and burying them on the moors – there's no justice' (Rush, 2013). Another family felt let down by the jury in a case where a woman's former partner launched a sustained attack on her in revenge for rejecting him. Family members were reported to have rushed distraught from the court when the jury foreman announced a unanimous verdict of not guilty to murder after two days' deliberation. An incredulous family friend was 'disgusted' at the outcome. She was 'not expecting that at all'. The family thanked the judge 'for coming to the only sentence suitable for this crime' – life with a minimum term of seven and a half years, but not to be released until he was no longer considered a danger to the public (read: women). As for the family friend, she remained perplexed: 'I'm just wondering, what is murder?' (Passant, 2015).

Tracy Kearns' partner told the court he had lost control and killed her because she had compared him unfavourably to her lover. The jury accepted his loss of control defence. The victim's family was 'devastated' by the manslaughter verdict and 13-year sentence, her mother declaring: 'I will never understand how this can be seen as justice. Nothing other than a life-sentence would ever be justice for what this man did to Tracy' (ITV Report,

2017). Karen Jacquet's killer pleaded guilty to her manslaughter by diminished responsibility. The plea was accepted and he was given a sentence of nine years and four months. In the family's view, 'diminished responsibility does not mean no responsibility', but while they hoped the court could assist the offender to get the treatment to ensure his 'safe release in time', there was 'little justice that can come from such a tragic situation' (Reid, 2018).

For some families even a murder conviction does not provide a sense of justice. Charmaine Macmuiris' family felt the life sentence for murder with a minimum term of 14 years for her jealous boyfriend failed to reflect the severity of what was described in court as a 'vicious attack on an entirely innocent victim' whom he falsely believed was seeing another man (Turner, 2013). Natalie Saunders' partner was sentenced to life with a 21-year minimum after being found guilty of her murder by a jury after less than two hours' deliberation. Her family wished they could say 'we have got justice for Natalie but we will never have justice' unless her killer 'suffers the same brutality he subjected Natalie to' (cited in Clark-Billings, 2019). And Tyler Denton's family wanted her former partner to get a longer sentence for murder than life with a 30-year minimum for killing her and stabbing three members of her family. She 'didn't get the justice she deserved' (Williams, 2018).

## Conclusion

Justice for intimate partner femicide victims in the form of murder convictions and longer sentences is what most families say they want and reformers promised. That is what most of them are getting in the post-reform era. Some acknowledge they will 'never have justice' however long the sentence. Others aspire for a different message to be taken from their loved one's slaughter. As I write in 2021, the family of 17-year-old Ellie Gould, killed by her boyfriend the day after she ended their relationship, is reacting to his life sentence with a 12-year minimum for murder. Ellie's grandmother wanted the death penalty – 'I believe it should be capital punishment – a life for a life'. In contrast, Ellie's mother wanted a 'life means life' sentence. He should never be freed. Why? Not because justice demanded it but because: 'He's a danger to society, he's a danger, particularly to women' (BBC, 2019). It's not only him. Seeing a man's killing of a departing woman not as a one-off occurrence and not as a question of getting justice for her but as a question of ensuring women's safety signals a growing awareness of a well-documented pattern of behaviour that endangers women – men are still killing their wives, women partners and especially their former partners at a rate of two a week in England and Wales. Criminal law reforms rebalancing law's traditional hierarchical offender–victim relationship in favour of the victims are a vital step towards getting intimate partner femicide recognized as a first-order social and political problem. Unquestionably, this has been a successful feminist intervention predicated on the evidence collected by feminist scholars and acted upon by law reformers committed to feminist praxis.

To conclude: the anti-feminist commentator who worried that feminist-inspired reforms would produce an 'unjust, feminist view of murder' was right to see the reforms as 'politically motivated'. The fight to deliver justice to victims and to abolish excuses for killing them is an intensely political fight, one that her own condemnation of the reforms and that of the reformers' parliamentary opponents made crystal clear. She was also right to predict that 'poor' Othello would 'get short shrift' from feminists. But significantly, it is not only feminist-identified reformers who condemn 'infidelity'-obsessed Othellos. Today English juries are convicting modern-day Othellos of murdering their Desdemonas and, hearteningly, so too are young audiences acting as juries at performances of my play, *Othello on Trial* (Howe, 2015). Shakespeare's *Othello, The Moor of Venice* has haunted the writing of this chapter as well it might. Its brilliant dissection of men's excuses for killing wives, excuses which have informed defences to murder in the 400 years since he wrote it, renders it the perfect vehicle for contesting the self-evidence of the excusatory force of so-called 'crimes of passion'. Justice at last for Desdemona? Maybe not, but breaching the self-evidence of male right is imperative and profoundly satisfying, though unfinished, feminist political work.

## Notes

[1] *Director of Public Prosecutions, Gauteng v Pistorius* (96/2015) [2015] ZASCA 204 (3 December 2015).

[2] There is a vast feminist literature on the operation of defences to murder in intimate partner femicide cases. See, for example, the reference lists in Howe (2002, 2019a, 2019b).

[3] The universal 'we' embedded in the notion of 'our sense of injustice' is at odds with Heinze's problemat izing approach to law's justice. See, for example, Heinze (2009). See also my review of his book (Howe, 2014a).

[4] See Howe (2013, 2019a) for accounts of men who killed wives, partners and former partners and then committed suicide or failed in suicide bids.

[5] *Bullard v The Queen* [1957] AC 635 at 644.

[6] *R v Coutts* [2007] 1 Cr App R 6.

[7] *Coutts* at 12.

[8] *R v Smith (Morgan)* [2001] 1 AC 146 at 173–4, my emphasis.

[9] *Berthill Fox v R* No 2 PC 2002. *Luc Thiet Thuan v R* [1997] AC 131 at 157.

[10] *Bertill Fox*, para 39.

[11] *Vinagre* (1979) 69 Cr App R 104 at 116.

[12] *R v Townsend* (1979) 1 Cr App R (S) 333 at 334–5.

[13] *R v Suratan, R v Humes and R v Wilkinson* (Attorney General's Reference No 74 of 2002, No 95 of 2002 and No 118 of 2002) [2002] EWCA Crim 2982.

[14] *R v Clinton, R v Parker, R v Evans* [2012] EWCA Crim 2. See Howe (2012: 774–8).

[15] In the following, the media item reporting the trial is provided as the source for all citations.

# References

Allison, S. (2015) 'Pistorius murder verdict gives respect to Reeva, say her mother', *The Guardian*, [online] available at: https://www.theguardian.com/world/2015/dec/04/oscar-pistorius-verdict-respect-reeva-june-steenkamp-interview-murder [accessed 13 July 2021].

Arkell, H. (2013) 'Father-of-two "stabbed adulterous wife to death in front of their young son in attack which was recorded on dictaphone he used to spy on her"' *Daily Mail*, [online] available at: www.dailymail.co.uk/news/article-2323868/Andrew-Parsons-stabbed-adulterous-wife-death-young-son-attack-recorded-spy-dictaphone.html [accessed 13 July 2021].

BBC (2013) 'Devendra Singh jailed for murder of wife Charlotte Smith', *BBC*, [online] available at: www.bbc.com/news/uk-england-stoke-staffordshire-23044637 [accessed 13 July 2021].

BBC (2019) 'Ellie Gould's "evil" killer should never be released, family says', *BBC*, [online] available at: https://www.bbc.co.uk/news/uk-england-wiltshire-50262657 [accessed 13 July 2021].

Calderwood, I. (2016) 'Jealous husband who stabbed wife to death is cleared of murder because she said she had a new lover and was leaving him', *Daily Mail*, [online] available at: www.dailymail.co.uk/news/article-3401586/Jealous-husband-stabbed-wife-death-cleared-murder-said-new-lover-leaving-him.html [accessed 13 July 2021].

Clark-Billings, L. (2019) 'Natalie Saunders murder: Man who strangled mum-of-five to death jailed for life', *Mirror*, [online] available at: https://www.mirror.co.uk/news/uk-news/breaking-natalie-saunders-murder-man-14395402 [accessed 13 July 2021].

Constable, M. (2005) *Just Silences: The Limits and Possibilities of Modern Law*, Princeton: Princeton University Press.

Gye, H. (2013) 'Jealous husband stabbed wife 15 times', *Daily Mail*, [online] available at: www.dailymail.co.uk/news/article-2524723/Jealous-husband-stabbed-wife-15-times-ran-sent-Christmas-card-lay-dying-hospital.html [accessed 13 July 2021].

Heinze, E. (2009) '"Were it not against our laws": Oppression and resistance in Shakespeare's *Comedy of Errors*', *Legal Studies*, 29(2): 230–63.

Heinze, E. (2013) *The Concept of Injustice*, Abingdon: Routledge.

Hinsliff, G. (2003) '"Crime of passion" is no defence', *The Guardian*, [online] available at: www.theguardian.com/politics/2003/jan/19/ukcrime.prisonsandprobation [accessed 13 July 2021].

Hinsliff, G. (2008) 'Harman and law lord clash over wife killers', *The Guardian*, [online] available at: https://www.theguardian.com/politics/2008/nov/09/harriet-harman-defence-of-provocation [accessed 13 July 2021].

Howe, A. (2002) 'Provoking polemic: Provoked killings and the ethical paradoxes of the postmodern feminist condition', *Feminist Legal Studies*, 10: 39–64.

Howe, A. (2012) 'Enduring fictions of possession: Sexual infidelity and homicidal rage in Shakespeare and late modernity (glossing *Othello*)', *Griffith Law Review*, 21(3): 772–96.

Howe, A. (2013) '"Red mist" homicide: Sexual infidelity and the English law of murder (glossing *Titus Andronicus*)', *Legal Studies*, 33(3): 407–30.

Howe, A. (2014a) 'Review: *The concept of injustice*', *Legal Studies*, 34(4): 736–48.

Howe, A. (2014b) 'Fatal love', *Griffith Journal of Law and Human Dignity*, 2(1): 4–24.

Howe, A. (2015) '*Othello on trial*: Engaging with the "extra-academic outside world"', *Queen Mary Human Rights Law Review*, 2(1): 133–44.

Howe, A. (2019a) 'Provocation by sexual infidelity: Diminishing returns?' in A. Howe and D. Alaattinoğlu (eds) *Contesting Femicide: Feminism and the Power of Law Revisited*, Abingdon: Routledge, pp 11–26.

Howe, A. (2019b) '"Being wrought, perplexed in the extreme": Othello and his syndrome' in A. Howe and D. Alaattinoğlu (eds) *Contesting Femicide: Feminism and the Power of Law Revisited*, Abingdon: Routledge, pp 55–72.

ITV Report (2017) 'Anthony Bird sentenced to 13 years for "sustained and prolonged attack" on partner Tracy Kearns', *ITV*, [online] available at: https://www.itv.com/news/wales/2017-11-29/anthony-bird-sentenced-to-13-years-for-sustained-and-prolonged-attack-on-partner-tracy-kearns [accessed 13 July 2021].

Larner, D. (1998) 'Justice in drama: Historical ties and "thick" relationship', *Legal Studies Forum*, 21(1–3): 3–19.

Larner, D. (1999a) 'Justice and drama: Conflict and advocacy', *Legal Studies Forum*, 23(1–2): 417–29.

Larner, D. (1999b) 'Teaching justice: The idea of justice in the structure of a drama', *Legal Studies Forum*, 23(1–2): 201–10.

Larner, D. (2001) 'Passions for justice: Fragmentation and union in tragedy, farce, comedy, and tragi-comedy', *Cardozo Studies in Law and Literature*, 13(1): 107–18.

Manderson, D. and Yachnin, P. (2010) 'Shakespeare and judgement: The renewal of law and literature', *The European Legacy*, 15(2): 195–213.

McCarthy, R. (2014) 'Luan Leigh murder: Obsessed husband killed wife after she removed his photos from her bedroom', *Birmingham Mail*, [online] available at: www.birminghammail.co.uk/news/midlands-news/luan-leigh-murder-husband-killed-8317195 [accessed 13 July 2021].

McDonagh, M. (2008) 'An unjust, feminist view of murder', *The Times*, [online] available at: https://www.thetimes.co.uk/article/an-unjust-feminist-view-of-murder-8gkk279tnf3 [accessed 13 July 2021].

Mihai, M. (2011) 'Socialising negative emotions: Transitional criminal trials in the service of democracy', *Oxford Journal of Legal Studies*, 31(1): 111–31.

Murdermap (2013) 'Stabbed by a former lover: Naudel Turner', [online] available at: www.murdermap.co.uk/pages/cases/case.asp?CID=85901908&VID=1050&Case=Stabbed-by-a-former-lover:-Naudel-Turner [accessed 16 October 2019].

Neill, M. (2006) *William Shakespeare: Othello, the Moor of Venice*, Oxford: Oxford University Press.

Osuh, C. (2012) 'Jailed for life: Man who knifed mother of his child to death at their Salford home', *Manchester Evening News*, [online] available at: www.manchestereveningnews.co.uk/news/local-news/jailed-for-life-man-who-knifed-698798 [accessed 13 July 2021].

Passant, A. (2015) 'Friend's disgust at Christine Henderson murder trial verdict', *GazetteLive*, [online] available at: www.gazettelive.co.uk/news/local-news/friends-disgust-christine-henderson-murder-3670131 [accessed 13 July 2021].

Reid, B. (2018) 'Man jailed for manslaughter of "defenceless" partner after attacking her with rolling pin and knife', *Nottingham Post*, [online] available at: https://www.nottinghampost.com/news/local-news/man-jailed-manslaughter-defenceless-partner-1911762 [accessed 13 July 2021].

Rush, R. (2013) 'Nine years for a man that's capable of killing someone', *Daily Mail*, [online] available at: www.dailymail.co.uk/news/article-2439304/Adrian-Muir-Pamela-Jacksons-sons-anger-unjust-sentence-given-manslaughter.html, [accessed 13 July 2021].

Spencer, J.R. (2009) 'Response to Ministry of Justice consultation paper murder, manslaughter and infanticide: Proposals for reform', [online] available at: http://www.docstoc.com/docs [accessed 13 July 2021].

Turner, R. (2013) 'David O'Sullivan jailed for life for Christmas day murder of Charmaine Macmuiris', *Wales Online*, [online] available at: www.walesonline.co.uk/news/wales-news/david-osullivan-pleads-guilty-christmas-4288041 [accessed 13 July 2021].

Valverde, M. (2002) 'Justice as irony: A queer ethical experiment', *Law and Literature*, 14(1): 85–102.

Van Dijk, J.J.M. (2008) 'In the shadow of Christ? On the use of the word "victim" for those affected by crime', *Criminal Justice Ethics*, 27(1): 13–24.

Verkaik, R. (2008) 'Judge backs infidelity defence for killers', *The Independent*, [online] available at: https://www.independent.co.uk/news/uk/crime/judge-backs-infidelity-defence-for-killers-998207.html [accessed 13 July 2021].

Williams, K. (2018) 'Tyler Denton "didn't get the justice she deserved", say family as killer is jailed for life', *Daily Post*, [online] available at: https://www.dailypost.co.uk/news/north-wales-news/tyler-denton-didnt-justice-deserved-14546917 [accessed 13 July 2021].

## 12

# An Anti-Carceral Feminist Response to Youth Justice Involved Girls

*Jodie Hodgson*

## Introduction

Girls have consistently represented a minority of the youth offending population and their involvement in the youth justice sphere has often developed from concerns in relation to displays of 'risky femininity', most prominently in relation to adolescent sexuality and sexual agency. This chapter, therefore, does not intend to enter into a debate concerning the prevention, management or reduction of girls' offending behaviour. This is not to say that girls don't break the law, but for those that do, it is established that their offending is often accompanied by profound experiences of victimization and social, economic and material injustice and inequality. The purpose of this chapter is, therefore, to critically explore and challenge the way in which girls' involvement in crime, and their criminalization, represents broader and more complex problems regarding their lived realities, which require a holistic and alternative response to the one currently facilitated by the youth justice service. Situating the structural inequalities and social injustice which disproportionately affect girls and young women, by virtue of age and gender (notwithstanding the intersections of class, ethnicity, disability or sexuality), at the centre of debate and discussion, the chapter advocates for the development and application of a 'girl-wise' penology, underpinned by an anti-carceral feminist response to the injustices girls experience at the hands of the penal estate.

In order to make the case for a 'girl-wise' penology, informed by an anti-carceral feminist logic, the chapter will provide contextual insight into the structural position of girls, their relationship with youth justice and the ways in which policy and practice, over the past two decades, has had particularly gendered consequences for those in conflict with the law. In doing so it will draw attention to the extent to which the experiences of girls continue to be marginalized within criminological discourse and academic scholarship. Moving forward, the chapter suggests that in order to overcome such marginalization, the experiences and needs of girls, and responses to them, need to be incorporated into abolitionist and feminist praxis.

Focusing on the relative absence of radical feminist responses from existing literature concerning girls embroiled in the youth justice system, the contributions from this chapter are intended to directly address the need for a radically informed shift in the existing treatment of, and responses to, girls in the justice system. The arguments presented form part of a broader discussion which contributes to the established and emerging arguments concerning abolitionist alternatives to state responses to criminalized women and girls, and the subsequent injustices to which they are subject. The intention is to build upon abolitionist perspectives on injustices perpetrated by the state, with a specific focus on the ways in which such arguments would extend to girls in order to improve the material and lived realities of their lives. In order to do this, it is first necessary to conceptualize the position of girls in the youth justice service and their experiences within it.

## Forsaken girls and youth justice

In England and Wales, girls represent only one-fifth of young people subject to youth justice intervention and their offending is predominantly considered less serious than boys' and their involvement in the system is often short-lived (Arnull et al, 2005; Bateman, 2008; Shepherd, 2015). In the context of criminological inquiry, they have remained largely absent in comparison to the attention given to their young male and adult female counterparts. There is, however, an established body of knowledge produced by feminist scholars, as a response to this inherent neglect of girls at the hands of the state and within criminological discourse, which has drawn attention to the ways in which the social construction of gender and the structural inequalities inherent within it, have served to shape girls' experiences in the social world and the responses to, and nature of, their offending (see, for example, Hudson, 1989; Worrall, 2001; Cox, 2003; Batchelor and Burman, 2004; Burman and Batchelor, 2009; Gelsthorpe and Worrall, 2009; Phoenix, 2012; Sharpe, 2012; Sharpe and Gelsthorpe, 2015).

In light of such knowledge which articulates girls' subordinate position in the social world, by virtue of their gender, feminist scholars have demonstrated the importance of challenging the culpability of girls' offending behaviour by repositioning the state, and informal agents of social control, as the subject of interrogation. As such, there is now an international body of empirical research which has revealed the 'importance of victimisation in the aetiology of young women's offending' (Sharpe, 2012: 18) and the disproportionate extent to which gendered violence and victimization shapes the lives of girls who enter the youth justice system (see, for example, Chesney-Lind, 1989; Howard League, 1997; Burman et al, 2000; Bloom et al, 2003; Batchelor, 2005; Goodkind, 2005; Belknap and Holsinger, 2006; Schaffner, 2006; Sharpe, 2012).

In addition to physical and sexual victimization, it is established that high levels of social exclusion, educational marginalization, social care intervention, neglect and poverty are also prevalent issues which characterize the formative experiences of girls in the justice system (Bateman and Hazel, 2014; Sharpe, 2015; Goodfellow, 2019). Concerns are also raised regarding much higher levels of mental health problems, compared to boys, particularly for girls detained in secure placements (Belknap and Holsinger, 2006; Ministry of Justice, 2017). Feminist incursions within criminology, which have challenged the gender-blindness inherent within the discipline, have revealed the gendered context of women and girls' formative experiences and the ways in which they intersect with their offending behaviour, alongside their differential treatment by criminal justice agencies. Drawing upon this research from scholars such as Smart (1976), Chesney-Lind (1989), Carlen (1990) and Heidensohn (1996), for example, it is now recognized that girls are subject to specific gendered risks and vulnerabilities. Despite the emergence of such critical and feminist scholarship concerning the experiences of women and girls, as victims and offenders, the core arguments of such work are yet to be expanded beyond the peripheries of criminological discourse into the exploration of radical social transformation of the material and lived realities of girls' lives. Accentuating such injustice is the persistent failure of youth policy and practice to respond appropriately to these risks and vulnerabilities and the deleterious impact this has had for girls will form the focus of the following critical discussion.

## (In)justice, welfarism and risk

The history of girls and their contact with youth justice reflects attempts to control their behaviour through criminal justice and welfare interventions that seek to enforce and communicate moral and behavioural expectations associated with ideological discourses of femininity (Worrall and Gelsthorpe, 2009). In the past girls 'have been socially constructed within a range of legal, welfare, and political discourses as, on the one hand, deeply maladjusted misfits and, on the other … dangerous folk devils, symbolic of postmodern adolescent femininity' (Worrall, 2004: 44). Despite such shifting discourses there does remain some 'historical continuities' (Worrall and Gelsthorpe, 2009: 211) most prominently in relation to expectations relating to appropriate female behaviour, emanating from dominant discourses of femininity that emphasize feminine ideals of domesticity, emotionality, fragility and sexuality (Carlen and Worrall, 1987). Therefore, attempts to regulate girls' behaviour in line with such discourses have been a principal theme represented within criminal justice and welfare responses that focus on girls' deviance (Hudson, 1989; Cox, 2003; Gelsthorpe and Worrall, 2009; Sharpe and Gelsthorpe, 2009, 2015). These responses, however, are not consistent and they have been subject to change in line with 'trends in youth justice policy and practice, criminological theorising and … socio-political concerns' (Sharpe and Gelsthorpe, 2015: 50).

Conflicting discourses of welfare and justice characterized much of the 20th- and 21st-century responses to girls, and despite the expectations of femininity being a consistent feature, shaping youth justice intervention into girls' lives, neither of these responses have been benign for girls. For example, policy and practice underpinned by welfarism were closely related to expectations associated with appropriate female behaviour (Sharpe and Gelsthorpe, 2009) and suggested to have acted as a basis on which to justify restrictions on girls' individual freedoms, most prominently due to concerns surrounding girls' sexuality and their demonstrations of sexual agency as being perceived as offending against their femininity (Worrall and Gelsthorpe, 2009). A shift to a justice-based model of intervention, prompted in part by the critique that girls' behaviour was being policed in relation to notions of respectability and appropriate femininity (Sharpe, 2012), was however no less problematic. Responding to girls through the welfare model of justice meant that girls were subject to the same forms of criminalization as those experienced by boys (Worrall, 2001). As such, there was a significant increase in the number of girls being incarcerated, 'not on spuriously benevolent welfare grounds but on spuriously equitable "justice" grounds' (Worrall, 2001: 86).

The emergence of a risk-based penology as a dominant paradigm in youth justice practice continued to produce gendered implications for girls involved in youth justice. Towards the end of the 20th century a central focus on risk management and crime prevention 'derived from developmental theories of criminality' (Pitts, 2001: 77) and empirical research focused on 'calculating risk' and the 'statistical probability of reoffending' (Muncie, 2004: 276) emerged. Such 'risk factor research' indicated that exposure to risk factors in 'psychosocial domains … at an early stage of life … can predict and even determine later offending' (Case and Haines, 2015: 101). This prompted a wide range of risk prevention interventions that ultimately led to young people being responded to in terms of risk factors associated with offending behaviour (Muncie, 1999). This shift from welfare and justice to crime prevention and risk management had 'particularly dramatic and criminalising consequences for girls and young women' (Worrall and

Gelsthorpe, 2009: 219). This was because the categorization of offending populations according to levels of risk resulted in identified needs of offending populations becoming conflated with risk. For young female offenders this served to frame their gender-specific needs as 'criminogenic problems' (Hannah-Moffat, 2005: 43). As a result, the social and structural inequalities girls experienced on the basis of their gender were reframed as 'individual problems or … individual inadequacies' (Hannah-Moffat, 2005: 43). In this context gender was no longer considered a predictive factor of offending behaviour, as actuarial discourses of risk management determined ethnicity and social class as more relevant to pre-empting offending behaviour. Girls thus became subject to the same risk-based calculations as boys resulting in a significant net-widening impact and a spike in recorded offences perpetrated by girls (Worrall, 2001). This increase in recorded offences committed by girls, in addition to the aforementioned development of a body of feminist research, has revealed how the prevalence of physical, emotional and sexual abuse characterize the lives of justice-involved girls (see, for example, Chesney-Lind, 1989). Further, this has 'prompted attempts to reconfigure criminal justice responses to them, through gender-specific programming' (Sharpe and Gelsthorpe, 2015: 49).

One of the central contributions and concerns emerging from feminist pathways research is the extent to which girls' formative experiences and their offending create a paradoxical status between their victimization and their criminalization (Chesney-Lind and Pasko, 2013). In addition, such research has also been pivotal in highlighting the prevalence of self-harm and other mental health problems and substance abuse among girls (Sharpe and Gelsthorpe, 2015). It is such contributions to knowledge concerning the social, structural and institutional injustices girls experience, that have been drawn upon in order to develop gender-specific programming for youth justice involved girls. Within England and Wales, such knowledge has been transferred into youth justice policy and practice through gender-specific crime prevention programmes influenced by the Oregon Guidelines for Effective Programming for Girls (Morgan and Patton, 2002; Youth Justice Board, 2009). The Oregon guidelines are underpinned by the evidence base informing feminist pathways research and focus on the delivery of relationship, health and strength based programming for girls, which seeks to address issues of trauma and victimization, physical, sexual and mental health and self-respect (Morgan and Patton, 2002). The development of such programming aimed to 'advance equitable treatment' within youth justice practice (Sharpe, 2015: 2).

The epistemological foundations, upon which gender-specific programming have been developed, begin with the understanding 'that girls and women are gendered subjects, with particular, gendered social experiences, who therefore require a holistic, therapeutic approach to intervention in recognition of the social origins of their troubles' (Sharpe and Gelsthorpe, 2015: 57). It is, therefore, now acknowledged that 'interventions for girls and young women should aim to provide a comprehensive ... service that addresses the complexity and multiplicity of their support needs [and] must also be explicitly gender responsive' (Bateman and Hazel, 2014: 4). Additionally, it is now also recognized that, in comparison to adult female offenders, girls 'have distinctive needs because of their younger age and stage of emotional development' (Burman and Batchelor, 2009: 279). Therefore, it is suggested that the 'real-life context of young women's offending demands a consideration of the key determinants of gender and age' (Burman and Batchelor, 2009: 281). While the emergence of gender-specific programming demonstrates the role of feminism in the development of youth justice policy and practice concerned with responding to the 'broader context of limiting social and structural conditions' (Burman and Barcheler, 2009: 279), which characterize girls' experiences, it has also been subject to critique, most prominently on the grounds of misconstrued assumptions concerning girls' offending.

For example, Sharpe (2015: 2) contends that 'the translation of feminist pathways research into gender-specific youth justice policy and practice is based on flawed assumptions about girls' pathways into and out of crime', and has the potential to result in 'iatrogenic consequences' for those subject to them. Goodkind (2005: 61) has also highlighted how attempts to implement gender-specific provision in the United States have failed to address 'institutional or structural change' and have instead focused on imputing individual responsibility on girls and their families.

Additional contributions concerning the relevance and rationale of gender-specific programmes and services for girls in conflict with the law have been challenged on the grounds that they are based upon a neoliberal appropriation of feminist values which materialize in the 'disempowerment' of girls (Goodkind, 2009: 398). Reflecting on findings from empirical research focused on two girls' programmes in North America, she contends that the emphasis gender-specific programming places on 'independence, self-esteem, choice and empowerment' (Goodkind, 2009: 403) fails to raise girls' awareness of the social injustice and oppression which shape and control their experiences. Further, it fails to recognize how they intersect with differences in terms of ethnicity, class and sexuality, while also failing to emphasize the need for collective resistance and transformative, radical change to disrupt such oppression. As such, the focus on individual aspects of self-development and change imputes upon girls an individual responsibility to effect change. It is this imputation of individualized notions of change and responsibilization within gender-specific programming which, according to Goodkind (2009: 397), reflects the 'intersection of neoliberalism with feminist values' and translates into the disempowerment of girls and a contradiction to feminist values which promote both individual and social change.

There also remains a series of salient questions which have yet to be addressed in the current literature and theorizing surrounding the contemporary state of youth justice and girls. These questions, unsurprisingly, given the systematic neglect of girls within youth justice policy and practice discourse, are concerned with determining the place of girls within the current youth justice sphere. What does their future look like within it? And what actions need to be taken to address the institutional injustices girls currently face?

Phoenix (2016: 135) contends that given the social, economic, 'material and cultural' inequalities, which feature prominently in the lives of those who form part of social divisions based upon gender, race, class, sexuality and disability, 'the ideals of justice are not capable of being realised'. Young people are already subject to structural inequalities by virtue of age and these inequalities are often compounded by experiences of 'victimisation and criminalisation' (Phoenix, 2016: 135). Drawing upon this argument, Phoenix (2016: 135) suggests that contemporary responses to young people's offending behaviour have the potential to be 'fundamentally unjust because they target the lawbreaking behaviour of young people already marginalized by class, gender and cultural inequalities while simultaneously practising a form of radical non-interventionism regarding the crimes … committed against them'.

Due to the extent to which the structural inequalities in relation to social divisions of gender, race, class, ethnicity, disability and sexuality continue to shape the social world and individual experiences within it, the practical transference of gender-responsive policy and practice is not straightforward nor adequate in responding to girls in conflict with the law. This is because the current arrangement of society, established upon a hetero-patriarchal order, creates a number of challenges and contradictions relating to the structural and material conditions affecting girls' lives, which gender-sensitive approaches are restricted in their ability to resolve. The crucial problem being that the principles upon which gender-specific provision for girls are based, specifically 'healthy relationships', 'self-esteem' and 'empowerment' (Sharpe, 2015: 6), do not address the structural conditions which perpetuate girls' marginalization and oppression within society.

In this context, the reality is that youth justice intervention, informed through a gender-specific provision, may actually serve to restore existing conditions of powerlessness, injustice and inequality. It is therefore crucially important to recognize the problematic nature of incorporating changes to process and practice, without being aware of, and endeavouring to respond to, the broader structures of unequal power relations operating within society. Restructuring power and instigating institutional and structural change is, therefore, first and foremost required, in order to provoke change within the micro and macro levels of social life. Thus, it is contended that in order to transform the current treatment of, and responses to, girls who offend, 'it is first necessary to critique patriarchal structures, redistribution and reconceptualisations of power' (Malloch, 2017: 155). The following discussion describes a practical account of how such a transformation might be achieved.

## Towards a girl-wise penology

As Carlen recognizes in her work on *Alternatives to Women's Imprisonment* (1990), the situation of girls must be understood within the larger social context of neoliberal penalty and society more broadly. The economic position of working-class families has plummeted, creating greater pathways to offending and criminalization. Instead of being recognized as a product of deteriorating social conditions, young people are actually being brought into the remit of the youth justice service through policy and intervention which emphasizes individual responsibility. Meanwhile, structural inequalities and violent forms of austerity continue to be unchallenged as a consequential factor of their offending behaviour.

Like Carlen (1990), this chapter supports a commitment to radical reform which is concerned with the criminalization of a small number of youth justice involved girls who have experienced social, economic and structural disadvantage and victimization. Ultimately, the force of the chapter lies in an anti-carceral feminist response to youth justice involvement in girls' lives. Such a positionality is determined on the grounds that girls who do break the law should not be required to endure further control, punishment and victimization, but should be provided with social support and assistance, something which the state currently deprives them of.

The examples discussed within this chapter emphasize that the harms inflicted upon girls through the current system endure, and thus they need addressing in a context that places the rights and protection of girls at the forefront of youth justice policy, practice, criminology and academic discourse. While a feminist jurisprudence would be welcomed in replacement of a hegemonic jurisprudence, it is not possible to state that broader social, political, economic and structural issues would not infiltrate the final version of such a penology in the same ways a 'non-feminist' jurisprudence transcends into penal policy in different, and detrimental, ways for girls.

As such, the chapter ultimately advocates for the abolishment of a youth justice jurisprudence for girls as it currently stands. A recommendation which is developed in line with a feminist conceptualization of justice underpinned by a commitment to radical and transformative societal change. It is not intended for this recommendation to be interpreted as an oversight of the injustices inflicted upon boys at the hands of the state. They too are not protected, nor exempt, from experiences of inequality and marginalization which render them more likely to be embroiled in a justice system that, ultimately, exacerbates their existing problems. However, there are profound policy implications which arise from the concerns raised with regards to the position of girls in the youth justice service. First, it is evident that the needs and experiences of girls who encounter the youth justice service are being relegated to the peripheries of youth justice discourse. Second, youth justice policy and practice has served to exacerbate gendered social control. Third, echoing the recommendations put forward by Corston (2007) in relation to adult female offenders over a decade ago, there is a need for a radical change to the treatment of girls who offend, one which requires an overhaul of youth justice policy and practice.

These implications, in addition to the material and lived realities of girls' lives, provide a basis and rationale in which to develop a feminist praxis which recognizes and responds to their social, economic and structural disadvantage that shapes their experiences in the social world. As a response to the injustice criminalized girls face, this chapter advocates for the development and application of a 'girl-wise penology'. It is intended that this recommendation mirrors the pioneering arguments put forward by Carlen (1990: 109) for a 'woman-wise penology' that incorporates the principles of 'remedial action', 'resistance' and 'democratic exploration' in the treatment of women (and girls) involved in the penal system. Overall, the intrinsic aim of a 'woman wise' penology, as Carlen advocated, was to ensure that the treatment of women offenders does not serve to exacerbate their social and structural oppression within society.

The arguments put forward with regards to lessons learnt from attempts to incorporate responsive policy into practice, emphasize the need to counter existing discourse that continues to reproduce the logic and practice of gender-specific reform as opposed to anti-carceral ideals. This is because punishment is 'criminogenic in its own right' having actually produced 'social, psychic, political, and economic harms of unprecedented proportions that are the conditions for current abolitionist projects' (Brown and Schept, 2016: 447). The adoption of a girl-wise penology would push forward an anti-carceral feminist agenda, and contribute towards the dismantling of the youth justice system as a fundamental contributor to the exercise of violence against children and young people. As such, this argument is not just about the development of radical alternatives to the youth justice service but following the arguments put forward by Brown and Schept (2016) this anti-carceral feminist positionality is also about establishing and making radical changes that ensure safe accessibility to education, healthcare and employment, in addition to the disestablishment of criminal justice. This requires the deconstruction of carceral ideology and the politics of punishment to enable new ways of thinking and acting that, ultimately, serve to ensure the safety of girls embroiled in the justice system, and a commitment to feminist praxis specifically concerned with raising consciousness and responding to the conditions of girls' oppression and their lived realities.

## 'Remedial action'

There are three components in which a girl-wise penology would progressively differ to the gender-responsivity which, initially emerging from the Oregon Guidelines for Effective Programming for Girls, currently informs the very limited policy response to girls in the justice system. First, 'girl-wise penology' challenges the ways in which gender-responsivity, developing from feminist pathways research, has been appropriated in ways that legitimize state-facilitated interventions. These interventions fail to acknowledge the systemic inequality that characterizes girls' experiences or challenge the injustice they face.

Current policy and practice shaping youth justice responses to young people in conflict with the law supports their diversion away from the formal justice system. Although this is a welcome, and to a certain extent a progressive, alternative to the straightforward criminalization of young people seen in previous responses, this approach is far from unproblematic. While it has contributed to a reduction in the number of girls criminalized, diversionary methods remain grounded in punitive interventionism. This is because diversion, as it is currently practised, filters young people into other welfare-based services which mirror formal youth justice intervention, as opposed to practising a form of non-interventionist diversion and keeping a child entirely away from system contact (Kelly and Armitage, 2015; Smith and Gray, 2019). I argue that those that have not avoided criminalization or regulation at the hands of the penal estate still require a different approach.

Such a different approach goes beyond gender-specific provision in policy and practice as it currently stands. What is required is a strategy for eradicating the social injustice of poverty, deprivation and marginalization which characterize the lives of girls who come to the attention of the justice service and an erosion of the social inequality and structural determinants, emanating from the social division of gender and the patriarchal system of control upon which society operates.

As Carlen (1990) states, remedial action should repair the 'present wrongs' that the criminal justice system has imposed upon women. For girls, I contend that addressing the inequity they have experienced from the penal system through remedial action is to engage in opposite action. There are two contexts, specific to girls, in which I suggest opposite action should be undertaken. These are the invisibility and neglect of girls and the ideology of austerity.

The system-wide neglect of girls is clearly illustrated in the publication of the most recent review of the youth justice system by Charlie Taylor (2016). The review, despite recommendations, did not address the specific needs of girls separately from boys, while the government's response to the review made 'no reference to the treatment of girls … other than in police custody' (Clinks, 2016: 13). Such negligence of girls' needs is more broadly symbolic of the forsaken position of girls throughout the youth justice landscape and the enduring lack of radical response to this issue. Moreover, invaluable developments to government policy aimed at reforming how the criminal justice system responds to women in conflict with the law, such as the Corston Report (2007) and the Female Offender Strategy (Ministry of Justice, 2018), have neglected to address issues specific to girls. Such neglect highlights a systemic failure within academic discourse and youth justice policy and practice to take seriously the needs and experiences of girls.

While there is emerging research which is centralizing the experiences of girls in the justice system, such as my own research on girls' experiences of restorative justice interventions (Hodgson, 2018, 2020), criminological discourse which addresses the issue of girls' invisibility continues to be scarce. Their offending pathways and the treatment of, and responses to, girls in contact with the system remains a neglected issue in relation to policy and practice. Opposite action in relation to girls' invisibility, first, would be to engage in social inquiry into the realities of girls' lives in order to gain a precise insight into the materiality of their lives. This would involve a review of girls' position in the social, political and economic organization of society. Further, this would draw upon the insight from front-line practitioners in both statutory and voluntary organizations and agencies, but most importantly, this would be taken from the subjective experiences of girls involved in the justice system. Such a holistic inquiry would pave the way for the exploration and implementation of legitimate social change for girls and the elimination of their invisibility.

The second opposite action concerns the reversal of austerity sanctions imposed on education provision, local government funding and welfare spending. The Social Metrics Commission (2019) found that a third of children in the UK are living in poverty, while estimated figures put forward in a research report published by the Equality and Human Rights Commission suggest that the figures for children living in poverty is set to rise to 41 per cent by 2022 (Portes and Reed, 2018). The two-child policy, benefit sanctions against parents, and reductions to social care services have meant that children (in addition to other marginalized groups) continue to be subject to significantly higher risks of poverty as a result of discriminatory austerity measures introduced since 2010. There are also the gendered aspects of poverty which require acknowledgement. Austerity measures have had a disproportionate impact on women. Given the structural disadvantage women experience, the gender pay gap and the cuts to welfare services, which unduly impact upon women as primary caregivers, highlights that the 'feminisation of poverty' (Pearce, 1978) is still a stark reality of contemporary society.

Opposite action in the context of austerity and impoverishment would mean reversing aggressive and regressive welfare reforms which have disproportionately impacted upon women and children by removing the welfare cap and increasing welfare expenditure on the most impacted categories, such as families and children, and unemployment and housing. In doing so, government funding should be provided to local authorities to reverse the impact of austerity at a local level. This is vital for youth justice involved girls who are a vulnerable group with significant mental health needs and whose offending pathways are shaped by high levels of poverty and prevalent experiences of victimization. By dismantling austerity measures and investing in impoverished communities through radical and transformative change, underpinned by feminist praxis, which explores the subjugated knowledge and experiences of girls impacted by austerity, this will centralize their voices in effecting social change and justice while also protecting them from oppressive system contact.

In the context of public services, austerity measures introduced since 2010 have resulted in education spending being severely reduced. The Institute for Fiscal Studies has identified that since 2009/10 there has been an 8 per cent reduction in school spending per pupil, while the largest cuts have been to further education and skills spending which have fallen by 12 per cent (Institute for Fiscal Studies, 2019). Such cuts include the abolishment of the Education Maintenance Allowance aimed at supporting young people in further education beyond the age of 16 with a financial incentive of up to £40 a week. The impact of this was effectively the withdrawal of educational support for those who come from poor and impoverished families (Kingston and Webster, 2015).

Despite cuts to education services many children still benefit from education or training in schools. However, for girls involved in the youth justice system whose backgrounds are blighted by prevalent experiences of victimization, mental health problems, substance misuse and poverty, many do not attend school (Sharpe and Gelsthorpe, 2015; Taylor, 2016). Greater inclusion in education made possible by the reversal of austere education spending has the potential to achieve positive change for girls in terms of breaking cycles of poverty and social exclusion. Furthermore, providing a space for consciousness-raising on conditions of oppression and collective empowerment.

The current austerity measures impacting education provision is a pressing issue for every child and young person, however for those who are already struggling and in need of additional support and opportunities, such resources are missing. Ensuring the safety net of education is vital for girls who are in conflict with the law and reversing the fiscal policies imposed on education spending is an imperative component of remedial action in order to achieve a radical and transformative change for girls.

While malevolent fiscal policies have had a detrimental impact upon masses of people since they began in 2010, writing this chapter comes at an unprecedented and critical time as the COVID-19 pandemic is having a devastating impact globally on all sectors of social and economic life. Therefore, a final point to make here is how the catastrophic impact of COVID-19 emphasizes the urgent need for remedial action as part of a 'girl-wise penology'.

So far, the Office for National Statistics (2020) has revealed that Black women are 4.3 times more likely than their White male and female counterparts to die from COVID-19. While social distancing and lockdown measures have put women and girls at heightened risks of gender-based violence (United Nations High Commissioner for Refugees, 2020). In the United Kingdom, the *Guardian* (Moore, 2020) reports that domestic violence deaths have doubled since the lockdown was introduced, while domestic violence support services have disclosed a 120 per cent rise in calls to their help line. Moreover, the World Economic Forum (2020) has raised concerns regarding a lack of access to contraception and the potential for an increase in girls subject to female genital mutilation. In recognizing how long-standing issues of social injustice, vulnerability and structural inequality intersect with, and are exacerbated by, the ramifications of the COVID-19 pandemic the claims made by senior cabinet ministers, such as Michael Gove, stating that 'the virus does not discriminate' are obviously fictitious.

It is clear that COVID-19 and the state response to it exacerbates the injustice to which the most vulnerable groups within society are already subject. While the future is uncertain with regards to how the brutal impact of the virus will unfold on the vulnerable and marginalized, we know that the effects of the virus are not short-term and it is inevitable that social and economic changes will persist. Reflecting critically on such changes, the likelihood is that they will not be uniform across society and the intersection between the pandemic and the powerless needs to be taken seriously. It is recommended that remedial action described as part of a 'girl-wise' penology forms part of a radical recourse to such harms through a political, social and cultural shift away from injustice and social divisions.

## 'Resistance'

In recognizing and responding to girls through remedial action which counteracts their relegation to the peripheries of criminological, and specifically youth justice discourse, it is also important to acknowledge girls' demonstrations of resistance and agency and the need to provide a salient space in which they can challenge and make recourse to alternative discourse, which positions them as active agents with the power to shape and define their own lives and experiences. The emphasis here is that the marginalization of girls' unique experiences at the hands of the carceral estate are not a complete process and that there are opportunities for contesting these injustices. These include resistance to tokenistic change that appropriates feminist values, but ultimately serves to maintain powerlessness and embed gender inequality.

Embodying and enabling 'resistance' in the context of a 'girl-wise' penology would comprise of challenging criminological discourse and youth justice policy and practice which responds to girls through responsibilization strategies that positions them as full agents, while simultaneously denying them their full agency through intervention which emphasizes ideals of femininity and moral integrity at the same time isolating their offending from the broader structural inequalities which are pivotal to the forms of oppression and victimization girls experience. In this context resistance would involve providing a voice to girls in relation to matters which are of significance to them and an opportunity to participate in the shaping of their experiences and simultaneously challenging the ways in which essentialized stereotypes of femininity, inherent within the social construction of gender, shape the governance of girls. By providing girls with a voice to share their own narratives and subjectivities, a space can be provided where the confines of power brought to bear on them can be resisted, and alternative narratives can be produced which challenge the exercise of patriarchal power and the formal and informal mechanisms of social control to which they are subject.

## 'Democratic exploration'

The final component of a 'girl-wise' penology is engaging in democratic exploration in order to respond to the current material and lived realities of girls' lives as they currently stand. I contend that a youth justice jurisprudence has not been effective in offering protection to girls from further trauma, distress and injustice. Many of the outcomes of such interventions hold the capacity to be experienced by girls in a penal context. For example, removal from homes, placement in secure accommodation and referrals to statutory welfare services have all been critiqued on the grounds that they deny girls due process of law, infringe their rights and are often underpinned by subtle mechanisms of social control which, intentionally or unintentionally, function to shape girls' attitudes and behaviours in line with dominant discourses of adolescent femininity.

As such, I suggest that such democratic exploration advocated by Carlen (1990) would consist of the exploration of the continuum of ways in which girls live and exist and a comprehensive consideration of how to accommodate the needs of girls and work with them in non-homogeneous ways that take account of conflicting and complex issues within an inclusive framework. As such, this would include democratic exploration of ways to support lesbian, gay, transgender, intersex and cisgender girls, those who are part of Black, Asian and minority ethnic groups, those who are looked after by the local authority, those who are mothers and those who are carers.

The three principles outlined are not new and there are many professionals, practitioners and academics already utilizing the principles of remedial action, resistance and democratic exploration to provide innovative and improved experiences for women and girls in the justice system. However, taking these principles forward I suggest that the values and practice underpinning them could be used as a starting point to envision the eradication of youth justice involvement for girls entirely.

## Towards abolition?

The final question this chapter poses is: what other alternatives are there for limiting the gendered harms inflicted upon girls who enter the justice service? The abolition of women's imprisonment is advocated for on the grounds that it has a devastating physical, psychological and social impact on those imprisoned. Might such abolitionist arguments, like those put forward by Carlen (1990) in relation to criminalized women, be extended to the incarceration of girls within the secure estate or youth justice intervention as a whole?

In support of Carlen's strategy for the abolition of women's imprisonment, I propose that there is a need for further exploration of feminist anti-carceral strategies and policies which offer 'girl-wise' interventions rooted in the delivery of social justice. It is suggested that given the very small number of girls who offend, in conjunction with the various social and penal injustices which characterize the lives of this group of girls, the following strategy offers a valuable opportunity to envision the practical realities of abolitionism in the context of youth justice.

This strategy, I suggest, is to be facilitated as a replacement of a youth justice jurisprudence for girls in conflict with the law, through a feminist-informed programme which recognizes, and endeavours to respond to, the social injustice girls who enter the youth justice system are faced with. Importantly, this would involve prioritizing the issues of power, agency and subjectivity, while also recognizing how each of these intersect with the wider functions of patriarchal state power.

I will now set out a strategy for the abolition of youth justice involvement in girls' lives and the development of anti-carceral 'girl-wise' justice. At the centre of this strategy is the development of a holistic package of support for girls which takes account of the material circumstances of their lives and connects their lived experiences to their offending and the opportunity for transformative change. A more diversified framework for responding to girls who offend would reconceptualize the treatment of, and responses to, offending girls as the responsibility of the youth justice sphere and, instead, provide a space in which alternatives to the governance of girls through a penal system can be established.

Following Angela Davis' (2011: 106) 'abolitionist alternatives' such a strategy would require a 'continuum of alternatives'. First, this would involve the removal of youth justice intervention for girls, as such the current wrongs perpetrated by the system would be eradicated. In practical terms this would mean intervention that, instead, combines exploration of the social, structural and personal causes of girls' offending with the disapproval of their offence.

We know from existing research that social and structural marginalization and physical, mental and emotional health problems are prevalent among the female offending population (Sharpe, 2012; Bateman and Hazel, 2014; Sharpe and Gelsthorpe, 2015). For this group it is recommended that they are provided with help through non-punitive measures of reconciliation and integration schemes. It is contended that the primary goal of these measures should be the reinvigoration of education, not just within school, but within community and recreational spaces. This would include continued access to a national health service that is adequately funded, and equally distributed, with an emphasis placed on ensuring high-speed, straightforward access to mental health care and access to reconciliation programmes, all of which must account for racial and class-based disparities as well as other structures of male domination. In a practical context, this would require a reversal of the current austerity measures that currently plague the most marginalized and vulnerable within society, and the deployment of professionals who are effectively trained and committed to instigating structural change for girls.

In the current system of youth justice, the impact of risk management, responsibilization and the continued conditions of austerity, have meant that the extent to which youth justice practitioners have the capacity to instigate structural change for girls is significantly limited. With relevant training, youth justice practitioners currently working with girls could be redeployed into alternative roles as part of a 'girl-wise' justice programme.

Ultimately it is suggested that education, health and social justice should be placed at the centre of such a progressive programme, with such provision being underpinned by a feminist praxis which creates a space for girls' voices and experiences to be heard, while recognizing and endeavouring to respond to the ways in which girls' offending, victimization and state responses to these experiences are inherently shaped by gendered relations of power. It is argued that such feminist-informed social policy would mobilize structural and systemic reform of the ways in which girls are currently treated in the context of criminal justice policy. Such radical reform would centralize a rhetoric of resistance and collective action to social injustice perpetrated by the state and empower girls by making gender, and their individual experiences, a visible factor responded to by social policy intervention.

## Conclusion

The approach to a 'girl-wise' penology outlined in this chapter is indicative of the principles and strategies which might replace youth justice responses to girls in conflict with the law with strategies of social justice, informed by an anti-carceral feminist logic. Through the exploration of feminist anti-carceral strategies and policies that need to be in place in order to prevent girls from being subject to further injustice, the chapter has sought to highlight that the injustices girls face at the hands of the justice service are profoundly connected to their structural position within patriarchal society. This means linking the gendered experiences of harm, control, marginalization and oppression, which shape girls and women's experiences in the social world, to the injustice distributed by state power.

By highlighting these experiences of oppression and injustice resulting from youth justice intervention and state power more broadly, the chapter has carved a space in which to argue for a new framework which abolishes the current youth justice governance of girls who offend, and replace it with new social policy that eliminates the inappropriate appropriation of feminist concerns, in order for the harms inflicted upon girls through the current system to continue to endure. As such the development and application of a 'girl-wise' penology, informed through feminist principles and logic and focused upon the need for democratic exploration, resistance and remedial action, provides a unique and progressive space in which the rights and protection of girls can be secured and placed at the centre of progressive social policy.

### References

Arnull, E., Archer, D., Eagle, S., Gammampila, A., Johnston, V., Miller, K. and Pitcher, J. (2005) *Persistent Young Offenders: A Retrospective Study*, London: Youth Justice Board.

Batchelor, S. (2005) '"Prove me the bam!": Victimization and agency in the lives of young women who commit violent offences', *Probation Journal*, 52(4): 358–75.

Batchelor, S. and Burman, M. (2004) 'Working with girls and young women' in G. McIvor (ed) *Women Who Offend*, London: Jessica Kingsley, pp 266–87.

Bateman, T. (2008) 'Target practice: Action detection and the criminalisation of children', *Criminal Justice Matters*, 73(1): 2–4.

Bateman, T. and Hazel, N. (2014) *Resettlement of Girls and Young Women: Research Report*, London: Beyond Youth Custody.

Belknap, J. and Holsinger, K. (2006) 'The gendered nature of risk factors for delinquency', *Feminist Criminology*, 1(1): 48–71.

Bloom, B., Owen, B., Rosenbaum, J. and Deschenes, E.P. (2003) 'Focusing on girls and young women: A gendered perspective on female delinquency', *Women and Criminal Justice*, 14(2/3): 117–36.

Brown, M. and Schept, J. (2016) 'New abolition, criminology and critical carceral studies', *Punishment and Society*, 19(4): 440–62.

Burman, M. and Batchelor, S. (2009) 'Between two stools? Responding to young women who offend', *Youth Justice*, 9(3): 270–85.

Burman, M., Brown, J., Tisdall, K. and Batchelor, S. (2000) 'A view from the girls: Exploring violence and violent behaviour', unpublished final report for ERSC.

Carlen, P. (1990) *Alternatives to Women's Imprisonment*, Milton Keynes: Open University Press.

Carlen, P. and Worrall, A. (eds) (1987) *Gender, Crime and Justice*, Milton Keynes: Open University Press.

Case, S. and Haines, K. (2015) 'Risk management and early intervention: A critical analysis' in B. Goldson and J. Muncie (eds) *Youth Crime and Justice*, London: SAGE, pp 100–18.

Chesney-Lind, M. (1989) 'Girls crime and woman's place: Toward a feminist model of female delinquency', *Crime and Delinquency*, 35(1): 5–29.

Chesney-Lind, M. and Pasko, L. (2013) *The Female Offender: Girls, Women and Crimes* (third edition), London: SAGE.

Clinks (2016) *Clinks Submission to the Review of the Youth Justice System*, [online] available at: http://www.clinks.org/sites/default/files/basic/files-downloads/clinks_taylorreview_final.pdf [accessed 21 October 2016].

Corston, J. (2007) *The Corston Report: A Review of Women with Particular Vulnerabilities in the Criminal Justice System*, London: Home Office. Available at: www.clinks.org/resources-reports/who-careswhere-next-women-offen der-services [accessed 19 August 2016].

Cox, P. (2003) *Gender, Justice and Welfare: Bad Girls in Britain, 1900–1950*, Basingstoke: Palgrave Macmillan.

Davis, A. (2011) *Are Prisons Obsolete*, New York: Seven Stories Press.

Gelsthorpe, L and Worrall, A. (2009) 'Looking for trouble: A recent history of girls, young women and youth justice', *Youth Justice*, 9(3): 209–23.

Goodfellow, P. (2019) *Outnumbered, Locked Up and Overlooked? The Use of Penal Custody for Girls in England and Wales*, London: Griffin Society. Available at: https://www.thegriffinssociety.org/outnumbered-locked-and-overlooked-use-penal-custody-girls-england-wales [accessed 5 January 2020].

Goodkind, S. (2005) 'Gender-specific services in the juvenile justice system: A critical examination', *Affilia*, 20(1): 52–70.

Goodkind, S. (2009) 'You can be anything you want, but you have to believe it: Commercialized feminism in gender-specific programs for girls', *Signs*, 34(2): 397–422.

Hannah-Moffat, K. (2005) 'Criminogenic needs and the transformative risk subject', *Punishment and Society*, 7(1): 29–51.

Heidensohn, F. (1996) *Women and Crime* (second edition), London: Macmillan Press.

Hodgson, J. (2018) *Feminising Restorative Justice: A Critical Exploration of Offending Girls' Experiences of Participating in Restorative Justice Conferences*, PhD thesis, Liverpool John Moores University.

Hodgson, J. (2020) 'Offending girls and restorative justice: A critical analysis', *Youth Justice*, doi: 10.1177/1473225420967751.

Howard League (1997) *Lost Inside: The Imprisonment of Teenage Girls*, London: The Howard League.

Hudson, A. (1989) 'Troublesome girls: Towards alternative definitions and policies' in M. Cain (ed) *Growing Up Good*, London: SAGE, pp 197–219.

Institute for Fiscal Studies (2019) *2019 Annual Report on Education Spending in England*, [online] available at: ifs.org.uk/publications/14369 [accessed 26 July 2021].

Kelly, L. and Armitage, V. (2015) 'Diverse diversions: Youth justice reform, localized practices, and a "new interventionist diversion"?', *Youth Justice*, 15(2): 117–33.

Kingston, S. and Webster, C. (2015) 'The most "undeserving" of all? How poverty drives young men to victimisation and crime', *Journal of Poverty and Social Justice*, 23(3): 215–27.

Malloch, M. (2017) 'Justice for women: A penal utopia', *Justice, Power and Resistance*, Foundation Volume, pp 151–61.

Ministry of Justice (2017) *Restorative Justice Action Plan for the Criminal Justice System for the Period to March 2018*, London: Ministry of Justice, [online] available at: https://www.gov.uk/government/uploads/system/uploads/attachment_data/file/596354/rj-action-plan-to-march-2018.pdf [accessed 29 July, 2017].

Ministry of Justice (2018) *Female Offender Strategy*, London: Ministry of Justice, [online] available at: https://assets.publishing.service.gov.uk/government/uploads/system/uploads/attachment_data/file/719819/female-offender-strategy.pdf [accessed 29 August 2018].

Moore, A. (2020) '"Every abuser is more volatile": The truth behind the shocking rise of domestic violence killings', *The Guardian*, [online] available at: https://www.theguardian.com/lifeandstyle/2020/apr/22/every-abuser-is-more-volatile-the-truth-behind-the-shocking-rise-of-domestic-violence-killings [accessed 9 May 2020].

Morgan, M. and Patton, P. (2002) 'Gender-responsive programming in the justice system: Oregon's guidelines for effective programming for girls', *Federal Probation*, 66(2): 57–65.

Muncie, J. (1999) 'Institutionalized intolerance: Youth justice and the 1998 Crime and Disorder Act', *Critical Social Policy*, 19(2): 147–75.

Muncie, J. (2004) *Youth and Crime* (second edition), London: SAGE.

Office for National Statistics (2020) *Coronavirus (COVID-19) Related Deaths by Ethnic Group, England and Wales: 2 March 2020 to 10 April 2020*, [online] available at: https://www.ons.gov.uk/peoplepopulationandcommun ity/birthsdeathsandmarriages/deaths/articles/coronavirusrelateddeathsb yethnicgroupenglandandwales/2march2020to10april2020 [accessed 7 May 2020].

Pearce, D. (1978) 'The feminization of poverty: Women, work and welfare', *Urban and Social Change Review*, 11(1–2): 28–36.

Phoenix, J. (2012) *Out of Place: The Policing and Criminalisation of Sexually Exploited Girls and Young Women*, London: The Howard League for Penal Reform, [online] available at: https://d19ylpo4aovc7m.cloudfront.net/ fileadmin/howard_league/user/pdf/Publications/Out_of_place.pdf [accessed 19 August 2016].

Phoenix, J. (2016) 'Against youth justice and youth governance, for youth penalty', *The British Journal of Criminology*, 56(11): 123–40.

Pitts, J. (2001) *The New Politics of Youth Crime: Discipline or Solidary?* Basingstoke: Palgrave.

Portes, J. and Reed, H. (2018) 'The cumulative impact of tax and welfare reforms', Equality and Human Rights Commission, [online] available at: https://www.equalityhumanrights.com/sites/default/files/cumulat ive-impact-assessment-report.pdf [accessed 4 April 2020].

Schaffner, L. (2006) *Girls in Trouble with the Law*, Piscataway: Rutgers University Press.

Sharpe, G. (2012) *Offending Girls: Young Women and Youth Justice*, Abingdon: Routledge.

Sharpe, G. (2015) 'Re-imagining justice for girls: A new agenda for research', *Youth Justice*, 16(1): 3–17.

Sharpe, G. and Gelsthorpe, L. (2009) 'Engendering the agenda: Girls, young women and youth justice', *Youth Justice*, 9(13): 195–208.

Sharpe, G. and Gelsthorpe, L. (2015) 'Girls, crime and justice' in B. Goldson and J. Muncie (eds) *Youth Crime and Justice*, London: SAGE, pp 49–64.

Shepherd, B. (2015) 'Youth justice practice with girls' in J. Annison, J. Brayford and J. Deering (eds) *Women and Criminal Justice*, Bristol: Policy Press, pp 99–118.

Smart, C. (1976) *Women, Crime and Criminology*, London: Routledge and Kegan Paul.

Smith, R. and Gray, P. (2019) 'The changing shape of youth justice: Models of practice', *Criminology & Criminal Justice*, 19(5): 554–71.

Social Metrics Commission (2019) *Measuring Poverty 2019*, [online] available at: https://socialmetricscommission.org.uk/wp-content/uplo ads/2019/07/SMC_measuring-poverty-201908_full-report.pdf [accessed 4 January 2020].

Taylor, C. (2016) *Review of the Youth Justice System in England and Wales*, London: Ministry of Justice.

United Nations High Commissioner for Refugees (2020) *Displaced and Stateless Women and Girls at Heightened Risk of Gender-based Violence in the Coronavirus Pandemic*, [online] available at: https://www.unhcr.org/uk/ news/press/2020/4/5e998aca4/displaced-stateless-women-girls-heighte ned-risk-gender-based-violence-coronavirus.html [accessed 10 May 2020].

World Economic Forum (2020) *UN: 3 Months of Lockdown Could Result in 15 Million Cases of Domestic Abuse Worldwide*, [online] available at: https:// www.weforum.org/agenda/2020/04/coronavirus-women-domestic- abuse/ [accessed 10 May 2020].

Worrall, A. (2001) 'Girls at risk? Reflections on changing attitudes to young women's offending', *Probation Journal*, 48(2): 86–92.

Worrall, A. (2004) 'Twisted sisters, ladettes and the new penology: The social construction of violent girls' in C. Alder and A. Worrall (eds) *Girls Violence: Myths and Realities*, New York: New York Press, pp 41–60.

Worrall, A. and Gelsthorpe, L. (2009) 'What works with women offenders: The past 30 years', *Probation Journal*, 56(4): 329–45.

Youth Justice Board (2009) *Girls and Offending: Patterns, Perceptions and Interventions*, London: Youth Justice Board.

# Afterword

*Pragna Patel*

Much of my work over the last four decades has grappled with questions that provide the central themes of this book: how do we ensure that the state protects the most vulnerable among us and guarantees their human rights without violating wider human rights and the rule of law itself? The urgent and contemporary challenges we face as feminists are encapsulated in our endeavours to address the role played by the criminal justice system and the state in a context of rising violence against women and girls. In addressing the issue, we are compelled to examine how power, race, class and sex intersect to reproduce inequality and injustice, raising profound questions about how and under what terms we engage as feminists with the state. This dilemma becomes all the more profound when situated in the wider context of an increasingly austerity driven and controlling state that makes progress difficult, threatening to wipe out the feminist gains that have been made by taking away the very tools needed to hold state and non-state power to account.

Over the years, much has been achieved through feminist struggles for state intervention in its protective capacity in respect of crimes of violence against women and girls. We have seen, for example, changes in criminal laws and policies around battered women who kill and the abolition of the law of provocation which was built on male norms of behaviour. There have been a plethora of laws, policies, strategies and action plans around violence against women which recognize that physical, sexual, financial and psychological abuse form part of a continuum of abuse and a wider dynamic of patriarchal control to which women are subjected in the private sphere. The 2019 case of Sally Challen led to a wider understanding of the concept of coercive control in reproducing gender inequality, while the 2018 Worboys case at the Supreme Court established that the police have a duty to investigate serious crimes of violence under the Human Rights Act. At the same time, incessant campaigning by Black and minority feminists has enabled us to put to bed the worst aspects of state policies on multiculturalism that failed to recognize forced marriage, female genital mutilation (FGM) and honour-based violence as forms of abuse and violence rather than as cultural practices that had to be tolerated. This led to the creation of new laws such as the Forced Marriage Civil Protection Act 2007 alongside statutory guidance and policies setting out good practice, all of which were unthinkable only a couple of decades ago.

Yet, these positive developments have failed to eliminate or even diminish the central tension that runs through our engagement with the state. On the one hand, we continue to grapple with state 'over-reach' or 'over-policing' which involves the intensification of state powers of coercion and control as highlighted so viscerally in the recent case of Child Q: the 15-year-old girl of African–Caribbean background who was subjected by the police to a strip search involving exposure of intimate body parts while she was menstruating and at school. No appropriate adult was present during the ordeal in December 2020, which had taken place without parental consent or knowledge. The police had been called by teachers at the school who claimed she strongly smelt of cannabis and suspected she was carrying drugs, but none were found during the subsequent search. An official investigation in March 2022 found that racism was likely to have been an 'influencing factor' in the actions of the police officers.

Arguably, nowhere is the tension arising from state over-reach more stark than in the growing nexus between the functions of the police and immigration authorities characterized by surveillance and brutal enforcement. In February 2020, for instance, we witnessed the acquittal of a Nigerian rape survivor of charges of assault. The case concerned events in May 2018 when she was subjected to an unlawful and forcible removal from Yarl's Wood Detention Centre, onto a plane by 11 private security guards hired by the Home Office. Ignoring a court order staying her removal, the guards had placed a blanket over her head, making it difficult for her to breathe so that she feared she would die. The judge said that the amount of force she used in defending herself while she was being restrained was reasonable.

On the other hand, we have seen cases like that of Banaz Mahmod, a 19-year-old woman of Iraqi Kurdish background, whose body was found in a suitcase buried in a Birmingham garden in 2006. She was the subject of an honour killing by her father and other male family members, who tortured and raped her before strangling her because they disapproved of her relationship with her boyfriend. Prior to her death, she had reported threats and attempts on her own life and that of her boyfriend on four separate occasions. She was dismissed by the police for being 'melodramatic', and on one occasion they even considered charging her with criminal damage for breaking her neighbour's windows in her effort to escape from an attempt by her father to kill her. Her experiences highlight how we continue to face the 'under-policing' of domestic and sexual violence, including specific cultural forms of harms that still attract little or no state intervention. This is one reason why the numbers of women killed by their abusive partners has not changed for decades – some would say they have increased – and why rape convictions are dismally low and diminishing.

In some minority communities, such 'under-policing' often goes hand in hand with the adoption of a culturally relativist approach to justice and rights: one based on the misguided view that religious and cultural practices, irrespective of the harms they may cause to women and children, must be tolerated and/or addressed through community and religious gatekeepers. In the process, the state ends up helping those gatekeepers achieve their key goal – to maintain the patriarchal status quo and retain their monopoly over power and resources – at the expense of the human rights and freedoms of women and children.

The need to simultaneously resist racism and state oppression while also struggling for women's rights in the family and community has involved adopting what is now widely recognized as an intersectional lens. Unfortunately, much of the debate and practice around intersectionality has reduced the concept to a simple matter of recognizing multiple identities of individuals rather than as a framework for deconstructing a woman's social positioning that captures both the structural and dynamic consequences of the interface between two or more systems of institutional discrimination and power.

For example, immigration laws and policies do not just create exclusionary and discriminatory racial processes that deny citizenship rights to migrant women facing abuse; they also reproduce and reinforce gender inequality and patriarchal power. By forcing migrant women into economic dependency on their spouses for their survival, immigration policies create conditions that are conducive to heightened forms of coercive control. Perpetrators routinely subject such women to domestic violence, imprisonment in the home, domestic servitude, cruelty, neglect and, in some cases, abandonment in countries of origin. They confiscate essential documents and keep women deliberately uninformed about their status. The denial of access for such women to key welfare services and benefits that form a crucial safety net for other abused women allows perpetrators to weaponize immigration laws to keep them in a permanent state of vulnerability and subjugation. The intersection of immigration controls and domestic abuse in effect gives rise to new techniques of patriarchal surveillance and control. The result for migrant women who face violence in the home is a continuum of private and state violence.

Most migrant women are too afraid to report their experiences of domestic abuse to the police for fear of retribution from perpetrators and from the state. When they do summon up the courage to report, they find that their accounts are dismissed, trivialized and discredited by the police. In some cases, far from being assisted and protected as victims of domestic abuse, they are subject to investigations and even arrested, cautioned, detained and charged with immigration offences. This state of affairs seriously undermines the protection principle, undercutting the overriding duty of the police and other statutory services to safeguard vulnerable adults and children. The problematic practice of data sharing between the police and immigration authorities for state surveillance purposes was the subject of considerable campaigning by Black and minority feminists during the passage of the Domestic Abuse Act 2021. However, in the face of findings by various police inspectorates and regulatory bodies that such data sharing causes 'significant public harm', the government has pressed ahead with the practice. In doing so, the government has chosen to prioritize the so-called 'integrity' of the immigration system over the protection of migrant women. The irony is not lost: guidance from the state acknowledges that insecure immigration status is a risk factor for domestic abuse.

In the face of unchecked institutionalized police racism, misogyny and brutality, and against the backdrop of the Black Lives Matter protests, we have witnessed the growing momentum of the anti-carceral movement which questions whether feminism has reached the limits of its engagement with the criminal justice system. These questions are based on the view that the feminist use of the criminal justice system serves not to empower or liberate but to further marginalize and criminalize women, especially those from the racial minorities who are disproportionately at risk of state-inflicted harm. For my part, while I agree with the urgent need to look beyond the criminal justice system towards a more holistic approach to justice that also addresses the economic and social conditions that shape gendered violence, I consider that anti-carceral politics also raise a series of other dilemmas and concerns that have yet to be properly addressed: in particular, who or what fills the space vacated by the police and the criminal justice system, given the fact of non-state actors who similarly wield systemic carceral power in the family and community; a power that manifests predominantly as intensified moral policing and coercive control that generates the very forms of gendered harms from which women need protection.

In the last three decades, the rise of neoliberalism – combined with the growth of religious fundamentalism and conservatism in minority communities – has brought with it increasingly violent mechanisms of female subjugation and the suppression of feminist dissent. It is well documented that all women share similar experiences of domestic and sexual violence/abuse but many minority women can also face additional and specific forms of harm arising from cultural and religious dynamics and values that reproduce highly rigid gender norms and sex inequality. Indeed, their experiences show that there is a direct link between regressive gender norms that circumscribe minority women's participation in public life and the incidence of violence against women and restrictions on their freedoms in the private sphere. In consequence, my work on violence against women has also been directed at wresting control and power away from religious leaderships and family and community elders that deny women and children the right to access the formal legal system or other institutions of the state in order to assert their rights to protection, choice and autonomy. I have seen how, in the face of a shrinking welfare state and cuts to services including legal aid, a large proportion of minority women are increasingly forced to resort to religious or community based forms of arbitration and dispute resolution. But these are dangerous patriarchal processes that serve to enhance religious and social control, and are ultimately even less amenable to accountability and gender justice.

For these reasons, we have no choice but to conceptualize and challenge the state to ensure that it serves as the ultimate guarantor of our human rights while also recognizing and challenging its increasingly coercive and punitive interventions that reproduce race, class and sex bias. Those who work on the front line know only too well that daily engagement with the criminal justice system is a necessity if women and children are to be protected from abuse and violence. This is why, in my view, the answer lies neither in abandoning the criminal justice system as a site of feminist resistance nor in putting all our faith in its ability to deliver justice and rights. The real challenge lies in working out how we strengthen mechanisms for legal and political accountability for the abuses of power that are routinely committed against women and girls in the public and private spheres and in how we continue with our political demands to that end.

I see many challenges looming ahead. We are faced with a government intent on legislative reforms that cast a dark shadow over the struggles that we have waged against violence against women. For instance, taken together, the Policing, Crime, Sentencing and Courts Bill, the Nationality and Borders Bill and the proposals to 'update' the Human Rights Act, represent a grave threat to feminism: at stake is our right to question, challenge, resist and dissent from political developments that have increasingly taken an alarmingly authoritarian turn made possible by the silent complicity of a large part of a disenchanted and disenfranchised population. But the political end game of such developments is systemic democratic exclusion and the exercise of power without consent, transparency or accountability – all of which should and must be central feminist concerns. The erosion of the rule of law and the retreat from international human rights law and standards is a real threat which will make life even more precarious for all women and girls who will be among the first casualties of abuses perpetrated by the state and non-state actors alike.

This book is the start of a long overdue conversation about feminism's engagement with the criminal justice system and, most importantly, with the broader question of how we bridge the gap between feminism, anti-racism, social justice and democracy.

# Index

References to endnotes show both the
page number and the note number (47n14).